MEET

Judd Wise, the co... among ropers as far back as Wyoming and Montana, and whose first-hand stories about Pete French make him the most venerable buckeroo in Burns.

The Chinese in the gold town of Jacksonville, whose mine twelve miles out of town supported an exotic way of life before they were shipped out to San Francisco *en masse* in 1915. But for many years on New Year's every child in town could count on pockets filled with nuts and candies, china lilies and glass bracelets, and the clap of fire-crackers in the night.

VISIT

Prineville, whose gold mine is a town-owned railway and is a haven for rockhounds who come searching for agates, obsidians and thunder eggs. These are not for sale in Prineville; they are there for the taking.

Maupin, on a naked plateau that slides down into the cavernous gorge of the Deschutes River, where the All Indian Rodeo rocks the town once a year, and a lovely river winds into a future where it may no longer exist.

FEEL

A TOUCH OF OREGON

A TOUCH
OF OREGON

Ralph Friedman

A COMSTOCK EDITION

SAUSALITO   ●   CALIFORNIA

Copyright © 1970 by the Pars Publishing Company

All rights reserved

Library of Congress Catalog Card Number: 74-132470

SBN 89174-005-8

First Printing: May 1974
Second Printing: July 1976
Third Printing: December 1984

Printed in the United States of America

Cover photo by Ray Atkeson

COMSTOCK EDITIONS, INC.
3030 Bridgeway, Sausalito, CA 94965

Contents

Again my love

This book is the latest verse in my continuing love song to Oregon.

The adoration began with *Oregon for the Curious* and was followed by *Tales Out of Oregon* and, in part, by *Northwest Passages: A Book of Travel.*

Let this book, however, not be construed as a huckster's pitch for Oregon. I am not uncritical of much that I have seen here. Years before it became popular, I was pointing to the many faces of pollution. I have seen beauty despoiled in every part of the state and in this book I have again sounded my feelings on this grim subject.

My writings on Oregon have never suggested that this is the most "beautiful" or "fascinating" of the 50 states. It happens that at this time of my life I know Oregon better than I do any other state. Had I lived, say, in Montana or Nevada or North Dakota I would probably have written about any of them with as much affection—and agony.

Still, I am glad I had Oregon as subject matter, because of the many dimensions the state possesses. How many other ocean-bordered states have great chunks of land stewing in the flavor of the Old West? How many wheat states have high mountain ranges? How many apple states have immense wastelands? This kind of list could fill a page.

A Touch of Oregon is indigenous Oregon—that which is so intimately related to the state as to stamp the character of Oregon on almost every page. At the same time, each of the stories has a universality which extends to every section of our country and, indeed, beyond our national borders. I remember chatting in Turkey with a desert-loving, soft-voiced camel driver who immediately reminded me of Reub Long, the Sage of Fort Rock. Judd Wise, the old cowpoke of Burns, brings back memories of a vaquero with whom I spent an afternoon in Mexico. If I close my eyes I can see Roy Stauffer of Union as a craggy Vermont farmer; Jack Steiwer of Fossil as a lanky guide in Nova Scotia; Jean and Ed Forsha, our beloved music-makers of Murphy, as an Oklahoma couple the depression had driven to the cottonfields of California. None of us is altogether unique; each of us encompasses multitudes.

The Oregon partisan will perhaps say of this book: This is Oregon, recognizing that it is but a representation of the state. In other states readers may say: Here are places and people worth going many miles to see because they are so interesting and different. Well, Westfall will not be found in Rhode Island nor the All-Indian Rodeo at Tygh Valley observed in Wisconsin. And at first glance the people, too, are not like those one encounters on the buses of Chicago or New Orleans. But viewed more closely they have much in common with people in all states, all lands, except that their experiences are Oregonian and their characters have been given a special expression by life in their small world of Oregon.

Here, too, in these pages, is an Oregon that is very real and deep to me. Preparation for the writing not only involved lengthy interviews, much of it providing new information about the pre-automobile days, but hundreds and hundreds of hours in historical research and thousands of miles in travel.

And out of it all, the laughter and the anguish, has come another verse in my love song, growing sadder and more poignant, to an Oregon we are watching disappear.

The hills of Owyhee

The moon swayed from its invisible rigging on the tallest peak in the width and length of the desert. Distorted by distance, dust of starlight and a cloud which bobbed as though it were riding waves, the peak appeared to be in motion, a needle-slender buoy in a phantom playa. The moon was an eye attached to this movable stalk, a silvery ommatophore warily scanning the crouching landscape below.

I was for a moment immured in that feral wasteland, somewhere in southeastern Oregon, above the sinuous Owyhee River. Time has shaped that moment into a dissoluble dream, so that the exactness of detail and the continuity of action are gone, long ago eroded, but the impressions remain, impaled on an hour beyond returning.

It happened in the young manhood of my life, when I was strong and fancy free.

A sawed-off rancher in a lop-sided jalopy had given me a lift and just before he turned off the main road had seriously suggested that I spend "a little time" at his spread. "Gotta get back to Jordan Valley in a few days," he said. "Putyuh on the road again."

No one anywhere was awaiting me so on we rambled, his rackety flivver lurching and coughing up a tire-chewing trail. Many miles later we reached a rocky splay, the front yard of a distended ashen-colored shanty that was home to the bantam-legged rancher and his wife, a long-board woman of precise speech, methodical movements, toil-marked hands and devout religious bent.

Both the man and woman made me welcome. Visitors were rare. Theirs was a lonely existence. From the cap of a small butte you could look over vast space without noting a single other dwelling. The couple knew the names of every family for miles around, so sparsely settled was the land.

I stayed at the homestead three days, helping the sedulous couple all I could. It wasn't much but at least I didn't feel guilty about eating. Neither of them com-

3

plained about my eager but ineffectual labors and both avouched they would be glad to have me stay on. But on the fourth day it was time for me to hit the road again. I was young and the West was brimming with faces I had not yet seen. "O.K.," the rancher grumbled. "I was thinkin' you'd stay over Sunday, but I'll take yuh in."

Unfortunately, a rancher from an even more remote homestead bumped in on a flatbed truck held together by bailing wire and declared in a nervous drawl that he badly needed help. His wife was sick and some of his stock had disappeared. Nobody in the Owyhee Hills then had a phone or a two-way radio; that part of Oregon was primitive in communication as the Willamette Valley had been a century before.

On the frontier all work halted when a neighbor was in trouble. So my friends took off with the worried man, she to nurse and he to round up stock.

"No need you comin' along," the rancher said to me. "I'll be back by nightfall to handle the chores. Might have to go back in the mornin'."

"Is there anything I can do while you're gone?" I asked. "No," he muttered, reaching for a flashlight. "I'll handle things when I git back. You know where the food is."

"Now it looks like you really don't know when you'll be going to Jordan Valley," I moaned, my disappointment visible. "Reckon not," he grumped. "What's your hurry?"

But I was in a hurry; more precisely, I was impatient. Summer had only so many days left. "In that case," I said, "I'll hike to the road."

The rancher stared at me. "It's a good piece back." He turned and I never saw the front of him again.

All afternoon I walked without seeing anything associated with the human race except faint tire scars and some barbed wire fencing that sagged wearily. Slivers of breeze swirled over the alkali and sage, twisting between rocks to nibble and slash at the lethargic earth, piranha winds scouring the glut of helpless hills. The rocky trail wambled through sickly wasteland that seemed stricken by wen and serpigo. Only a sort of desert awn, fibering and bearding the parched earth, gave any semblance of vegetation to some of the hummocks. Others were as bare as thunder eggs.

In the first few hours, grinding up and down one wrinkly, dusty, stony slope after another, without seeming to advance an inch upon a hag-butte I had fixed as a landmark, I began to despair. What idiocy had impelled me to trek back on foot? Why had I thrust myself into this egregious wilderness, stark and hostile? Perhaps somewhere, somehow, I had wandered far from the main trail. Perhaps I was stumbling into the maw of the desert. Whichever way I turned the land was alien; I would never find my way out. Facing ineluctable doom I scourged myself with harsh words for my anxiety to move on. Why had I not stayed at the homestead as the rancher had advised? The desert was miserable; you could have it. If hell was nothing and nowhere, the desert was a damn good pastiche of it. I was alone, forsaken by everyone but Apollyon, that jesting angel of the bottomless pit.

Later, under the incessant downpour of the unclouded sun, I felt as torpid as the land appeared; by late afternoon we were both comatose, I within and the land through my eyes.

Then, suddenly, where the trail twisted downhill below a brambled bank, I saw the gray branches of cottonwood trees, two of them, O Joy! Out here, I thought, the cottonwoods should be called alamos, as they are known in Mexico, where they are shelters on the desert. An arroyo squirmed from the trees until it outran my eyes but I did not follow it with my feet. I was caked by an agglutination of dust and sweat, my mouth choked with scurf, the strap of my packsack knifed my shoulders.

I plopped under the branches. Swigged from my canteen. Sponged my forehead. Dampened the back of my neck. Sat under the buzzing branches until the ache oozed out of my limbs. Sat there at home with the scrags and fardels of the desert. Rested there until my heart was again adventurous.

From that point on, refreshed, I saw the desert through different eyes. It was no longer a mask of death but a body with many faces. It was cruel, harsh, taciturn and stoic, but it could be diffusive, too, with subtle surprises. Above all it was life, mutable as life, and if its beauty was not that which fell in cliches, like apple from a windshaken tree, it lay itself open to the imagery of every poet.

Somehow the desert beyond the cottonwoods also

changed, as though to confirm my new appraisal of it or to reward me for kindness of thought. It was now filled with furtive exotic excitement, tingling in the silence of the eerie.

Leaning toward sundown the land was so still it seemed under the sea. From rises on the trail I saw on the benches and aretes of mystic hills, yellows and purples as deep in tones as coral on the ocean bed.

The phlegmatic hills, bent by the weight of the heat, wore curled sideburns of chaparral. On one hill a lone tree, forlorn as a naked sinner in a circle of hypocrites, cast a drip of shadow the color of dried blood. On another hill in the western yonder the frozen forms of three pines, enlarged by the distortion of light waves, looked like Spanish bayonets, or tall vaqueros standing in a triangle.

A haze of sagebrush budded on an indolent wave of the desert sea and pullulated on a swell beyond. Two specks circled over the swell, dropped into an oval, and moved elliptically toward a target in an owl-feathered clump of sage.

Twilight found me still some miles from the highway. My camp would have to be on the open wasteland, and I vulnerable to whatever came along. So I climbed the beveled side of a chalky hillock to its crinkly mesa and couched myself on the torrefied ground. All about, the ghostly parchment seemed devoid of movement. Yet in a moment I heard a rustle in the sage below the hill and overhead two birds raced, one pursuing the other.

Darkness brought stars, tripping daintily onto the stage of night like feather-footed ballerinas. First one, and then another, and then in torch-bearing crowds. I lay supine on my blanket, bewitched by the most pellucid and regal of heavens.

It was a gala performance. The queen sky wore her best parure; dazzling earrings, bracelet and necklace. No city dweller had ever witnessed such celestial magnificence.

Still awake, I watched the moon sway on its invisible rigging. For a moment I was startled by the wail of a coyote; later by the scream of a desert feline. The sounds were whiffled into murmurs by a rising wind—and I contemplated my surroundings.

If the desert showed rage it was only reflecting wrathful men; if it seemed uncommonly cruel it was acting in quick reprisal to pusilanimous freebooters. The desert could break on its molten wheel even the bravest and stubbornest of resolute pilgrims but it broke these slowly, or it molded them into flesh forms of the wasteland; terse and enduring. The angry and the cowardly it swiftly drove away or destroyed wholemeal.

After a while I heard bells ringing, or fancied I did, and they came perhaps from unseen sheep grazed on a range beyond a web of eroded humps. The bells rang softly from the flocculent hills: softly, slowly, lazily, hypnotically, and to this soothing tintinnabulation I sank into sleep.

Hours later I opened my eyes to see the moon, now a stale macaroon nibbled at the edges, disappear behind a purple mountain until its pale silver was drowned in the bluish mist of fetal dawn.

I kept to my blankets until the flames of morning leaped to the tops of the hills and were carried by a romping breeze over the ridges. Then I arose and larked along the mesa to warm my blood.

It was a glorious morning. What did I care if I had only a small chunk of cheese left in my packsack? The price of a soul-cleansing was worth a meal or two. It was good to be alive. I felt both serene and excited.

Yesterday, at despairing points on the trail, only a mad sort of gumption prevented me from turning back to the homestead. Now I was glad I had continued on. You don't see country from a car, even at 10 miles an hour, as you do on foot. My shoes were the worse for wear and my feet were sore but I had no regrets. Not now. The worst was over. The road could not be far away.

A cloud drifted around the corner of a butte, skimming lightly as a sailboat. The flame of sun tinged its edges and the cloud made a starboard turn toward a protective hill. The butte glared at the hill, a crone cheated of her fancies. It was time to gather my things.

All packed, I stood on the mesa for one more round of eye-quaffing. Memories from the hillock to last forever—however long forever is. To the south a patch of withering grass hung over the shoulder of a hill, like a dull green serape. South by east a hoyden wind rubbed against indifferent chaparral. Northward, mountains rose upon mountains to the end of the world. And somewhere between the beginning and the end the Owyhee River rose from cached canyons to breathe free upon the plain before plunging in dithyrambic cry down into another gorge. The last glimpse I had of it, from my private aerie, showed a blue-gray riata snarled in a chocolate-colored fissure.

So I climbed down and took up the hike again. Though the morning was cool I did not set a brisk pace. The desert had trapped me. It was iridescent, plastic, mutable. I paused for a moment to fix for the camera in my mind's eye a single scene and it was half an hour before I moved again. But eventually I brought myself along the stumbly trail to another stream—Jordan River, flashing its sunlit tail around a bend, like a ruffed grouse.

It's Jordan Creek on the maps but I still call it Jordan River. Any stream on the desert deserves the name of river, even if it's a wadi that only fills up twice a year. That's how I see it now and that's how I saw it then, when I set my pack down on the silky lanugo grass curled out of the river hem, removed my shoes and socks, and bathed my battered feet.

My legs, with pants rolled to the knees, were still in the soothing current when along the bank thudded a piebald mare. The rider and I saw each other at the same time and hollered hello simultaneously. Alongside me he dismounted with remarkable grace, considering his girth. His belly heaved out over his belt and quivered like jello as he touched the ground. Once he straightened, though, he looked more barrel-chested than fat.

His eyes, slate blue and wide, were piercing, except for his first focus, surprised and droll. You could tell right away he was wondering what you were doing here and planning his next move. His eyes reminded me of a cure-all-oil drummer I had seen a few weeks back at a county fair. He, too, was rotund and broad-shouldered, and I paid him special close heed because a pastor's wife, knotted at my elbow, called him a quacksalver, and I didn't know then what kind of critter that was.

There were, offhand, two differences between the drummer and the mare rider. The first man was whey-faced, with a thin, conniving mouth. The second was healthily tanned and his mouth ingenuous.

"Water taste pretty good," he began.

"Great," I replied.

"Always good in these parts," he probed.

It could have been an interesting game but I did not care to play it so I told him where I had been and where I was heading.

He heard me out, never shifting his eyes from mine. What concerned him most was the plight of the remote ranch family and he said he would try to get up there later that day.

"You need every friend you've got out here," he said. "You might like to live it alone but you can't make it alone."

He skewed at his horse and asked if I had had my breakfast yet. A piece of cheese, I told him. "Well," he drawled, reaching into a saddle bag, "I took these along to munch on but the missus says I'm too fat." And he handed me two hardboiled eggs and a couple of small apples. I ate them, devoured them, to the discontent of the mare, who kept nuzzling at me until the rancher pulled out a third apple and put it up to her mouth.

"You got about two miles to the road," the rancher said. "Good thing I was in no hurry today. Climb on and I'll give you a lift."

So I mounted the horse, balancing myself behind the saddle, and we bumped along until we reached the highway.

"Stay on," he directed. "I'll get you a hitch." He geed the mare to the side of the road and waved down the first vehicle. The driver was someone he knew, of course, a farmer going to town. They had to chew the fat first, not having seen each other for a few weeks. By then I had slid off the horse, who squinted at me with skeptical orbs, and waited for the outcome. By and by the rancher said to the farmer in the fender-scraped pickup: "Can you take this fellow to town, Ed? He's been up to the hills for a few days."

Ed motioned me to the pickup. As he started up he waved and the rancher, leaning over the mare's neck, hollered, "You take care of yourself, hear?"

That's the way, though I have been to Jordan Valley several times since, I remember best the desert of southeastern Oregon.

The Buckeroo

If you're looking for old cowpokes, go to Burns. That town has more venerable buckeroos than anywhere else in Oregon. Every time we go through Burns we discover another one. On our last trip we found Judd Wise, whose range days rolled back to the turn of the century, when Harney County was still a frontier.

Put a white beard on Judd Wise and he'd look like Santa Claus. He had Santa's ample belly, merry eyes, pink cheeks, round face, good nature and hearty laugh. I told him so and he chortled, "Ho, ho, ho."

Judd Wise was the son of a Warner Valley homesteader who sold out to start a store in Plush. In 1893, when Judd was three, he was put on a horse. But he had to walk to school, four miles each way, "through the snow, too," he chuckled. At 10, when he had advanced to the sixth grade, his schooling ended. He found work at the famous P-Ranch, wrangling horses. Three years later he was a full-fledged cowboy. At 20 he was a ranch foreman and at 28 was put in charge of the entire P-Ranch, one of the largest stock operations in the West. ("We ran 45,000 cattle, 10,000 sheep and 5,000 horses," Judd recalled.) In 1928, when Judd was 38, the company that owned the P-Ranch sold out and Judd was given his choice of land to buy. He purchased the Riddle Ranch, on the other side of Diamond, for $42,000. Everybody said he'd go broke, giving that much for six sections, and during the depression he almost did. "It was pretty rough goin'," he said. "Usually keep three men, I couldn't hardly board myself at that time." So in 1936 he sold the ranch for what he had paid for it and moved into Burns, from where he roamed around the country as a cattle buyer. A few years ago, Judd noted, the present owners of the Riddle Ranch turned down an offer of $500,000 for it. He shook his head when he mentioned it, maybe thinking that if he had held on to it for 30 more years he'd have

10

made the big money. But how can a man tell what lies so far ahead?

Pete French, Oregon's greatest range legend, and the founder of the P-Ranch, was gunned down by a homesteader in 1897. The vaqueros who rode with French were still on the ranch when Judd Wise started horse wrangling in 1900 and often spoke of French, relating stories and bits of information which Wise vividly remembered seven decades later.

"Oh, all them Mexicans was there, 25 of them, and there was some Basquos there, practically the whole outfit was there that worked for Pete French. Oh, they liked him. He was awful good to his help. Treated them good, took care of them, and they just thought he was God Almighty Himself. Especially them Mexicans. They were awfully loyal to him."

French imported the vaqueros with the understanding that he would file a homestead claim for each and then buy each claim for $300, Judd said. It was the way of the Western baron, range land east of the Cascades and timber west of it.

Then came trouble with the true homesteaders, who were flocking into the rimrock valley that flowed sheen grass and rippling from the tight corridor of the Narrows to where the silent Steens Mountain, in its last bulky throb, spent itself on the bunchgrass of Skull Creek, its spiny fingers groping for the scurf of Catlow Rim.

"What was the matter," Judd Wise explained, "was Pete French claimed he owned all this land they were settling on. He was makin' it pretty rough for them, trying to run 'em out of there."

The vaqueros told young Judd that the homesteaders "drawed straws to see who'd kill Peter." He described the assassination as he had heard it from the Mexicans who were there. "Pete was up along the cattle, this fellow come up and he said, 'Where's Pete French?' and they said, 'He's up there,' and he just deliberately rode up to the side of French and shot him right there, shot him in the head, and run off. That's all they was to it."

Judd remembered his wrangling years, when he had the remuda, as though they were still with him. At three in the morning he arose to get the horses, who had been turned loose in the field. Bringing them in, he said, would have been impossible without a bell mare. "You could go out in this field and just go hollerin' and that old bell mare'd take to the corral just as hard as she could run and then you'd just go round and pick up the back end of them and push 'em towards the bell mare and they all went to the corral. Well, then the boss come out and got every man his horse. You had ten horses that belonged to you, nobody else rode 'em but just you, but he'd pick out one and catch him and you'd ride him. It was up to you to ride what he told you to. He knew all those 300 horses, know'd 'em just better than he did people."

Later, when he was a buckeroo, he broke horses. His eyes gleamed as he talked about it. "Well, what we used to do, is just catch 'em and throw 'em down, and put a saddle on them, and when they got up, well, we was on 'em, and ride 'em around that way and then, maybe ride him for a week, get him to goin' good, and then turn him over to somebody else."

That little rill of a smile which pursed through his lips bulged into a grin when he reflected on being tossed by cantankerous broncs. "I've been throwed, and pawed, and bit, and kicked and run over and fell down, and I've been lucky or I wouldn't be here."

He took everything in good-humored stride, from busting broncs to his wife, whom he had married in 1914, and for whom, it was obvious, he had a very deep attachment. More than half a century of sharing the problems each dawn deposited had agglutinated them, so there was between them an unspoken concord of spirit, but each retained an individuality upon which the other did not trespass. It was, perhaps, a compensation of the lonely for having no children.

"I met her down here at the Narrows, to a dance," he recalled. "Her father owned a homestead there and she taught school. She started in when she was 18 and she taught up to the time we was married. We went together five years before we was tied. I seen her oncet every two or three months, maybe. No oftener. That's the reason we got along so good." And he laughed until the room was filled with the warm melodies of his mirth.

Life for a buckeroo around 1900 was pretty rough, Judd said, and he dipped into memory for details. He had a long dipper and the well was full.

"Well, we slept out where we was, about ten months of the year. Just had a bedroll, is all. Once in a while, in summer, you'd take your overalls and boots off, that'd be about all. I've slept with my boots on months at a time. You'd go to bed and then you'd have to get up and guard the cattle, guard the horses, you'd be so tired you'd lay down and go to sleep. A couple—three hours, they'd get you up, start you over. After a hard day's work you'd be so tired you wouldn't notice if the ground was hard. Oh, oncet in a while you'd make camp, you'd gather some sage brush and put it under your bunk and make it a little softer. Use that for feathers. Break the tops off 'em. Make a place to put your bed."

Two months of the year the buckeroos returned to the ranch, where they had wooden bunks. "We slept practically the same way, a whole lot the same way, only we took our clothes off, and usually put some hay or something under us."

Meals were at the chuckwagon, which Judd called the buckeroo wagon—"Was just a wagon with four mules, just had a big cover on the back, just had a big table you let down there to eat, mostly prunes and beef, a few potatoes, didn't know what canned stuff was, nor butter nor eggs nor nothin'.

"You was lucky to get two meals a day. You had one about four o'clock in the morning, and then you worked all day without any dinner, then you got supper sometimes, oh! sometimes four o'clock and sometimes nine o'clock. And it was seven days a week. I didn't know there was such a thing as Sunday."

Judd's first wages were 50 cents a day. He laughed when he said it and he laughed some more when he added that he sent most of his earnings to his mother.

Out of that 50 cents a day, and the dollar a day he received later, when he was a buckeroo, he had to buy his clothes. "These old blue duckin' shirts we mostly wore, we give 50 cents apiece for them, and a pair of boots cost five dollars."

The cowboys dressed simply, he said. "You just had levis, straws and boots, and that's all. The hat was usually pretty big. We didn't know what a kerchief was." And he shrugged off the wearing of guns as another piece of Western fiction.

Judd talked about the routine of cowboy life in sweeping terms, leaving particulars to other moments. "Well, you'd leave in the spring of the year, you'd take your buckeroo wagon and go clear over here in Warner Valley, and clear around down in Nevada, and clear around on the Steen Mountain, and get back the first of July. And you didn't have no fields, and no fences, and no nothin'. You'd just go out in the spring of the year and you'd brand calves and then you'd go back in July and go out to get in the beef and brand calves and then the only time we was ever at the ranch was along about the first of December, about two months in the winter."

For fiction writers, the great excitement on the range was the roundup. Judd Wise saw it as simply more hard work. "You'd just go out, 25 of us could circle a big country, just bunch 'em all up out there in the flat, some of 'em hold them up there, and the others of us'd go in and lasso 'em and drag 'em out and brand 'em."

He did not say a word about his lariat skill. Even today old-time cowpokes around Burns remember Judd Wise as being the best man with a riata they ever saw. As far back as Montana and Wyoming he was a legend among ropers.

The cattle drives, which could start as early as August or as late as November, lasted 21 days, whether the drive was to Winnemucca, in Nevada, or to Ontario, on the Snake River.

"We didn't try to make many miles on the drive," Judd said. "Just kind of herded them along where there was grass. Only time we pushed them was when we were short of water, and then you sat up with them and guarded them nights, you know."

When the drovers returned to the P-Ranch they went back to the desert, to gather the cattle left behind, and to bring them into the various ranches owned by the company. "We couldn't leave them out there," Judd explained. "Snow got deep then. They'd all starve to death. We herded them into the ranches and put 'em on feed."

Practically every cowboy movie has a stampede in it. Judd could recall only one. It happened in Vale, on a drive to Ontario.

"Well, them times they sold all the big steers, nothin' under three years old. We had two bunches o' steers, and the main boss come along and said, 'Just put 'em all together, take 'em on down,' and we just got 'em all together and the train comes along and they tored down all the fences and we was three days tryin' to gather 'em up and never did get them all. Why they just, Gee Whizz! I tell you, you had to get out of the way and stay out of the way because you'd get killed."

Sometimes, to break the monotony of the daily grind, the cowboys would play tricks on each other, mostly doing things that would get a man's horse to bucking, and it was a good joke when the rider was thrown. Once, as Judd recalled, the trick went sour. "The horse fell right on that man's head. We got a span of mules and a buckboard and loaded him in the hind end and carried him to Burns. He's still alive, I think, but he's kinda crazy, always, after that."

Judd Wise remembered the cowboys of his youth as a special breed. "All of them were good fellows. Kind of a rough class of people, I'll tell you that. They was just plenty rough. But they'd never get drunk or fight on the ranch. They could ride anybody's horse, and they never growled, even when they come in and was give out they was always in good humor. It was a pretty rough time. I know that people wouldn't do those things that we done in them days. Oh, the cuts that they sew up now, the boys would just tie a rag over it and go on."

For all the camaraderie of the range, the cowboys led a lonesome life, Judd remarked. "You'd average goin' to town maybe once, twice, every two-three years. We come to town most of the time to get drunk."

It is no big feat today to drive from Burns to Frenchglen, where the P-Ranch was headquartered, in an hour. It took the buckeroos, using horse and buggy, three days. The first night was spent at the Narrows and the second at a homestead between the Narrows and Burns. There was little to Burns then: "A few houses up there on the hill and then an old blacksmith's shop and a couple of old saloons and that was about the size of it."

If he had his life to live again, Judd Wise observed, he wouldn't change his buckeroo days. He could look back and see where he had a lot of fun out of it. And the times were happier than the present. "Everybody was like one family, today they ain't," he declared, looking wistful.

"If you went to anybody's house you went right in, and if they wasn't there you went and got something to eat, and put your horse in the barn, and stayed all night, but today they don't do that."

Judd Wise saw his first automobile, a Model T Ford, when he was three or four years past voting age. "I didn't know there was such a thing," he said, putting his hand to his forehead.

He could look up now and see jet planes, and television brought him pictures of men walking on the moon. Such a far cry from his early cowpoke days, when the sky was unassailable and only the very sophisticated in Burns had heard rumors of a machine that moved without being pulled by horses or mules.

Judd laughed and slapped his knees. "You just think you're living in a different world, that's all. There's just that much difference."

The juices of life still surged strong in Judd Wise. He was not yet ready for the final rockingchair. He had just finished two months of work in the hayfields and was looking forward to helping a friend fix a house. It wasn't the money, he noted. To live is to function and Judd Wise, at the door of 80, was too alive to quit functioning. So he had rebelled at retirement and gone off to run a haybuck in the fields he had thundered over on a swift stallion 60 years ago.

"Oh," and his shoulders quivered restlessly, "I just get tired settin' around, you know, and nothin' to do, and I just look at the television and read the paper and when you've worked all your life you feel like you want to do somethin'!"

"I wonder why I like it"

Twenty-two miles west of Vale we turned north off US 20, crossed the Malheur River, and less than two minutes later were parked smack in the center of Harper.

There must be at least a hundred colorful settlements within a few miles of national or state roads in Oregon. Almost everyone rockets past the turnoffs, hell-bent for the famous places, but being a natural born bum, I follow the gypsy trails to the other side of the hill. If I had my choice of where to spend a day I'd take Arock over Salem, Lookingglass over Eugene, Broadbent over Albany, Elk City over Coos Bay and Harper over Portland.

You might remark that there isn't anything to do at these shriveled map points, but my idea of a satisfactory doing is to enjoy the scenery, turn my mind back to when the land was new, galumph down the dirt cuts that wiggle away into the woods and desert until they run out of incentive, sing at the top of my lungs without people staring at me, and palaver with the folks who have a little kindling time to spare.

So here we were in Harper: no billboards, parking meters, sidewalks, traffic lights, factories or pollution. The town squatted on one side of the road, drawn up like a last line of retreat. We counted a store, garage, tavern and post office. There were also three churches in town, each of which drew parishioners from the gullied hills of the deep hinterland.

Harper was just a couple of ranches when the railroad came through in 1912. Right away it boomed. Within a year there were three stores, a barber shop and two hotels. When the railroad eliminated Harper as a stop, the town started downhill. (Anyway, completion of US 20 would have whittled Harper to its present size.) The depot stood empty, gathering dust and cobwebs, until someone had the bright idea that it could be converted into a church building. So it was moved a couple of blocks and was now the property of the Church of Christ.

It seems that every hamlet, even if its population is limited to playing solitaire, claims some tremendous distinction. Harper was no exception. The storekeeper boasted that Don Gregg, who operated an apiary close by, was, and I quote exactly, "the biggest beekeeper in the whole world." Gregg wasn't in so I never did learn whether he was the foremost beekeeper of the planet or just Malheur County.

Having reached Harper we decided to push on to Westfall, 12 more miles off the highway. It was an easy drive, but lonely and strange. In the first few minutes we passed several ranch houses but after that we saw no dwelling until we came to Westfall and, as it turned out, we scanned none there.

We paused five or six times, to photograph spectacular rock formations, which appeared from afar as broken battlements, and to imagine prairie schooners tossing on a choppy sea of sagebrush. Across this thorny, bone-dry wasteland the ill-fated emigrants of Meek's Cutoff Party strained and gasped in 1845.

Spring brings wildflowers, popping out of the ground like prairie dogs, bobbing their heads and sniffing at the feet of the sun-painted rocks. That's the best time to see this country, when the desert is transformed into a great ballroom of lavishly-hued flora dancing with verve and merriment to the cotillion strains of the lively zephyrs. But even in summer and early fall, any day is good to visit Westfall.

For all practical purposes there was only one building in Westfall: the post office, which Rachel Looney kept open from 9:45 A.M. to 11:45 A.M. Her home was outside the town limits, making Westfall the only post office in Oregon, and perhaps all 50 states, that didn't have a single resident.

There was little for Mrs. Looney to do. The mail came in, she put it up in 24 boxes, completed the rest of her chores, and read a newspaper until closing time. The only people to come into the tiny post office were ranchers, some of whom drove many miles to pick up their mail.

Mrs. Looney was at first reticent to talk to me. She had good grounds for suspicion: somebody coming all the way from Harper to see Westfall when there was hardly any Westfall left. But eventually, through the diplomacy of my wife, the tension eased and Mrs. Looney chatted about herself and the town.

She was two years old when she arrived here, in 1902. The town was going strong then, the small valley below the wind-scoured hills filled with homesteaders who did their shopping in Westfall. As she grew into girlhood the town matured and expanded, and she described it in its heyday.

"There were 100 schoolchildren at one time. Now there are none. There was two general stores, a blacksmith shop, a telephone system, two hotels, three saloons, a bank, a confectionery, a church, a dance hall—yes, and we had a barber shop at one time.

"It was a busy town, lots of activity. It had to be: this was a freight stage stop on the road from Vale to Burns. And we had dwelling houses all up and down—40 of them."

The best-known house was built about a mile from the post office by Mose Hart in the 1890s. It was a large two-story building and was the residential showplace of the valley. Mose might have been a little disappointed in the care it was receiving: it didn't have a complete window pane or foot of wallpaper that wasn't peeling off or inch of porch that wasn't rotting. But even in its hollow and banshee-ridden eeriness it made a formidable impression upon us.

"Pacific Livestock Company from California was here," Mrs. Looney continued, speaking soft and slow. "They ran a lot of cattle. And bands of sheep. Then they barred sheep. Pacific Livestock sold out to the ranchers. And the homesteaders couldn't make it and sold their places to bigger outfits."

The final blow came when the railroad bypassed Westfall and laid tracks through Harper. "After that," said Mrs. Looney, her voice not changing tone, "Westfall was a goner."

Where there had once been homes and barns and corrals and sheds there was now only open field upon which stock nibbled and munched. "Even the town is grazing land," Mrs. Looney said. "There just isn't much here." And her voice now sounded tired.

Rachel Looney had been postmaster since 1946. Years

ago it was a full-time job. But as the number of boxes declined, so did post office hours, and now it was down to two a day.

Until 1964 Mrs. Looney and her husband, Primrose, also operated the general store, in the same creaky frame building. For 75 years, under one owner or another, the store had served the families of sheepmen, cattlemen, farmers and people who worked in town. It was longest known as the Jones and Company store and Mrs. Looney remembered when it had five clerks. The post office was part of the former store in which Primrose and Rachel Looney ran their mercantile business.

With its pot-bellied stove and 19th century air, the store was a museum piece. Few of the old trade articles were still around but, together with the early fixtures, there was enough to warm our fancy, and with Mrs. Looney reminiscing about what was sold when she was a girl and how the customers dressed, we were drawn decades back in time.

After the Looneys closed their store they moved from their quarters in the rear of the building to a house beyond the edge of town. "We were the last ones in Westfall and when we moved we took the total population with us," Mrs. Looney said with a slight smile.

Some days she could walk out to the groaning porch of the building and stand there for an hour or more, if she chose, without seeing hide nor hair of another human. Few people came by. Some of the ranchers dropped in for their mail only once or twice a week. But Mrs. Looney did not feel isolated.

"Between the post office and home I'm too busy to get lonely," she asserted. "There's everything to do at home. Now we have cows and chickens and a yard and a garden and sewing and cooking and making butter."

She had no plans for leaving. "I like it here," she said firmly. "It's just home to me—because I've lived here so long.

"Sometimes," she added pensively, "I wonder why I like it. It's so hot and dry and dusty. But it's home."

We drove back to Harper, the road to ourselves. Our original intention was to keep on going until we found a restaurant, but after Westfall Harper looked mighty big, so we hied ourselves to the tavern and ordered sandwiches and soda pop.

Spending our money in Harper was the least we could do to keep it from becoming another Westfall.

Sodbusters and Bill Brown

There are still Oregon maps around which show the town of Stauffer. One of these is a relief, made by a Denver company in 1957. Somebody should have told them that Stauffer faded out of existence more than a third of a century before the map was made. One of those who knows for sure is Roy Stauffer, a Union rancher. The locals wanted to call the hamlet Lost Creek but the U.S. Post Office, for reasons of its own, chose to name it after the first postmaster, J. C. Stauffer, Roy's father.

J. C. came out from Nebraska in 1910 and took claim on a homestead in the Lost Creek Valley, south of Glass Buttes. The next year, when Roy was 10, the rest of the family followed.

From 1911 to 1914 about 40 families moved into Lost Creek Valley. (The post office was established in September, 1913.) By 1916 only three or four families were left. The Stauffers pulled stakes in 1918, retreating to Bend, where J. C. found work in a sawmill.

In 1921 Roy quit home for the woods around Klamath Falls, where he logged until the depression of the 1930s. After that he knocked around the state, spending some years in Eugene as a home builder. Since 1954 he had been operating a farm about a mile out of Union, living with his wife and daughter, now a teenager, on land which was willed to Frieda Brown Stauffer by her folks, who settled here in 1901.

Settled back, in a rumpled, relaxed mood, Roy Stauffer talked about his homestead days on the high desert and some of the colorful folks he knew then, particularly the legendary Bill Brown.

"Well," Roy began, in a drawl as comfortable to him as an old shoe and with a burry twang of sagebrush flavor, "we came to Oregon in 1911, and in March, we landed about March the tenth at Madras, Oregon. That was as far as the railroad run at that time. We shipped a carload of horses and wagons and we put our gear together,

22

covered our wagons, and started out for the high desert, which was about an eight day trip. I suppose you could drive it in three hours now without pushing on the gas.

"There was four families that came from Nebraska at the same time and we all put the covers on our wagons and started out in a caravan. We camped the first night at Metolius and the second day we reached Bend; we camped there for two or three days in the bend of the river where the Pilot Butte now stands. And then we went on to the high desert. We arrived some four or five days later at our homestead and our closest neighbor at that time was a man by the name of Smith and he lived four miles from us, and the next closest was my uncle, Horace Brookings, they lived 20 miles. We cleared the sagebrush the first year, about 160 acres, and we plowed and seeded that to rye and that fall we had a fairly good crop and my Dad brought a thrash machine clear out from Bend to thrash our rye.

"Now, I think I'm getting ahead of myself," Roy said, remembering something. "I'd better backtrack to when we got to the homestead.

"We put up three tents and then we went, my Dad and I, to Maury Mountain to get lumber. I was then 10 years old and I drove one team and my Dad drove another team; he had four horses and I had two. We were about a day and a half getting to Maury Mountain and I think probably about two days coming home. My Dad had a runaway coming down the mountain and I didn't expect that he'd come out of it alive but he somehow managed to reach the bottom and still be on the wagon. I had a big team and they never let the wagon get started going down there. We had brake sticks which was pretty hard to hold; you had to hold it with a rope over your shoulder and that was quite a job with a load of lumber on. When we got home we started immediately to build our house. It was two stories, 24 by 12, and the boards run up and down. Then on the inside we tacked paper on, and we had a stove right in the middle of the building which we cooked on and used for heat. We all slept upstairs. Then my Dad built on another wing on the house and had the post office in there. My Dad also was a notary public and he notarized perhaps nearly all of the homesteaders that proved up on their claims.

"Well," continued Roy, catching up to where he had left off, "the harvest. I imagine we probably had about a ton to a ton and a half an acre of rye, that's all we raised was rye. Rye was supposed to grow in a drier climate. We had a lot of rain in the spring of 1911, a lot of rain and a good crop, and in the spring of 1912 we also had a good crop, but the rabbits was the pest and they practically ate our field up, they were by the thousands in there. Other counties had rabbit drives, and Lake County did, a place or two. They'd kill four or five thousand rabbits in a drive but they were so numerous that it didn't seem to affect the amount of rabbits to any extent.

"Yeah, the first and second year was pretty good, and then the third year there come a dry cycle and we planted our rye and it was so dry in the spring the wind blew and it blew the rye out. Then we reseeded it again, but we had very little luck in getting the crop and the weather was too dry. And it seemed like we went into a dry cycle then for about four or five years, and practically all of the families left. We started a school, all the homesteaders got together and built it, in 1913, and in a couple of years there was hardly no kids around to go there.

"I tell you," Roy went on, a bite of ire cutting into the nostalgia, "the government made a complete mistake by allowing the homesteaders to go in and plow up the bunch grass, which was the best single feed for stock I've ever seen. Range cattle could be turned out poor and skinny and within two weeks a person wouldn't know them for the change because of the bunch grass.

"Most of the people in Lost Creek Valley, they gave up farming when they left. They started in jobs again—a lot of them went to California and some to Portland and some Seattle. I don't know whether it was the government or the promoters, had big ads in the papers about all this land that would grow anything, and of course people thought they were getting a farm for nothing, when actually all they were getting was a lot of trouble. I think it was a complete mistake for the government to have allowed that to have happened, but then these promoters —why, anything to get a little money. The people who located these settlers on the land used to drive them out there, some of them had a little old car then, or a team and buggy—I think the first ones had a team and buggy

—and they'd probably be three or four days and they charged about $300 to locate a family on; well, three hundred and twenty was a homestead, and then you had your right of the desert claim of a hundred and sixty acres. Most of the homesteaders had three-twenty; my Dad, he took a desert claim also and had another hundred and sixty acres.

"Most of the homesteaders didn't have much money. They built little shacks, most of them not bigger than 12 by 14. That was the average home. We had eight head of horses, so we done a lot of trading for most of the settlers. Those that came in without stock, they intended to stay there; I think you had to stay seven months out of twelve, and so they'd come in the winter and leave in the summer, or vice versa; whatever work they were doing outside, why, they'd go back and work and then they'd come and stay the seven months. I think perhaps some of them didn't stay that long but nobody objected to them proving up on the land.

"When the settlers left, they mostly just let the land go back, there was no sale for it. When my Dad finally left he sold out to a fellow by the name of Forbes for a thousand dollars. I think he sold the horses, which we had about 75 head, he sold the horses and the land both for one thousand dollars."

Roy didn't think there was anything left now to Stauffer. He had been back some years before and had a hard time finding any of the shacks. The government had the land now and leased it to cattlemen and Roy figured that maybe the cattlemen had torn down the majority of the shacks and concentrated the lumber at a headquarters post.

On a warm May day in 1912 all the families living in Lost Creek Valley got together on Glass Buttes for a day that is still clear in Roy Stauffer's mind.

"There was a spring halfway up the butte, and we all went to the top, and the men carried a big, long pole, and we all signed a piece of paper and put it in a tobacco can, and we all agreed to come back there again in 20 years but I haven't heard that anyone ever came back. It would have been interesting if we had a-put it in a glass jar so that it wouldn't deteriorate and had gone back and witnessed the names that was on there and tried to find out where the people were that signed that slip of paper."

But Roy really wasn't as interested in reminiscing about the homestead days as he was in telling of Bill Brown, for whom he worked at one time.

William Walter Brown—none of the old timers knew him by that name—was educated at San Jose Normal School, in California, and at Willamette University, in Salem. He taught school for a while, until he had saved enough money to head out for Eastern Oregon and the stock raising business. Overcoming adversities that would have broken the hearts of weaker and more conventional men, he gradually amassed holdings that covered almost 40,000 acres in four counties and more stock than anyone in the state. He died penniless, leaving a memory that has proliferated into a hundred anecdotes. There are few people living today who knew him in his prime, when he acquired the reputation of being an eccentric. One of these is Roy Stauffer.

"Well, Bill Brown and his brother came to the high desert in about 1880 with a band of sheep, four or five hundred, to Buck Creek. They didn't own any land but they ranged their sheep wherever the grass was green. They finally split 'em up and had two or three bands and then in 1889 they had what was called a double winter. They had a hard winter early in the season, it probably started in October or November, and then along about February they got a Chinook wind that took nearly all of the snow off, and then came another big snow and the stock was weak from the early winter, so a lot of them didn't survive. When spring came at last Bill Brown and his brother lost all but 500 of their 10,000 sheep and then the brother left and Bill Brown stayed with it and he herded the sheep himself.

"There was a story that Bill Brown had only one sock during those hard times and he wore it on one foot one day and the other foot the next day.

"Well, Bill Brown stayed with sheep and expanded and filed a lot of claims and bought Buck Creek and the Gap Ranch and other places, filed on most of the water rights on the springs, so that he'd have water for his stock. He got more sheep and he got herders and then he bought a bunch o' horses; I'm not familiar with whether he bought them from somebody who was running them there or whether he brought them in. And he hired buckeroos.

They'd start riding in the spring and ride until September, building corrals to round the horses up in. He had more horses at one time—maybe 25,000 head running there—than any other individual west of the Rockies. In 1916 or 17 they rounded up 10,000 head of horses at Benjamin Lake, which was about 10 miles from our homestead, and the Army personnel came out there and picked out the horses they wanted, and they bought a thousand head at 95 dollars a head.

"Well, Bill then, he bought some new stallions and he put them in with his horses, and he had a pretty good bunch, his brand was a horseshoe bar on the jaw, and he also expanded his sheep operation. He gained his reputation as a horse owner but he actually had more sheep.

"Bill had about 25 men to ride for him during the summer and every morning it'd be just like being in the rodeo. The foreman would say: 'Which one you want to set today?' The guy would point him a horse and the foreman would lasso him and bring him out. Guys would be bucked off and nobody would think anything of it.

"The horses ranged back as far as 35 miles for water. They'd always go to water at sunup, at break of day. You'd see big dust clouds, there'd be trails eight to 12 inches deep. The horses would trot, single file, the stallion bringing up the back, seeing that they stayed in line, just an easy trot. They'd wade out into the water and drink a little at a time—drink a few swallows, lift their heads, take a few more swallows. It'd take an hour for them to tank up. The buckeroos would like to catch them there because they were so full of water they couldn't run. When they'd run, they'd throw the water up—just puke it up. After they left the water they'd take all day to get back to the range. They'd stay two days; on the third day they'd go back to water again.

"I was a horse wrangler for Bill. There's no one sport in the world as exciting as rounding up wild horses. If you're raised in that country you feel a certain attachment to the wild horses. When you've got a good saddle horse and you take off after a wild horse, I tell you, it's fun, it's a chase. There's something about a man on horseback that makes that horse feel superior and when you have a saddle on a horse he can really fly and he'll run the wild horse down.

"Well, at the end of the war, or just before the war was over, two fellas came out to buy Bill Brown out and his headquarters was at Buck Creek, and they tried for several days to get in contact with him, but Bill didn't want to sell and so he evaded them and he stayed away from home until they had gone. He didn't want to sell, and still he didn't want to face them with the prospect that he might sell. So he kept on, and in the early 1920s, when we had a recession, why the horses, when the automobile came in, the horses dropped almost to nothing, five or 10 dollars a head, and sheep dropped way down, and he borrowed quite a lot of money, so he finally went broke.

"He had given money to some kind of church group that had a retired people's home down in the valley, and he finally ended up there, broke. He came back to the desert a couple of times, riding the bus, imagining he could get started again. He must have been in his seventies then. But he never got going." (Brown died in the Methodist Old People's Home at Salem in 1941, at the age of 85.)

"I can remember Bill Brown like he was sitting in front of me all the time," Roy Stauffer continued. "He was about six feet tall and weighed probably 200 pounds. He never drank or smoked. He never swore or used profane language of any kind. If he got mad at one of his hands he'd just write him out a check and say, 'You're fired.' His strongest statement, best as I can remember it, was 'Mortally certain you shouldn't do that.'

"There was a lot of legends about the way he wrote checks. He wrote them on anything and they were always honored. Sometimes when the herders would quit out on the high desert, a long way from home, Bill would just tear a wrapper off a tomato can or a corn can or something, even a piece of board, and write an order to the bank to pay the sheep herder off, and the bank would O.K. it.

"Brown was real active. He was always out in the field lookin' after his sheep and horses. He worked harder than probably any man he had workin' for him. In lambin' time, why, he'd be out night and day with the lambs. After that bad winter of '89 he herded the sheep alone, and looked after 'em, and he moved his camp all by himself; he didn't even have a camp tender till he got on his feet again. He was a very hardy man; I can't remember him ever bein' sick and doubt if he ever was. Everybody got along pretty good with him and everybody had a lot of stories to tell about him.

"One story was that he carried strychnine and raisins, strychnine to kill the coyotes and raisins to eat for lunch, in his shirt pockets. Everybody ate raisins, that was their fruit. Once he got the strychnine and raisins mixed up in the same pocket. He just took the raisins out and blowed the strychnine off from them, and ate 'em, but I suppose that's just a story that went around.

"Bill Brown started a store on Buck Creek. Jimmy McEwan, a little Scotsman, worked for Brown and the two would fight and have spats and McEwan would quit and then he'd come back and it went on like that for years. Jimmy lived about four miles from us—right down close to Lost Creek. So we knew him. One day he went down to Buck Creek to get some flour and ham and bacon and Brown wouldn't let him have them so Jimmy McEwan smuggled them out and put them in his buggy. Bill seen them and put the goods back in his store. Jimmy went back and snuck them out again and took off.

"Bill once gave my Dad 25 sheep. He said: 'Well, I guess you need a livelihood and, anyway, we're eating up your grass.'

"Once he told my Dad he hadn't gotten out of life what he thought he should. I guess he wanted a wife and kids.

"Maybe he was thinking of Mickey Hutton. He fell deeply in love with her. I don't think that story's been told. Bill Brown came to our house once and stayed about three hours and was telling my Dad all about his love affair. He said that when he was out herding the sheep he could see her flying above them, like an angel. He thought that it was quite a tragedy that his love affair had to end bad.

"Mickey Hutton was at least 20 years younger than Bill. She was the daughter of Samuel Hutton, an early pioneer on the east side of Wagontire Mountain. There was some fairly good springs then and a fair amount of families.

"After Mickey jilted Bill she married a fellow by the

name of Foster. She was a mail carrier long before she married. She carried mail from Silver Creek to Wagontire and then she went clear to the post office at Butte, about 20 miles south of Stauffer. That post office was run by Mr. and Mrs. Joe E. Pope.

"She carried the mail in a buckboard or sled, or cutter, when the snow was deep. She would leave Silver Creek early in the morning and she'd go through Wagontire and deliver mail to all the people along the route and bring the mail to Butte. Then she'd start back and stay at her brother, Link Hutton's house, overnight, and the next day go back to her house at Silver Creek. She made the route once a week.

"Bill was mighty stuck on Mickey Hutton. He had quite a crush on her. One day, when he came to see her, he had a nice suit, which he bought in Burns, over his old clothes. But his work pants showed. He had one suspender over the new suit and one over the old clothes.

"He had a diamond brooch made in the shape of his brand and he went to Mickey and tied it around her neck and said, 'Anything that wears the horseshoe bar brand belongs to me.' She took it off and threw it on the ground. Tom Hutton, her brother, told me this story. I worked for Tom.

"You know, it's a kind of funny thing about Bill Brown. He was a mighty independent man and didn't like anybody to put a halter on him. He could appreciate wild horses wanting to be free. And here he's treating Mickey Hutton, who was as independent in spirit as he was, just like a stock animal: 'Anything that wears the horseshoe bar brand belongs to me.'

"I s'pect," said Roy Stauffer, standing up as Frieda called us to supper, "Bill just didn't know better. Maybe that was the biggest tragedy in his life—being too close to sheep to know how to deal with a woman."

A serving paleface

The Indian Festival of Arts was headquartered in the lobby of the Sacajawea Hotel in La Grande. That seemed logical, Sacajawea being a Shoshone. However, while the hostelry had been defunct for almost a decade, the Festival of Arts had just completed its most successful year, and Gladys Bibee Price, a white woman, was looking ahead to an even brighter future.

I can see already that I have displeased the sweet and gentle Mrs. Price, who repeatedly asked to be kept out of the story. "Just write about the Indian people and the Festival," she urged. But there weren't any Indians around, and Mrs. Price, the executive director of the association, knew as much about the festival as anyone.

It is a mistake, she italicized, for whites to be given credit for Indian efforts. "The white people have been thinking and doing things for the Indians long enough and while there are white people involved in the Indian Festival of Arts we are very careful to take a back seat. We hope that the Indian people will more and more assert themselves and decide things for themselves and for this reason the board of directors is composed of, quote, a majority plus two Indians, so that the Indian people make all major decisions and set all policy. The white people are there only to be of assistance and this is especially true in my case. I run interference for the Indian people and do the bragging about them—really a public relations thing."

Still, agreeing as I do, this gives Mrs. Price a uniqueness, for most whites, no matter how loudly they sing the praises of the Indians, do not essentially believe the Indians possess the capabilities to organize their own ventures and to speak articulately for themselves. This kind of paternalism has a chauvinism of its own, no matter how lavishly disguised by philanthropic postures. So I was anxious to learn something about Gladys Price before she inundated me with Festival information.

31

In 1910, when she was two, her family moved from Laramie, Wyoming, her birthplace, to the Flathead Reservation of Montana, where her father took up a homestead. "Montana schools are for the most part integrated and I was never in a class of any kind or in any year that didn't have Indians. I learned to admire them and to realize they were like anybody else."

And that, despite my best efforts, was all she would disclose about the first half-century of her life.

She and her husband, a school administrator, moved to La Grande in 1958. The next year, as part of the Oregon Centennial, the National Indian Encampment was held in Pendleton. Gladys Price wrote and compiled a booklet for the Encampment, titled *Nun-Mip-Ni-Sheek,* Nez Perce for "We Remember." It is a beautiful collection of photography, old and new, and legend and history in poetry and prose. Most such "commemoratives" are not worth more than a cursory glance spent during an idle moment. This one was a keepsake.

Back in La Grande, *Nun-Mip-Ni-Sheek* stirred some latent interest in Indians and several persons, including the president of Eastern Oregon College and a prominent clergyman, "started talking about it being a shame that Indians were not recognized as individuals for what they had accomplished." It seems, Mrs. Price told us, that when Indians are introduced at public gatherings they are generally summoned as members of collectives—tribes or other groups—but not as individuals. "That's wrong and we wondered what we could do to correct it."

Discussions soon involved Indian men and women in the Pacific Northwest and in June of 1960 the first Indian Festival of Arts was held, at the Sacajawea Hotel. Since then, the annual four-day festival had been staged in La Grande each June, with later festivals sited at the high school, the football field being used for a tepee village.

If there hadn't been overflowing audiences, at least a beginning had been made in dignifying Indian culture. "The Festival was created for the purpose of giving the American Indian people the opportunity for showing their talents in the whole rainbow of arts. That's why it got started in the first place. Our premise is that talent, intelligence and integrity are not measured by pigment of skin."

Any Indian of any tribe on the North American continent was eligible to participate—which meant about 200 tribes. More than 150 tribes had been represented by at least one individual each. Mrs. Price spoke with lyrical enthusiasm of the visit by Princess Wild Cranberry. "A real hereditary princess of the Wampanoag tribe of Massachusetts—the farthest any Indian has come. She explained her tribal customs and history and was a very good speaker. I like her very much."

The festival, said Gladys Price, beating on air with a tightened fist to express her intentness, "is so different, so very, so wonderfully different. We encompass the traditional arts and culture of the American Indian people and give awards in all of these arts and then, in addition, we give awards in the contemporary capabilities and talents. This makes the Indian Festival of Arts very unique in Indian gatherings all over the United States."

But soon she was back to carrying on about the project being the work of the Indians, of many Indians, from many areas. "Twenty tribes are represented on the board of directors. The Indians control the board. This we would like to emphasize."

The president was Benjamin Pease, Jr., a Crow with an M.A. in Education, and Director of the Job Corps Center at Moses Lake, Wash. The treasurer was William Minthorn, a Cayuse, who lived in Pendleton. He was a retired civil engineer. As treasurer he wrote the checks and kept the accounts. The bylaws of the organization stated that the job of executive director should be salaried but there wasn't enough money in the treasury for Mr. Minthorn to pay the executive director, so Mrs. Price still remained in the "volunteer" status. "We're operating on a shoestring," she sighed.

We asked what had been her greatest satisfaction in working with the festival. She bubbled in laughter. "Satisfaction? Frustration!

"Actually," she said, "it was more or less a hobby, or something. You know, once in a while someone has a terrific urge, something that you just have to do, whether you have time to do it or not, and this has been the case here. It was satisfying in the beginning because it was something that I'd probably been getting ready for all my life, so my association with the Indians, and this type of thing, prepared me. But we've had setbacks, difficulties along the way. However, we've had a feasibility survey and we've been told that if properly developed the potential is unlimited."

The dreams of the dedicated included an area, outside the city of La Grande, which would have on it a museum, art gallery, theater-in-the-round, Indian-theme restaurant, a convention-type motel, and a broad grassy spread for a tepee village.

It seemed to us the dreams might be some time in coming. The first festival brought gate receipts of less than $2000. Nine years later this modest figure had been barely doubled. But Mrs. Price was not at all discouraged. "We've made such a lot of progress!" she exclaimed. "We really have." And she laughed. "I've got a wildcat by the tail; I've got to hang on. You know, we're just about to make it, so here I am."

After I had put my notebook away, Gladys Price appeared disturbed. She was looking inside herself and feeling, I could sense, that she had given us the wrong impression. She was obviously not happy with the tenor of the interview and wanted to rectify matters. Over a cup of coffee she pleaded: "Write about the Festival and the Indians. Please! It's the Indians who are important. It's their Festival. They're the really important people. Don't say what the whites are doing for them. Tell the true story of what they accomplished and can accomplish."

Well, Gladys, I have been writing sympathetically about the American Indian for 30 years, so I feel that my credentials are pretty good. Don't be upset if I devoted some lines to you. You're something special, too.

Homesteader ghost

At Ruggs, which is made up of a grain elevator and a small store, we turned south, onto Oregon 207, and drove nine miles over a whorled plateau, largely vacant, to Hardman. Along the way we did not meet a single car.

There had been one business open in Hardman the last time we were there: a grocery-post office-gas pump complex. The building still stood but on it there was nailed a sign: CLOSED.

Main street, the state road, was lined by a seedy litter of parched wooden structures. My first image: a neglected cemetery of plots with sagging grave markers. Not a soul lived in any of these buildings.

We tramped through high grass east of the pavement to inspect abandoned dwellings, a store, and a barn. What appeared to be the skeleton of a windmill had been toppled; its beak pressed down on the peeling roof of a wind-scoured house. If you exclude the swishing of a cow tail behind a wire fence across the highway there was not a breath of life where the heart of a town once beat strongly.

The only evidence that people lived hereabouts was the row of mail boxes outside the building that had been the store and post office. We had retraced our steps there when a pickup truck pulled in and a man climbed out. His name was Harold Stevens, he told us, and he had lived all his life, since his birth in 1912, on farms near Hardman.

At one time, about 50 years back, he said, there was a family on every 160 acres. And there were men up in the hills, cutting trees down for cordwood that warmed the homes of Hardman and the farmers who shopped in town.

"The small farmers sold out and they became big farms and the people moved away, that's all," Harold Stevens explained simply. "The land wasn't meant for small farms." He pushed back his hat, squinted at the frozen waves of

35

the plateau rolling in on Hardman, and added: "The woodchoppers left, too."

Stevens strolled with us around town, chatting about the Hardman he had known in his youth.

"There used to be two hotels; I don't know whether they was actually named or just known by the people who run it. There were two groceries, there used to be a hardware store, a drug store and a Pastime. There was a flour mill, settin' right over there. And there's an old lodge hall. The freight—the wagon freight, teams—used to go through here, to Monument and that country. And there used to be two schools, a grade and a high. I imagine there was 50 kids going to school when I started. I guess there's just one family with kids here now. Altogether, maybe seven families around, old timers who retired and folks who work someplace else."

Stevens wiped his brow. He had seen a lot of summers and sweated through every one. "The store and post office went out in the fall of '68 and there's no business here at all." He pulled out his mail, tossed it into the cab of his pickup, and opened the door. "You hate to see any place go," he remarked wistfully. "It's quiet now; no place to meet your friends in like the store. I just come into town to pick up my mail."

Across the pasture where the cow was swishing her tail we took a second look at a solidly built house. It seemed to be occupied so we found a rocky street that led around to it and went calling on the brothers Bechdolt, Adrain— correct spelling—and Archie. Their parents had homesteaded at the fringe of Hardman in 1899. Archie was born in 1901 and Adrain in 1906. They were burly men, dressed in overalls, and looking like they really belonged in the house, which must have been at least 60 years old and had a turn-of-the-century atmosphere.

The Bechdolts had sold their ranch in October, 1968— 5,760 acres, cattle and wheat; 1,000 in farmland and the remainder pasture. For almost 70 years they had been farmers. Why had they quit? They answered gruffly: "Too damn old and no descendants."

They thought they'd stay on in Hardman until their bloodrills ran dry. "The only reason we would think of moving away is that in the winter time the road gets bad and when you get old it becomes a concern," Adrain said.

"It's kind of isolated and there's nothing to do for old people, but it's nice," Archie added.

Adrain tacked on another comment: "Outside of the cold winters I don't know any other place I'd want to live in."

That's the way it went with the brothers talking. They had lived so long together their minds had orchestrated. The two tongues spoke with one voice.

For a few moments they palavered about Hardman. Adrain said: "Between fires and houses torn down for lumber, there isn't much of the town survived."

"There's too many families left to make Hardman a real ghost town and not enough to give it life," grunted Archie, with a hoarse chuckle.

"The town had everything but a newspaper and a bank," Adrain declared.

"Had a doctor here until the first World War," Archie added with a prideful snort.

My daughter asked if she could go through any of the old houses, to see what interesting things she could find.

"Oh," said Adrain, "they've been picked over clean."

"And robbed," emphasized Archie. "A lot of the houses are still owned by the families that used to live in them. They used the houses as storage. And they got robbed."

Adrain nodded to the truth of his brother's statement. "A house we had was broken into and robbed twice."

Archie immediately carried on. "The family portraits were taken off the walls, old albums were hauled away. What the robbers didn't take, they wrecked. They took things that had no value to them, to anybody but us, like my mother's picture, and they destroyed what they didn't take. Useless destruction."

"No reason to it," Adrain added bitterly.

The brothers declined to be photographed. "We're run down just like the town is," explained Adrain, with a wave of his big hand. "Run down, played out and all the pretty bones dried up." And Archie roared in laughter that shook the room.

Somehow, for all its robustness, the laughter sounded ghostly.

To break a horse

Hampton Station, half-way between Bend and Burns, is probably the only cafe in the United States that publishes a newspaper. At least I have a copy: Volume 1—Number 1. The masthead states it is "published occasionally" and its front page, which shows an ox-drawn covered wagon, bears the red-printed slogan, "In the Heart of the High Desert."

Well, Hampton, the biggest settlement in the 129 miles between Bend and Hines, even though it's too small to be listed in the Index of the Oregon highway department map, is on the high desert, and that's for sure. Sage and wasteland wash to the shoulders of the highway, a strip of island in a sea that is strange and hostile to people who do not know the desert.

At one time, say about 60 years ago, homesteader settlements were scattered all around Hampton, including a few back of Glass Buttes, where the Indians went for obsidian, which made good arrow heads. Glass Buttes is 11 miles east of Hampton and is in Lake County, but on a direct line Lake County is only five miles south of Hampton. If you wanted to get into Crook County, you'd only have to walk a couple of miles north.

Anyway, all those homesteader hamlets back of Glass Buttes and most of the sodbreaker villages that were within practical wagoning distance of Hampton are gone. Some are so completely gone that even people who lived in these towns as children have a hard time locating where they stood.

Few of the tourists who pause at Hampton to gas up or grab a bite pay more than casual attention to Hampton Butte, a group of dissected hills northwest of the station. It is some sort of oddity that part of the hills are in Crook County and the peak, at 6,365 feet, is in Deschutes County. At least, a couple of ranchers from the butte country said the peak is in Deschutes County. Weeks later I asked a highway department fellow down in Salem about it and he replied, "The next time I'm around there I'll climb to the top and let you know." He was a great help.

Personally, I don't care one way or the other. I just like to pass on earth-shaking information that may change the course of your life. For me, Hampton Butte has deep historical significance and I kept staring at it through my field glasses, trying to imagine wagon trains grinding northeast of these hills. That's what a section of the Meek Cutoff Party of 1845 did. Lost and dispirited they wandered all over the high desert, searching for water and a way to the Deschutes River. Somewhere east of Glass Buttes, on a straight line north of Wagontire Mountain, they crossed the sage the highway now runs over, and beyond Buck Creek they turned west toward Hampton Butte.

This is Reub Long country. Everybody around here knows Reub, who comes from Fort Rock and Hole-In-The-Ground way, about 50 miles southwest of Hampton and back of Christmas Valley and Lost Forest. Reub moseys up to Hampton once in a while to sell autographed copies of *The Oregon Desert*, which he co-authored with the late Russell Jackman. When the Hampton *Tribune* was planned, Reub was asked to write a piece for it and he agreed. But, while Reub is a great talker, probably the best story teller in the state, he doesn't take merrily to writing. So he telephoned his old friend, Phil Brogan, in Bend, and sounded a request Phil had heard before: "You write a piece and I'll break a horse for you." Phil, who doesn't ride, laughed, and wrote the piece, and it takes up the whole back page of the four-page Hampton *Tribune*.

Phil told us this little anecdote when we saw him in Bend, and the way Phil chuckled you could tell he was very fond of Reub Long.

The two inside pages of the tabloid contained the menu. I asked a waitress how many people bought the breakfast rib eye steak with one egg, priced at $2.50, and she replied, "We get some hungry people around here."

Maybe what impressed me most about the paper were the circular announcements on the front page, informing the readers that coffee was "15¢ per hour." I asked the waitress if she timed people. She looked at me kind of funny-like and said, "I just work here."

Anyway, I have Volume 1, Number 1 of the Hampton *Tribune*, which is more than Phil Brogan had when I last saw him. "I ought to get a copy, especially since I didn't charge them for the article," Phil said. I knew it was selfish of me not to give him my copy but I looked at it this way: Phil lives closer to Hampton than I do, and if he can't get there, he ought to tell Reub Long. Any man who is willing to break a horse for a friend would think nothing of driving 50 miles across sage, sand dunes, dry lakes and rocky gullies to pick up something they give away for free at Hampton Station.

The lively booster of Fossil

No man had deeper roots in Wheeler County than lanky Jack Steiwer, whose great grandfather, Thomas Benton Hoover, founded the town of Fossil, now the county seat.

Jack's grandfather was a state senator and so was his father and Jack himself served a term in the legislature but he'd never do it again. The broad shoulders of his rangy frame shuddered as he thought about it. "No sir, not ever again. You have to run for the legislature and that's, well," and he made a sour face.

Being mayor of Fossil was different. Jack was mayor for three terms, six years in all, but he didn't run for office, he was drafted. After his third term he put his foot down. "Enough is enough," he declared firmly, so the voters drafted Ed Asher, who ran the variety store.

While Jack was mayor he conferred the title of honorary citizens of Fossil upon my wife and me, but Ed Asher didn't write us to say he was going to continue that exalted distinction so I reckon we're back to being plain folks again.

The Steiwers had been stockmen since the 1890s but Jack had other interests, too. He was an insurance agent and for a long time I thought he was the only one in all of Wheeler County. "Not quite," he corrected. "There are two. The district attorney is the other one."

There was hardly a civic service or improvement around Fossil in the past 20 years that Jack hadn't had a hand in. He helped organize a volunteer ambulance service (Fossil had no doctor), worked hard to build the volunteer fire department, was a prime mover in establishing a town museum, and when Wheeler County celebrated its 75th anniversary Jack ballyhooed the festivities all over the state.

He'd been involved in a lot of other things as well but I always thought of Jack as Wheeler County's unofficial ambassador to the world. It was hard for him to talk 60 seconds without bringing in something nice about the county, and the funny part is that he never seemed to be bragging. It was all enthusiastic matter-of-fact and if you didn't care to listen, well, that was your loss. So you'd miss out on Oregon's most interesting county. Not everyone can be perfect.

There were probably three times as many hills in Wheeler County as there were people, the population being 1,800. Fossil numbered about 550, which was just right for Jack Steiwer, who sometimes felt a little crowded when he drove 20 miles down to Condon, which was twice as big as Fossil.

What's so wonderful about Wheeler County, I asked him once.

"Well," drawled Jack, with a trace of a twang only a sharp-eared sagebrusher like me could detect, "I'll tell you.

"First, it has many geological wonders. Everybody knows about our fossils.

"We've got some of the finest scenery in the whole state, including the Painted Hills, which is the easiest place anywhere to pick up fossils.

"The John Day River is one of the last remaining major rivers in Oregon that is still undammed and below Service Creek it is pretty well in its natural state, and there are no highways along the river.

"Finally, air pollution is unheard of in Wheeler County."

The last time we were in Fossil Jack acquainted us with a tour enterprise he had started, called The Weekend. He planned to launch float trips down the John Day River and to offer horseback rides on trails along the stream or into the timber.

We pointed out that if he succeeded in enticing a lot of people to the county it might become too crowded for his liking.

He didn't think so, explaining that tourists didn't stay put and the tourist season wasn't long enough to do the county any damage.

Wheeler County had three motels—one each in Fossil, Mitchell and Spray. "Some people here say that's three too many," Jack smiled. He was willing to settle for a few more but he was absolutely against anything like a Hilton Fossil. "Heavens no!" he exclaimed. "God forbid!" And for a moment he really looked scared.

I hope I haven't lent the impression that Jack Steiwer was a hayseed who hadn't been around. He attended high school in Canada, studied two years at Stanford, and graduated from the University of Oregon. He drove to Portland more often than I traveled to Gresham and Fossil is 13 times as far from Portland as Portland is from Gresham.

"When you're driving back to Fossil," I asked him, "when do you feel that you're really in your home country?"

Jack stretched out his long legs and pondered. "After I leave The Dalles. When you're on the freeway you might as well be in Portland. Just about Wasco I know that I'm back in Eastern Oregon, and that's when I begin to relax."

Jack Steiwer had numerous opportunities to settle in one of Oregon's larger cities but the faintest suggestion that he leave Fossil gave him the shivers. "I couldn't stand the urban pressures," he said. "I like an easy style of living. Another thing, I know just about everyone who has lived in Wheeler County for any length of time and I can honestly say that there isn't a person in the county I don't like. That's important, isn't it?"

Life wasn't all dull in Fossil but the times were creeping up on Jack, who was past 40 and still single. For years he had been a regular attender at the Saturday night dances, held in the community hall, but he didn't go there anymore. "It's all rock music," he winced, "and I can't take it."

Jack and the district attorney teamed up once to bring culture, with a capital C, to Fossil. They rented the hall and hired a progressive jazz band from Portland. It cost the two of them $500 and they lost four-fifths of it.

"That was a night," said Jack, shaking his head. "First off, the band was two hours late and they weren't in good shape when they arrived. They played fine, though nobody seemed to understand them. They showed a movie, as background to their music, and halfway through the movie the film got snarled up and the screen had a sunburst effect. Everybody thought that was great, the real mood for the music. It was the one thing everyone enjoyed."

Well, we remarked, if it was that good, what went wrong to lose you all that money?

"Hardly anybody came," he replied. "I don't know where I got the idea that the people in Wheeler County would dig progressive jazz. I tell you, that was some night," and he laughed and laughed, getting at least two hundred dollars worth of laughter out of the story.

Condon: In a sea of grain

A block from the motel, the only one in Condon, the elevator of the Condon Grain Growers was still receiving shipments. The hour was halfway between seven and eight in the twilight but the tankers continued to arrive, cargoing the fruit of the crop in from the great ranches which enfolded Condon in ripples of sheared fields.

This was Gilliam County, one of the deep breadbaskets of Oregon, and Condon was the county seat. It wasn't big, Condon wasn't, maybe 1200 people, with little flair and few pretensions.

There was one plain and simple truth here: as went the wheat harvest, so went Condon. A poor harvest and the cash registers in the stores were on lean diet; a good harvest and the mercantile tills tinkled. Condon rose and fell by the price and quantity of wheat.

From the corner of Washington and Wall, near the grain elevator, you could look east and west out to the golden wheatlands. Two blocks north was another reminder of what was important around here, the facility of a farm equipment dealer. In Gilliam County farm equipment was more important than color television consoles, souped-up motorcycles, side by side refrigeration and even fancy automobiles.

About two blocks northeast of Washington and Wall the grounds of the Gilliam County Fair lay fallow. But in a couple of weeks, when the wheat harvest was wrapped up, the fair would start and Condon would see its liveliest days of the year.

Condon had no suburbs, no drifting away of the town. It was bounded by wheat fields. The streets that ran east and west deadended at the fringes of grain.

"There's no lumber here and no industry," declared a young school teacher who was manning the weigh station at the elevator. "There's just grain."

But cattle were also important. "There's a hell of a lot of cattle in Gilliam County," insisted the grey-haired

45

grocer who ran HJ's store, at the corner of Main and Gilliam.

"I don't know if I could cut it without cattle," pondered the ruddy-cheeked rancher who grazed about 150 head. "And cattle is a chore, too," he added. "After the harvest we take a breather. Go somewhere and rest up. Then it's back to the farm and taking care of cattle."

Still, he admitted, as did everyone else, that wheat was the base of the economy. "In Gilliam County," he observed, "wheat is king."

The next morning, about ten minutes after eight, with Condon already flooded by sun, we drove downtown for breakfast. About a dozen cars were parked along Main Street, but not a soul in sight. Then a merchant stepped out of his store and remarked, with a pleased smile, "It looks like it's going to be another beautiful day." The quiet that followed was shaken by a tanker rumbling toward the elevator. "And a good year," said the merchant, his eyes following the vehicle until it turned. "The harvest is coming along fine."

Clarno is just the right size

Herb McKay, who lived with his wife and two kids in the only house in Clarno, on the John Day River, laughed at the idea that he might be lonesome or bored, especially without television.

Some folks can't endure the prospect of life without TV—the very thought of no-tube existence hurtles them into traumatic shivers—but not Herb McKay.

"It would cost quite a bit to get in here and it would cost a lot anyway," he said.

His eyes followed four young people, two of them long-haired men bare to their levis, as they halted their car on the bank of the John Day and unloaded their gear for sunbathing and splashing around.

"Gosh," he mused to himself, "that's a crowd for sure." They were the only sign of humanity we saw on the river.

McKay returned to the subject of television. "It's a waste of time anyway. Nights aren't dull. There's always something to do, read or visit a neighbor or just sit around."

By neighbor, a term which might mystify urbanites, who define a neighbor as someone who resides on the same block, Herb meant anyone who lived within a 10-mile radius.

At one time, before Herb was born, there were farm families much closer to Herb's house. Indeed, there was once a Clarno post office. Its location depended upon who could be induced to be the postmaster, so sometimes the post office was in Wasco County and sometimes in Wheeler County. Herb McKay was glad the post office and the little settlement that was clustered around the bridge across the John Day had faded away long ago. He was of the mold of pioneer stockman Andrew Clarno, who settled on the river when there wasn't a soul around within two day's travel. Later, when Andy Clarno heard that a friend had filed claim on a homestead 20 miles off, he rode over on horseback and asked, in a hurt and slightly indignant voice, "Bill, don't you think you're crowding me a little?"

The 28-year-old McKay, who farmed 11,000 acres and ran about 200 cows, had come to Clarno from Antelope, where his father also operated a ranch. Antelope, 15 miles west, had a population of 30, which McKay thought was just about the right size for a town. Fossil, 20 miles east, numbered 550, and that was as large a metropolitan center as Herb cared to visit.

"I went to high school in Madras and that's way too big for me," he said, smiling. He was a friendly fellow, merry-eyed, and with a nimble mind.

"I don't feel isolated," he continued. "There's a mob of people around here—coming by all the time. Hunting season and nights there's a lot of traffic—a lot of traffic at night, but it doesn't lose me any sleep. It would take a lot to disturb my sleep."

"Where do you get this business about a lot of traffic?" I challenged. "All the way from Antelope we passed only one car."

"That's one car too many," he retorted. "I told you the road was getting crowded."

At Celilo Village the road runs out

The paved road ended abruptly at Celilo Village. Beyond it there was not an inch of pavement. It was probably the only settlement in Oregon, certainly the only one I had ever seen, that was in this shape. The road through the village was no road at all, by any decent standards. At best it was a rough trace, partly gravel and all washboard. Mostly you drove over rocks, pebbles, bumps and chuckholes.

Perhaps there was no pavement here because Celilo Village was an all-Indian hamlet, owned, in one manner or another, by its occupants, but it seemed to us that Wasco County could have paved the rocky tire-trail or at least maintained it as a good gravel street.

The village lay inert under tawny rock cliffs, scowling down upon rusty sage which sagged, dusty and exhausted, all through the settlement. Weathered rocks, looking like mud had drip-dried on their faces, were glazed eyes fixed upon junked cars dragged into the open to die and be stripped of their organs. If they had been flesh, the buzzards would have picked them clean to the bone. There appeared to be at least two junked cars to every residence.

About 100 people lived in the village, in dwellings which ranged from modestly poor to ramshackle livable. None of the houses suggested that they had been recently painted or reroofed or remodeled in any way. You had the feeling that the people were doing the best with what they had but were too tired or too poor, or perhaps both, to improve their dwellings. The village was an island neglected, running down of its own weight and time, with frustration and fatigue too deep and far gone to be turned back. It was the drab postscript of a dismal chapter, and those still here, except for the children, were weary footnotes of one more broken promise.

I remember the village when I first saw it in the 1930s. Crowded, alive, crackling with laughter, humming with the healthy sounds of happy work. That was when Indians were still fishing, as they had for centuries, from the cliffs above Celilo Falls, where part of the Columbia boiled through a trough. Salmon was the harvest and in the sheds of the village the salmon were dried and packed. Salmon was the big money crop for most of the Indians; for them everything revolved around the success of the run. If the salmon were plenty, the long house shook with the beat of drums, the jangle of bells, the thud of dancing feet, the measured striking of hands, and the warm gales of laughter. If the salmon were few the long house was a hollow gathering place for dreary lament.

The Indians had long been suspicious of the white man's word, but, they were assured in the solemnest of pledges that Celilo Falls was theirs to fish forever—"until the sun no longer arose," which is the same as forever. Then came the blueprints for The Dalles dam and forever passed into yesterday. Before the river was turned into a lake, drowning Celilo Falls, the Indians had been paid off and their platforms on the cliffs removed.

If it had been white businessmen who had received the paltry sums the government dispensed to the Indians, the cries of outrage would have resounded across the nation and the federal courts would have been full of demanding lawyers. But Indians—at that time, in the early 1950s, it was still considered sound history for every red man in the settling of the West to have been a varmint and proper movie fare for the cavalry to gun down the sneaky savages.

We bounced down the trace, that lay curled like a parched snakeskin, past the slumbering long house and the hunched drying sheds to the cabin of John Wynookie, who had lived in the village for about half of his 72 years.

Mr. Wynookie, a short, thin, gnarled man, who spoke so low I often had to ask him to repeat his words, first came to Celilo to fish in 1927.

He was born on the Yakima Reservation where, as a young boy, he "ran, rode horseback, chased horses around, went up into the hills, dug roots, had a lot of fun chasing wild horses around. I'd ride 'em once in a while; had to break my own horse."

After some elementary schooling on the Reservation he

went to work: "Haying, thrashing, picking potatoes, working for white fellows. Got 75 cents a day for haying and thrashing."

It was readily apparent that John Wynookie was not overflowing with love for the whites. There was a built-in bitterness in his short, under-the-breath chuckles, the frowns that creased into the corner of his lips, and the way he shrugged his shoulders when he talked about the whites. But he had lived to the point where bitterness had settled as a pool and he was too old to stir it into waves.

When John Wynookie came to fish, most of the places on the cliffs were taken by the ancestral families, whose positions had been secured so far back no one could remember, and passed on from one generation to the next. But there were several spots open to the unpossessing. "Any Indian could fish at these places," he said. "They would take turns. Fellas would sit around and when one catches a fish another fella takes his turn. They fished from spring to fall. Had to quit when high water came. I got married and then comes depression and nothing to do so I stayed here."

Before Mr. Wynookie took up fishing at the falls he had acquired a small farm in the Yakima Valley. When the lean years blew in like a swarm of locusts, agricultural prices dropped to rock bottom. "I fall behind, so I quit farming," he continued with his narrative, droning on in a low, patient voice that seemed to dwell in limbo. "I leased my place east of Toppenish, come back here, stay here, built a little shack. Then my house burn up, the farm burn up, everything gone. I stay here."

So he remained at Celilo Village, earning a living at fishing. He had his own drying shed, with family quarters in the rear. When he ran out of money he could borrow from fish buyers.

We asked him about his children. He coughed up a little laugh and continued to chew snuff and spit it onto the acrid ground. "I got one daughter," he replied neutrally. "Married to a Filipino, living somewhere in California." He glanced at us. That's the way of the world, he seemed to be saying.

We tried to turn his thoughts back to the old days: was there a lot of fun then? His mouth parted in a stump-toothed grin. "Oh yeah, they'd joke around, laugh around, tell a funny story of some kind while they were waiting for a fish.

"I guess there was a lot of fun or they wouldn't have it," he reasoned, and told of the dances in the long house: the War dance, for men; and the dances for men and women: Circle, Owl, and Rabbit.

"Men would dress up in buckskin outfits and the women in the beaded dresses. In Rabbit dance, Owl dance, mostly girls dance. Older people, they dress up but they sit around the drum mostly. Maybe in Circle dance they join in."

The biggest event of the year was when the first salmon was caught, around April or May, generally the last part of April, Mr. Wynookie recalled, as we stood outside his cabin, he talking mostly with his head down or cocked to one side and my wife and I listening intently.

He described the salmon festival in the long house. "They have big feast, eat salmon, and roots, and things like that, all different kind of roots, and they have War dance. Just about the time roots good in the hills, and the women dig them up. When the first roots come out they eat them, all in a bunch for everybody, before they pick them for themselves.

"They dry roots and put them away for winter, whenever they feel like eating roots, and the same with the salmon," he went on, telling now how salmon was processed.

"They got rock, big, round, and they dry the salmon and pound it, and they get steelhead oil and mix it with pounded salmon and keep it and make it taste good. They dry salmon, salt salmon, put it in barrels."

He was most relaxed and fluid when he talked of the village in its prime. "Oh, in the old days, there were so many people here they couldn't find a place to park. And there was a lot of gambling—stick games, poker, monte —outside the long house. They had shade fixed up for the gamblers. They had all the gambling during the salmon festival. Sometimes during the salmon season, after work, I gambled once in a while—nothing serious. I stayed for a while and then had to go rest for the fishing. It started at daybreak and I tried to be the first one out there, so I could have more turns. Sometimes they'd fish at night, but I didn't like it. You never catch too much at night anyway. Salmon don't run much at night, they start moving in the early morning."

So his life went on, until the government decreed that the sun would no longer arise. "The people here were pretty mad when they had to quit fishing at Celilo Falls," John Wynookie said, shaking his head grimly. "I was one of them mad—but I couldn't do anything. No one could. I got a little over three thousand dollars—not much. I could make that much in a year fishing.

"When they closed the falls most people go away," he added, chucking more snuff spit on the dun-colored ground. "They go back to their reservations—Umatilla, Warm Springs, Yakima, they come from all over. Only the people who live here year round stay.

"It has been 15 years, something like that, since they close falls. I haven't done very much. I used to fish down by where the dam is, on the Oregon side, but I've been sick quite a lot. Sometimes I've gone to Sherar's Bridge, near Tygh Valley, but Warm Springs Indians, they made a ruling only Warm Springs can fish there, so I can't go there anymore. I get rent money from Toppenish farm through Indian Agency. Wife gets forty dollars a month since last year—for old age."

There were about 20 families in the village then, Mr. Wynookie estimated. "Most of them go around wherever there's work—berry picking and something like that."

We asked him what was the happiest time of his life. He laughed softly, the laughter circling in his throat like a breeze which chases its tail in the grass but collapses when it tries to climb a tree.

"Fishing—having a lots of fun—making money," he replied, and for the first and only time there was a spark in his eye.

Then his head dropped and he muttered: "No more, no more." For him the past was dead, the present a wasteland, the future one weary day fastened to another. We shook hands and he shuffled into his shack.

As we walked toward the long house to take some pictures, three little boys followed us. We asked the tallest his name and age. He said he was Olin Don Charley, 10 years old, and the grandson of the late Tommy Thompson, the venerated chief of the Celilo Indians.

"My Indian name is Soo-La-Hik!" Olin exclaimed, with a big, beaming smile.

That's a real neat name, we said. Do you like it?

"Oh yes! And this is my brother, Isadore Kevin Charley. He's six. And this is our half-brother, Ian Moses Towhead. He's two."

Neither of the two other boys had Indian names, Olin said ruefully.

Well, I said squatting, with the boys around me, I'll give you Indian names in English. For Isadore, Tree-That-Will-Grow Tall; and for Ian, Bright Morning.

Olin good-naturedly approved the names. Then he told us a bit about himself. He was in the fourth grade, he did not seem to like school, and said he failed the second grade. Why? we asked. It was obvious he had a good mind. "I don't know." Didn't the teacher tell you why you failed second grade? "No." We felt sick.

God knows, enough white children have been ruined by insensitive teachers. What happens when an Indian child, coming from a depressed culture, from a world that is torn in at least two parts, and who grows up in a home where the parents speak their native tongues to their own parents, the ancients of another era—what happens to that child when he or she is judged by the standards applied to middle-class whites? Pity all the lovely bits of humanity called Olin Don Charley and weep for their uncomprehending teachers.

At the other end of the village—actually, at the beginning of it, near the entrance—we found 27-year-old Mary Jane Cook. She could trace her Celilo ancestry back 10 generations—"and there were more before them" —and she was born here, in a drying shed.

Mrs. Cook, a full-faced, swift-talking woman, with flashy eyes and an on-target tongue, was as sharp and breezy as John Wynookie was glum and reserved. She had an agile mind that let nothing get past her; forceful, energetic, the matriarch of her family, I could envision many situations where she could properly have assumed a leadership role. And here she was in Celilo Village, with no opportunity to put her excellent attributes into play.

She had left the village at the age of six, spending most of her years on the Warm Springs Reservation, but had come back, near the river of her lifestream, "to be near my people, before the old people forget me, to speak my tongue again. This is my home, this is where I belong; my people are here; I returned to my roots."

Home was shared with her four children, who had ambled down to the river; her second husband, a quiet Indian from British Columbia, now employed as a truck driver; and her uncle, a jovial, rotund, middle-aged veteran of World War II. Both husband and uncle left the talking to her, and they smiled sad agreement when she spoke of wanting to become a beauty operator. There was only one obstacle: money.

Since she was born, Mrs. Cook declared, only four children from Celilo Village had graduated from high school—four in 27 years. And just one, the year before, had gone on to college.

"I was one of the four to graduate high school," she said. "I wish I could have gone on. I wish I had the money to go to beauty school. But one started college— the first in the history of the village. Maybe there will be more. Maybe." And she clenched her fists.

Saddlemakers and steamboat days

Every once in a while some febrile home-town booster of The Dalles, feckless in an unguarded moment, would proclaim the city to be the most historic or the oldest in Oregon. But the more judicious elements limited their pride to sloganizing The Dalles as "End of the Oregon Trail."

A plaque on a rock in City Park bore that inscription, followed by "1843-1906."

The 1843 I could understand; it was the year the first wagon train came to Oregon. The 1906 was less explicit. Prairie schooners were clopping into The Dalles even later. But, since any year that marks the last usage of the Oregon Trail is arbitrary, I would not quarrel with 1906.

Anyway, many pioneer touches remained in The Dalles. For instance, Pulpit Rock, a natural altar at 12th and Court. Prayer meetings were held here and when there weren't whites around the Methodist preachers tried to build fires under Indian souls.

Then there was the first county courthouse, built in 1859, when The Dalles was the seat of the largest county in the nation. It originally stood where the city hall was now located downtown but some years ago was carted to an unattractive snub of weedy ground a block west of the natatorium. It was supposed to have been refurbished but nobody had done a lick of work on it yet when we were there and not a person we met had any idea when this pioneer structure would be returned to a semblance of its early life. It seemed a shame to have it just stand there, abandoned and helpless, like a feeble elder turned out of home without coat or money.

The second county courthouse was now part of the Smith Callaway Chapel, also downtown. Once considered doomed, the courthouse had been activated by the funeral parlor: a mortuary resurrecting the dead.

Nearby we found St. Peter's Church, a patrician edifice

frocked by the bearings of opulence. The moralizing palace of merchants and bankers on the rise, it provided eloquent clues to the social history of the town. A poor community could not have afforded so grand a church.

The gothic edifice, built in 1897 of local red brick, still boasted the tallest spire in The Dalles. And atop the spire there continued to perch the figure of a rooster, in commemoration of the cock that crowed "after Peter's denial of his Lord."

There were other interesting mementos of the early days, including the Old Government Mint and the Fort Dalles Museum. The mint was completed in 1868 but never put into production. It did not turn out a single coin. We discovered it at 710 E. 2nd St., as the rear section of a storage warehouse. Some of the local folks thought it deserved a kindlier fate.

Fort Dalles Museum was really the Surgeons Quarters, only remaining structure of the U.S. Army post established in 1850 as a crude stockade. Six years later the command passed to Captain Thomas Jordan, who drew freely on Army funds to erect a military village more to the style of country squires than field officers. He was scorched by his critics for his luxuriant and showy "mansions" on the edge of the wilderness but the doughty Jordan was not for practicing the spartan life while waiting for the Indians to "make trouble." Of course he could have used the "large sums" for more philanthropic aims, such as fluming food and supplies to hungry emigrants and Indians, but hadn't the aristocrats of Rome raised their costly Coliseum while thousands of their countrymen were impecunious? And has the knowledge that poor Americans rot in rat-infested slums ever stopped a millionaire from investing in a dwelling commensurate with his mental image?

The Dalles had three other museums. Winquatt, housed in a former cannery near the bridge linking Oregon to Washington, was loaded with artifacts of the mid-Columbia River Indians. Carpenters, downtown, exhibited a collection of early American hand tools, especially those used by a carpenter of the 19th century. And Nichols, on Union Street, contained geologic and paleontologic specimens chiefly uncovered by museum operator Lewis Nichols. He showed us a Pleistocene age mammoth tusk and tooth and a rock which he said was 500,000,000 years old. Being a bit before my time, I could not readily place it.

The Nichols Museum occupied the rear of the no-longer-used St. Paul's Episcopal Church, erected in 1875, and admission included a tour of the chapel. Actually, if I had my choice of seeing Nichols' collection or the chapel I would unhesitatingly opt for the latter. It was the most exquisite small old church I had seen in Oregon, its gorgeous stained glass windows reflecting sunlight upon the austere straightback pews; an ancient organ; and a pulpit whose simplicity set the tone of the historic atmosphere of the chapel. I could visualize the first generation of settlers, in their glossy Sunday best, turning the pages of their hymnbooks; I could hear their earnest singing, the off-contraltos and the grainy basses, properly spirited, as befitted staunch Episcopalians; I could see them leaving, with rulebook decorum, to walk to their buggies or, if they lived closed by, stroll righteously along the wooden sidewalks. "I do hope St. Paul's isn't turned into a funeral parlor," I said aloud, to no one in particular.

A lot of people in Portland looked upon The Dalles as the western border of Oregon's Old West country. We found a nuance of the Old West in the Bonney Saddle Shop, at 205 Court St. Here Garth Bonney was making a saddle while his mother, Mrs. Ralph Bonney, widow of Garth's father, managed the leather goods shop.

Garth was the third in a succession of Bonney saddlemakers, dating back 100 years to C. R. Bonney, who was born of Oregon Trail pioneers in 1853. Garth's son, Garth Jr., the fourth generation of his trade, had his own saddle shop in Beaverton.

It took Garth Bonney about 30 hours to make a plain saddle, which sold for $285, and about 40 hours to finish a hand-tooled saddle, whose lowest price was $350. "It took my father and grandfather the same time," he noted. "It's been hard work ever since it started. It's never been revolutionized much since the beginning."

He also made "bridles and halters and shifts and things like that" but his specialty was saddles and he had received individual orders from many parts of the country.

"The biggest kick in making saddles is the self-satisfaction in creating something," he said. "You'll never get rich at it, I'll tell you that."

Still, Garth Bonney was turning out far fewer saddles than his father or grandfather had. "I don't imagine I have over 15 orders a year any more. We sell a lot of TexTan saddles, that are factory made. A lot of men work on the production line so there's no personal stamp of craftsmanship."

TexTan saddles started at $95. They were manufactured in Yoakum, Texas by workers who, the Bonneys suspected, were not paid good wages.

When Mrs. Bonney was a girl, before the farmers had seen a thingamajig called the automobile, she lived in Stanfield and rode a horse to school in Echo. She hadn't been on a horse in decades. Garth Bonney mounted up "maybe once a year, in a parade." Neither of them felt you had to ride a horse to be a saddlemaker.

Bonney's shop lay between the Columbia River and Hans Blaser's house, up on the heights, but Blaser could relate the river to the days of the horse better than Bonney could.

Hans Blaser's parents preceded the Bonney family to The Dalles, arriving in 1879. His father was a wagonmaker and blacksmith "but Studebaker came along and put him out of business," said Mr. Blaser, a big, solid man. "Studebaker started to turn out wagons and all the little wagonmasters went out of business."

Born in 1894, Hans Blaser was helping around his father's shop when the 20th century still wore diapers. "When I was a kid," he recalled heartily, "we had to learn how to make horeshoes, fix spokes and just anything that was to be done around the wagon shop—painting, repairing, setting tires. There was a lot of teaming going on then, but The Dalles was small. There was nothing up on the hill, everything was downtown."

Most travel to Portland was by boat, he mentioned, and that set him off on a long discourse about the Columbia and the importance of The Dalles as a river town. This part of the city's history had been overlooked, he insisted, and emphasized that in the early part of this century boats played a larger role in the social and economic life of The Dalles than did the railroad or automotive conveyances.

"Why," he exampled, "there were seven or eight steamboats a day to Portland." He could still name some: The Dalles City, Bailey Gatzert, Tacoma, the Simons.

"Some steamers made a round trip a day, going down early in the morning and returning late at night. The only delay was at Cascade Locks. Summer time, with high water, they could shoot the rapids. In winter they had to go through Cascade Locks: a small set of locks—two, I suppose.

"Some boats would go one way one day and return the next day. These were the only ones hauling heavy freight. The boats that carried freight and passengers, they were the most modern things you ever saw. Talk about a deluxe restaurant! they had everything skinned. Finest meals ever served. Morning was ham and eggs, all you could eat, 20 cents or 25 cents. The river was always full of boats. It was unbelievable how they shoved the people on them. They'd have everything under the sun on those boats."

Hans Blaser had a ruddy complexion and when he hit full steam recalling the river boats his cheeks tingled and glowed. His wife, sitting starchly at his side, was a stickler for accuracy of detail and often checked him on dates and names, inhibiting his flow of narrative and colorful description. I didn't blame her; she wanted everything in apple pie order; but there are times when I am more of a professional romanticist than an amateur historian and I was a real pro now, listening wide-eared to Blaser rhapsodize about those river scenes as though he were on the Columbia himself then, the wind tangling his hair and the stream churning out music like a jolly Calliope. So I urged him not to worry about dotting each i and crossing the ts and just to go on reminiscing.

He smiled appreciatively and continued:

"There weren't many towns but there were a lot of landing places. If a fellow stood on the bank and waved his hand the boat would come in and a gangplank would be thrown out. If a farmer had a load of hay he'd bring it down to the river and it'd be loaded up. Those boats had big crews. They'd put the hay on with a couple of hand trucks in no time.

"And there was a lot of scows that operated by sail. When they went downstream they threw the sails into the water and the current pulled them along and when they went upstream they put the sails up.

"There were three or four docks. All the kids in town would go down to the boats and unload wheat or cement or sheep or anything and make two bits or half a buck. We'd get spending money that way."

That was all Hans Blaser had to say about the river for a while. He was never a riverman himself, being a locomotive machinist until he entered the soda pop business. In 1911 he became the first man west of the Mississippi to bottle Pepsi-Cola. His sons were carrying on with a plant in Pendleton.

Half a century ago Blaser shipped soda pop to Alaska in wooden barrels. They were carried up on crusty windjammers, along with an assortment of other freight. Returning, the jammers were piled high with salmon.

It was time for us to leave but Hans Blaser had a last word to say about the Columbia. "The river is all different. Barges come up and a Navy boat, a destroyed, makes a trip here about once a year, but outside of that there are just rowboats and powerboats—stuff like that, nothing to make your head swim. It was sure different in the old days. That's when the river was a river!"

A motorcycle on Mount Hood

The old man in the gray bathrobe, cheeks thin and sallow, reclines facing the window. He cannot walk to it; he has just a few days ago come out of the hospital and is propped in a convalescent chair, but his eyes reach to the window and beyond it. To a barn built at the turn of the century and now creaking at the joints. To a splash of green meadow and the blur of a dell. To wooded slopes climbing southward. And above all, big as life, to the peak of Mt. Hood.

Off its eastern face the white peak slopes to a knobby ridge called Cooper Spur. Its elevation is 8500 feet. The old man knows the fact well, as well as he knows the ridge. Once, many years ago, he drove a motorcycle to Cooper Spur. It was an amazing feat then—and it must remain so today. For no motorcyclist has ever climbed higher up a mountain than Wells Bennett did in early July of 1924.

Now it is apple blossom time in the Hood River Valley. The trees are sprigs of delicate snow and thousands of visitors have come from Portland and elsewhere to see them. From Hood River the sightseers motor to a brace of stores called the town of Mt. Hood, where they turn right for Parkdale and then, on another road, return to the freeway.

Beyond the junction, in a small frame house reached from the road by a foot path rutted across a tufting lawn, Wells Bennett looks out the window, paying no heed to the sounds of the tourist caravans. He has been through apple blossom time before—many times before. The apples are born, they ripen and they are picked. The trees are planted, they mature, grow old, and are pulled out. But the mountain stands as it has since man has known it. At least since then. And Cooper Spur is deep in his memory.

He was only 33 when he set his 4-cylinder Henderson up the mountain from Timberline. His finest hours of competitive glory were behind him, those years when he was "King of the Road" and the greatest cross-country cyclist America has ever known. The November, 1968 issue of *Cycle World* stated without exaggeration:

"If it had two wheels, Wells Bennett could ride it. If it had an engine he'd travel faster, and farther, across mountains, deserts or mud, to more miles of cross-country records than any man since motorcycles were invented."

He started riding a long time before he ever saw Mt. Hood or his wife, Beulah Ann, or her first husband, the late Mark Weygandt, the legendary guide who climbed to the summit of Mt. Hood far more times than anyone else.

"A long, long time ago," the old man recalls, stringing his words slowly into sentences as an elbow brushes the tray at his side. One of the bottles tips over and his wife stands it straight again, cautioning her husband, "Now don't you strain yourself." Then she shuffles sleepily out of the room, explaining quietly and with no trace of self-pity or rancor before she leaves. "I've been up day and night taking care of him since he came back from the hospital. We could all do with a nap, but if Wells is up to it, you go on talking to him."

The sparse figure in the gray flannel bathrobe nods, more with his eyes than his head, and starts again. "I was born in Kansas, Wichita, in 1891, and when I was thirteen I had my first motorcycle, an Indian, and when I was fifteen I was racing."

So began a career that was, as *Cycle World* put it, "to compile a fantastic lifetime total of nearly 50,000 miles of road records."

"Those days," says Wells Bennett, "there weren't many paved roads, or good ones of any kind. Fact is, you could go across most of the country and not touch any paved road at all. In the prairie states the rain turned the dirt roads to mud and the dry powdery silt you'd run into some places was a lot harder than sand to push through. I'd ride down the railroad tracks if that was the best available, and there were times when it was."

At 22 Bennett was riding the rough motordrome circuit, whose billboards accurately advertised: "Neck and Neck With Death."

In 1968, for *Cycle World*, Wells Bennett recalled the motordrome days:

"You could expect about a half-dozen spills at 90 every summer. Some got killed; some quit after one spill and went home; but those like myself just pulled the slivers out and got ready for the next race."

The year 1914 found Bennett, fresh from motrodrome triumphs, in Los Angeles. Someone had hatched an idea for a ticket-selling stunt at the Ascot Mile speedway: a race between an automobile, a plane and a motorcycle. Barney Oldfield drove the car, in his landspeed record "Blitzen Benz." Lincoln Beachey, the country's ace trick pilot, flew his Curtis Pusher. And 23-year-old Wells Bennett, on an Excelsior, was chosen to represent the speed demons of the motordromes.

"Barney Oldfield," and the old man chuckles with his eyes and pushes his lips into the hope of a smile, "he was a big heavy set blustering sort of good sport. Lincoln Beachey, he was a fine chap and a wonderful pilot. He'd nudge my helmet with his wheel and one race he set a wheel on my shoulder.

"We had lots of races, the three of us. Beachey always won—but it was exciting."

He sighs back against the tilted chair and locks his gnarling fingers. "Beachey always won," he repeats, "but it was exciting." And there is satisfaction in his voice.

Now he looks out the window again, a habit look not attached to what he is saying. "I drove very fast at times. You had to, to eat, and you had to win to get ahead. The fastest was one hundred and eleven miles an hour." And he leaves it at that: a footnote of his life.

From 1917 to 1919 he was a movie stunt man. If there was any glamour in picture-making he does not speak of it. "It was a job," he says, his voice flat, "and I was on a motorcycle, so I knew what I was doing."

In 1923 Bennett invested his motorcycle earnings in an Excelsior-Henderson sales agency in Portland. Almost 10 years late he would still be competing but his days as a full-time motorcyclist were over. Now it was time for him to settle down to the business of being a businessman. But his most famous thrust on a motorcycle was yet ahead.

Sometime in the spring of 1924 his good friend, Mark Weygandt, approached Bennett about a scheme that would provide national publicity to a mass assault upon Mt. Hood. "It was for the annual American Legion hill climb on July Fourth," Bennett says, looking like a weary teacher straining himself to deliver a lecture he has given often before. "Mark knew I had done a lot of driving up mountains all over the West, places where no other cyclists had reached, and places where I was the only rider in the pack to reach the top. Mark knew that. We were close friends."

The old man points with a gaze to Mt. Hood. "I didn't think the climb to the top would be too difficult, although I had never gone that high. So I thought about it a lot and planned on it and organized a team. I drove to Timberline on my cycle and two pack horses carried spare wheels and other parts up there. They were to follow me on my run.

"I let the air out of the tires so they were mostly soft and then put a wide band of metal with cleats on them that were two-and-a-half inches high. Then I put air back into the tires.

"There was a big crowd of people up at Timberline ready to go. I promised those foot climbers I'd climb the mountain at the same time they went up it. I was the only climber on motorcycle."

Bennett pushed off from Timberline before dawn on July 4. When there was sufficient light for photography, Fox-Movietone cameras began grinding. They followed Bennett as he churned across two glaciers and battled his way toward Cooper Spur. The foot climbers made it in a day but it took Bennett five days to reach the 8500-foot high east ridge.

"The rocks were big as pianos," Bennett explains, his voice serious and pedantic. "I had to go around and around the rocks. Big as pianos. I'd go up a bit and then I had to swing back to try and find another opening. The foot climbers just walked on the rocks and up them and over them but I couldn't do it. Those rocks were too huge."

Wells Bennett reached Cooper Spur through the sheer engine power of his Henderson. But it was obvious he needed help for the steep ascent ahead. Bennett had the solution: a 600-foot-rope would be anchored to wind on a rear wheel pulley.

"But there came up suddenly a mighty wind and a stinging snow storm and my pack horses couldn't get up there, so we called it off."

He recalls the experience matter-of-factly, without regret, and there is no point now, 45 years after the event, to ask if he really could have reached the summit had not the wind and the snow shattered his plans. The important point is: no motorcyclist had ever gone so high up the side of a mountain, and his feat was acclaimed from coast to coast.

The next year, in 1925, Bennett accompanied another climb part of the way and, according to a dispatch in a Portland paper, "performed some remarkable stunts with his motorbike on the snow fields."

But his cavorting was anti-climactic to Cooper Spur, and Bennett makes short shrift of it. "Just a bit of fun," he remarks, and presses his lips together.

Mark Weygandt died in 1944. Six years later Wells Bennett married the widow, Beulah Ann. They lived on a ranch Bennett owned on the Cooper Spur road, the last ranch on the lonesome road and the spread closest to Mt. Hood. The place was no stranger to Beulah Ann. She and Mark Weygandt had once owned it.

Spring comes late here, the thaw still struggling for victory when the apple trees are white, just five or six miles north. Even in late April and early May there is the taste of snow in the air. The snow arrives early in autumn and continues to lay under the shade of the pines until June. Some winters the temperature does not rise above the freezing point.

By 1961 the brittling bones of Wells Bennett had become too soft for the icy winds and the blinding storms that lash down from the high slopes. So he and Beulah Ann moved about seven miles northeast, to the gentler climate at the roadside hamlet of Mt. Hood.

"I don't know when I'll be fit again," the old man says now, fatigue pinching his pale cheeks. His hands tumble to his lap. All of him seems worn, except his eyes, which remain steady. He bids goodbye with them and his eyelids droop.

Outside, Beulah Ann, her lovely wrinkled face smothered in homefolk gentleness, exclaims cheerfully, in a voice that for the moment throws off 20 years, "The most beautiful view of the mountain anywhere is from here. You know, I never get tired of looking at it, after all the years, and," she points to the house, "neither does he."

Within a month, Wells Bennett passed away. In July, driving south from Hood River to Timberline, we paused at the frame house in Mt. Hood. Mrs. Bennett came plodding out to greet us. She was heavy on her feet and squinting hard.

"Have you been sick?" we asked.

She peered at us and came closer. "My hearing is bad," she said. "I can't hear well at all."

We told her we had interviewed her husband.

"He's dead," she said.

We said we knew, and expressed our sorrow.

"And this house is so lonesome now," she said. There was a lament in her voice that made the words painful for all of us.

"The house is so big without him," she went on. "So big and so empty and I'm lonely all the time, It isn't a home anymore. It's just a big empty house."

"Why don't you move into town," we suggested. "Portland, be near your children. They love you."

"If I could get the price," she replied, glancing at the house. "I'd sell. It's a good house, worth every penny."

"It's a fine house," we agreed, "and the location is beautiful."

She shook her head slowly. "It's so empty in there. I'd take a few hundred dollars less if I could sell."

Just then one of our dogs ambled up and sniffed Mrs. Bennett. She bent, stiffly and with much effort, to pet its head. "I had a little black dog just like that once," she said, her voice lighter but poignant and her eyes brightening but misting, in bitter-sweet reminiscing. "A fine little dog and oh, how I loved him. I named him Togo. Don't know why. I don't know where I heard the name. Togo, that's a funny name for a little black dog, isn't it, but I loved it."

"What happened to your dog?" my daughter asked.

"He was killed," Mrs. Bennett replied.

"How?" my daughter asked.

"Run over by a car," Mrs. Bennett said simply. "Togo, what a funny name for a little black dog. Now how do you think I got that name?"

The clouds were lifting from Mt. Hood and the great peak was now exposed to the noon-day sun.

"Did you ever climb the mountain?" we asked.

Mrs. Bennett came very close to us. "What did you say?"

We repeated our question in raised voice.

"Oh," said Mrs. Bennett. "My first husband, Mark Weygandt, he climbed the mountain more times than anyone else. He was a professional guide. Do you know how many times he was to the top of the mountain?" And she gave us the exact figure. Almost 600 times.

"But were you ever to the peak?"

She smiled gently, as her voice livened. "No, my husband wouldn't let me."

"He wouldn't?"

"Oh, I've been on the mountain year after year. I worked at Timberline. But I've never climbed to the top. He wouldn't let me. He said, 'I don't want to take a chance on anything happening to you.' 'Why not?' I asked him. 'Because you're my wife,' he said, 'and I care for you.' 'Don't you care for all the people you've guided to the top?' I said. 'Sure,' he said, 'I watch out for all of them.' 'Then, why won't you take me up there?' 'Because you're my wife,' he said, 'and I don't want to take any chances.' And that's the way it was."

The last time we were here, we remarked, you told us that the most beautiful view of Mt. Hood was from your house.

"It isn't any comfort anymore," she said, her eyes cast downward and her voice filling with grief again. "I'm very lonely. This big house is so empty now."

Tollgate on the Oregon Trail

Here, where the trembling wind quivers on the face of the woods beyond the eastern arm of present Rhododendron, the emigrants of the Oregon Trail who had taken the Barlow Road across the Cascades were confronted by a tollgate.

The mountain cutoff was a toll road, initiated by Samuel Barlow and Philip Foster, and toll was collected at a guarded gate which came to be known as a place, Tollgate. The name was now preserved by Tollgate Forest Camp, near the final passageway.

Tollgate marked the end of all that was rugged on the Oregon Trail. Behind the emigrants were the plains, the deserts, the deep rivers and the mountains. Their long ordeal had reached its climax with the hazardous descent of Laurel Hill, which sweeps up from Rhododendron toward the top of Mt. Hood.

"The road on this hill is something terrible," wrote Enoch W. Conyers in his journal of 1852. "It is worn down into the soil from five to seven feet, leaving steep banks on both sides, and so narrow that it is almost impossible to walk alongside of the cattle without leaning against the cattle . . . Our wagon was in all shapes coming down the hill; sometimes one fore wheel would drop nearly three feet from a boulder in the road, while at the same time the opposite rear wheel dropped two feet or more into another hole."

Wagons would have plunged down the hill, to be smashed into kindling wood, if the pioneers had not shown some innovation. They cut down trees about 10 inches in diameter and 40 feet long, "and the more limbs it has on it, so much the better," observed Conyers.

Using chains or ropes, whichever they had, the emigrants attached the fallen trees, top-end foremost, to the rear axles. Each tree served as an "excellent" brake, slowing the descent.

When a wagoner arrived at the foot of Laurel Hill he

detached his lead yoke of cattle, hitched them to the tree left by the previous wagon, hauled the tree off the road, and left "the tree in the road that he used on his own wagon for the next fellow to look after."

So the wagons, jarred but still rolling, groaned away from the fearsome slope and, all hands now in better spirits, pulled up at the tollgate.

There are, unfortunately, few toll records remaining. The most substantial I could find was a small, well-worn ledger which covered, among other accounts of the Barlow and Foster Company, approximately 120 entries.

The toll for wagons was $5 each; there was evidently no charge for persons. Some emigrants didn't have enough money to cover the fee. Christian Cline was five cents short. Mr. Willow, whose bill was $10, dug up only $4.84. Joe Patterson, assessed the same rate, did better, $9.68.

There is an item that Henry Roberts had 2½ wagons and paid $12.50. Matthias Sweegle, with 4½ wagons, parted with $22.50. What is a half wagon? A buggy perhaps? The pocket-sized ledger hints this possibility because D. S. Baker, who passed through the gate with a buggy, was charged $2.50.

Goods were accepted for partial or complete payment. C. P. Chetman left a blanket and $2.50; Thomas Donca parted with a coat, pants and shirt; J. M. Blachaby, a quilt and $1.50; Sam Tucker, $5 and a bedspread; William Boman, a quilt.

Even at casual glance it is plain as day that the records were not meticulously kept. The tollkeepers evidently exercised a lot of discretion and differed amongst themselves in determinig the price of goods and what they would consider in lieu of monetary payment. One gets the feeling, studying the entries, that regulations were often superseded by whim.

It is difficult now to understand the charge for stock. Samuel Barlow's son, William, recalled it, many years later, as $1 a head and almost all writers have accepted this figure. But the Barlow and Foster Company record book contains an item listing a total charge of $1 for 10 horses. This would fix the toll on stock at 10 cents a head which, to me, seems a reasonable figure to accept. There was evidently no assessment on animals pulling the wagons and buggies.

Having passed the tollgate the schooners moved on, through a flowery corridor that opened as a horn of plenty into rolling meadows. First Zigzag River, normally a low stream, was crossed. It was child's play compared to a score of other fordings that were now chill memory. A few miles further the Sandy River was met and followed until the wagoners reined southward.

In the early years of the Barlow Road most of the emigrants reached Oregon City by way of Eagle Creek, where Philip Foster operated a campground, restaurant, grist mill and general merchandise store. The most traveled route to Eagle Creek from the Sandy River began at present Sandy and was followed, in approximate measure, by Oregon 211.

"Did the pioneers really come here, right where I'm standing," my daughter asked.

"Yes," I said. "Right where you're standing. All over the place."

"And did children come through with dogs?"

"With dogs and ponies and sheep and all kinds of pets."

She picked up the leashes of our two dogs and trotted them about 50 yards toward Laurel Hill. Then she turned and, leading the dogs, strode very stately toward the tollgate, the mood of history making in her eyes. When she reached the gate she halted and looking as though she was saying, Now I am really in Oregon.

Then, quickly breaking mood, she slouched and scuffed toward us. She had crossed her Rubicon and it was back to behavior as usual.

I wondered, as she discarded her dramatic bearing to romp with the dogs toward the Zigzag, if maybe this wasn't the way most kids her age acted about 120 years ago.

The chute boss

Outside a small chute a lanky farmhand crouched at the gate, awaiting the signal from a pint-sized official with upraised flag, while two men gripping the rails inside the slatted pen tensed to put the boot into a moaning calf.

Benny Herrera's eyes trailed the calf as it scurried across the sodded floor of the scurfy arena, an overweight rider in hot pursuit. The lariat, missing its mark, sagged to earth like a wet noodle and Herrera shrugged. "Oh well," he muttered, and looked back to where another trial run was being readied.

A quarter horse skittered nervously past a corral of steamy cattle and Benny Herrera frowned at the rider, too rigid in the saddle.

Now the crowds were pouring in. "It'll be time soon, huh Benny?" A copper-skinned gangly youth, cradling a saddle, repeated: "Pretty soon, huh Benny?"

Herrera nodded amicably and turned to two men who had galloped up on sturdy cow ponies. He laid a big hand on the left backside of a sorrel, stroking the animal gently, and listened carefully to the horsemen, smiling as they spoke.

The husky, hurly-shouldered, square-pawed, open-faced man that was Benny Herrera paid no heed to the people filling the grandstand and climbing the gravel paths to squat on the May-green hill above the backless wooden benches.

Other comers were shuffling and stubbing up the chalk-dust rocky and from the already strained parking area, pushing through the lane of trailers that had settled for the weekend, stepping over beer bottles and beer cans, sweating already in the early afternoon of humid spring in Wasco County.

Hundreds of more cars were on the highway, one line coming down from Maupin, the other up from The Dalles. Patiently the drivers awaited their turn to be waved into the grounds. But scores of cars, their people impatient, were parked on the gray and green shoulders along the road, some as far as two miles from the entrance.

From the highway the strange mosaic in the bowl of the ripening wheatlands looked like a giant carnival or old-fashioned camp revival that had overnight mushroomed. For two days a year, three at most, the half-hidden hollow was a sprawl of trailers, trucks, cars, herds of stock animals, food and souvenir booths, and people, all flecked by dust. Almost 20,000 persons journeyed to the All-Indian Rodeo grounds a mile below Tygh Valley. The rest of the year the amphitheater lay silent, a sluggish cove in a choppy sea of many-waved hills: green, gold, blond, brown, black and white, depending on the season. And naked, except for the arena, the corrals, and the hall of the Tywama Saddle Club.

Outside the wooden hall a plump-faced ranchwoman pointed to a long upthrust of shimmery green across the road and explained to a visitor from New York: "That's Tygh Ridge. The covered wagons of the Lost Emigrant Party came by this way, up there, in 1845. You've heard of the Blue Bucket Mine. They were the one." Retreating from the sun, they sidestepped a couple of beefy stockmen to find shelter in the clubhouse. About 30 other whites were inside, jowls working over a buffet lunch.

Benny Herrera, full Navajo, wasn't upset about all the Tywamans being white. They did a good job for the Indians, promoting the rodeo, making money for the Indians, and that's all he cared about them. If they also made a good chunk of money for themselves, that was their business.

Herrera now had more important things to concern him. As chute boss, a job he had held for 10 years, he was the ramrod of the arena. A mountain of responsibility lay on his shoulders. He had a hundred problems to face before the first event was announced. Not all of them had to do with the chutes.

"You better take that thing in your hand someplace else," he admonished a blotchy-faced young buck.

A sniveling grin. "Aw, c'mon Benny, I'm O.K. You know me."

"What kind of cowboy are you?" Herrera taunted quietly.

The young man lurched a step forward. "Now Benny, it's O.K."

Herrera stood firm and shook his head. "What kind of example do you want to set?" he mocked with a disarming smile. "Is that the way a cowboy acts? You know better than that."

Grinning sheepishly, the glaze-eyed brave wobbily turned and wambled toward a gate, bubbles of beer falling like spit on his trouser leg.

"There's always one or two like that, ain't there?" said a man at Herrera's elbow.

The chute boss shrugged. "Most of 'em are pretty good boys."

"They respect you, they sure do," the man remarked.

"I'm an old cowboy," Benny replied. "I was ridin' rodeo before some of 'em were born."

He was put on a horse, on his father's ranch, near Las Vegas, New Mexico, before he could walk, and sometimes it seemed to him he had never dismounted. "I was raised around rodeos. My dad was a team roper with that old man Bob Crosby from Carlsbad, New Mexico, at that time. They team roped together, and I followed rodeos with my dad, just like I bring my kids with me today."

At 15 he entered his first competition, riding bucking horses at a junior rodeo in Montana. He participated in junior rodeos until he enrolled at New Mexico A&M; then he switched to college meets. In 1947, when he was 19, he joined the Rodeo Cowboys Association. Now he was with the pros.

Herrera stayed with the RCA for 12 years. His biggest purse was $2700, first place for bull riding at Boston in 1949. Still though, "I made a pretty good livin', anywhere from three to five, eight thousand a year for a whole year, when I was in . . ."

This was in addition to other work: "I do a lot of breakin' horses and I pack horses, and, well, I do anything that comes along."

His three years of engineering at New Mexico A&M had qualified him for construction work. Early in the winter he had been called up to Little Goose Dam to boss the job. Recently he had returned to his ranch at Dayton, Wash., about 50 miles above the Oregon line.

In 1959 Benny Herrera left the RCA. "I was getting

older and the competition was getting better. Now I just work the Indian rodeos and some of the Northwest."

He rode his last brahma bull in 1968, at the All-Indian Rodeo at White Swan, Wash., when he was 40. That was the end of the line for the really dangerous rodeo work.

"As long as I can help rodeo I'm gonna be the chute boss," he said. "I do a lotta ropin', bull-doggin', and I ride buckin' horses, but bein' a chute boss I found I better stick to it and let the young boys do the ridin'."

A shrill of terror whirled Herrera about in time to see a feisty horse, rearing abruptly, almost stumble into a huddle of spectators. The rider, shaken by the sudden move, angrily jerked his mount away from the fleeing people. Herrera strode to the group, regathering in nervous giggles, and urged, with a touch of perturbed anxiety, "Now please clear the arena. You've seen how accidents can happen. Please find a place outside."

A judge called down from a loft above the chutes, "How are things goin', Benny?"

"Fine," Herrera answered calmly.

"No problems?"

The chute boss propped up his massive shoulders. "The usual. Nothing serious."

Back of the arena the people, horses and vehicles making up the parade that would open the rodeo began to form. They gobbled up so much space that latecomers had to squeeze between horse rumps to reach the bleachers and the hill. "We've got another great crowd this year," the announcer exulted, and his amplified words, rolling up to the crest of the hummock, brought a ripple of applause.

Benny Herrera had just finished assuring a slope-shoul-dered lad, with boots twitching in the film of dust, that he'd be all right.

"A lot of the boys is comin' in green," he told us a moment later, "and they get on a horse, and I don' know, maybe like you said, they may be a little scared, and it takes them a long time to get ready, that's always a prob-lem. My biggest job is to get them guys ready and to get 'em out.

"You have to talk to them like a father to a son," he went on, while two or three men awaited a word with him. "You have to help 'em. You'll see here, there'll be half a dozen, there'll be eight chutes, and there'll be two on each chute come up and call me and say, 'Benny, what kind of a rein shall I use on this horse?' and I sure give him my best, the best of my knowledge, and some of them call on me and tell me to help 'em put the saddle on, which I will."

Hearing muffled thuds, Herrera skewed at a file of broncs being led into the corrals. He smiled wistfully to himself and turned his attention to a potato grower from the Yakima Reservation who played rodeo cowboy three or four times a year.

They shook hands. Herrera thumbed back the brim of his black Stetson and beamed down on the shorter, leaner man. They were more than two Indians: in a tribal sense they were brothers-in-law, Herrera's wife being a Yakima. There was only one problem in intertribal relationships— the lack of a common Indian tongue. Benny and his wife didn't mind speaking English but their children, who clamored to learn a language of their forebears, often expressed frustration.

Now Herrera sprang on his horse, a powerful-looking beast, and sprinted off to the far side of the arena to check on a couple of ropers who seemed to be having some trouble. When he returned he dismounted in one fluid movement. As soon as his feet reached the ground an old copperskin, with wrinkled cheeks and sun-tinted spectacles, pulled up on a sneezing bay and teased: "Hey Benny! You gonna ride a brahma today?"

Herrera grinned back. "No more."

The old man cackled, "Maybe you don' like brahma riding no more."

Herrera laughed quietly.

"Maybe it get too dull for you."

Herrera shook his head and the old man rode off with an open-mouthed chuckle.

For Benny Herrera, nothing in all the world was as exciting as riding a brahma. "It's a great thrill, a great sport. It's in your blood. I rode bulls for 20 years and right now, if I didn't have my boys countin' on me to make a livin', take 'em through school, college, I'd still ride 'em. But now, like I say, I'm a little older, and I made my wife a promise that when I was 40 years old I'd quit, and that was last year, so this year I'm never goin' to ride a bull. I've never been hurt, but it's finished."

It was all over except the memories—so recent, so vivid.

"You're out there to compete against the cowboy. You see a good ride and what you've got in mind is you're gonna go out there and beat that good ride that boy makes.

"You gotta think—you gotta. After so many years o' seein' bulls buck you just about know what they gonna do, they'll—well, you take that Snowfall, they call 'im, that great bull; one guy rode him in eight years; then cowboys have seen 'im and then when they make their first two or three jumps you know just about what he's gonna do.

"You gotta think ahead of a bull. Yeah. When you get a new bull and you haven't rode him, well, you ask the guy that's rode him, 'Well, what does he do? Does he turn to the left? Does he turn to the right? Well, what does he do?' And he'll tell you. Ain't no cowboy that's ever told you a lie."

He always knew riding a brahma was no creampuff job but once in the chute and ready to preform he was eager for action.

"You just gotta think about gettin' on him, show 'im that you can ride 'im, show the rest of the cowboys that you can get out there and ride a bull just as good as they can. You're not scared, you're nervous. I don't think there's a man that hasn't been nervous to get on a bull because it's—like you say, they're dangerous, but you don't think *too* much on it, but I guess everybody could be, I guess everybody's gotta be nervous. If they wasn't they wouldn't be human." And he throated a small laugh.

He could remember the other cowboys rooting him on when he was in the chute. "Benny, ride 'im!" "Get on him and ride 'im!" "Show the bull you can ride him!" And that's all Herrera had in mind—to ride the bull.

A complete brahma ride is supposed to last 10 seconds. I could see it as 10 seconds of earthquake, twisters turning the hills around, the earth tilting, the sky sliding, the spectators a smear of freakish color whirling and somersaulting against a world spinning madly and breaking up in fury. For Benny Herrera it was different. "You don't have much feeling. You gotta concentrate, just like when you're playing ball or boxin'. You gotta think when you're riding a bull; if you're not thinkin' you ain't gonna ride him long. All you're doin' is ridin' him and waitin' up there, and when you hear the whistle you know you got him!"

Still, there was always the possibility of being thrown. "You gotta stay right in the middle there. If you see you're hangin' up to one side and you ain't got a chance, the thing you gotta do is let go and get outa the way. You get on one side too far and you see you're not gonna get back on, you just automatically turn loose and get outa the way.

"You gotta hit, you gotta roll—you never stand up underneath the bull. When you hit the ground you gotta roll away just like playing football. You don't jump right up, you gotta roll away from 'em on your hands and knees, and—they'll tell you what to do; once you walk off a bull you're automatically gone." And he laughed the laugh of the seasoned warrior.

The arena had been cleared and the gate thrown open. The long parade filed in, led by a sparse, tight-lipped Chief. He was sallow and anemic compared to the dark, massive Navajo.

Benny Herrera leaned his broad back against a chute post, past which flame-nostriled broncs would leap and twist into arcs as the first event of the rodeo, and waited patiently for his real chores to start.

He had only brief advice for anyone who wanted to be a rodeo rider: "Stay in good shape, don't do any drinkin' when you're gonna compete, and keep one foot on one side and one on the other."

As the parade serpentined around the arena a paleface spectator arose from his bench seat and, in a voice that rang across the clodded oval, plumed by dust spumes, cried, "Ole!"

Benny Herrera smiled and shook his head. "Never a dull moment," he sighed happily.

There's more to Wamic than meets the eye

A rooster crowed and a horse was drinking out of a bathtub and that's all the sign of life there was in Wamic on that hot Sunday afternoon in August.

We didn't spot the rooster, and the horse, taking its fill from the bathtub parked in somebody's front yard, didn't see us.

No one was tending the gas pump outside the Wamic Store, which was itself closed. The school grounds were deserted. Not a sound strayed from a house. And the wind slept.

We had come to Wamic to find Mrs. Lenore Walters, who had told us, at the All-Indian Rodeo at Tygh Valley, that she would lead us to some interesting pioneer locations around Wamic. It did not occur to us that Wamic could mean way out in the country, which is where Mrs. Walters lived. It turned out, too, that she couldn't help us, being up to her ears with the County Fair, which was opening the next week.

How did we latch on to this information? By knocking on doors until we found a couple at home. Mr. and Mrs. Massie Ashley were their names and they treated us as hospitably as though we were some kind of kin.

When I mentioned that I was a gadabout reporter they asked my name and when they heard it they exclaimed: "Oh sure! We've got that book of yours, *Tales Out Of Oregon!*" So it pay to be known, even a little bit, because the Ashleys gave us a few hours of their restful afternoon, a precious commodity to part with when you're tired and have more important things to do.

The Ashleys had been farmers for a long time but rising costs and low prices had discouraged them to the point where they sold out and moved "into town," which is what any tiny hamlet is called by farm folks.

Now Massie Ashley worked the night shift in the saw mill at Tygh Valley and was relaxing on the sofa, with his shoes off, when we tapped on his door. He was working up enough energy to lie down for a nap, so he could store up some fuel for the mill job that night, but he put off his snooze while we phoned Mrs. Walters. When we learned that she couldn't go out with us, Mr. Ashley sighed, put on his shoes, and agreed to take us around.

It was a very nice thing for him to do and I told him so at least a dozen times but he shrugged off my appreciations. "I could use a drive in the country myself," he drawled, and his wife, a peppy woman with a winsome smile, offered, with welcomed enthusiasm, "I haven't been out to the Barlow Road for a long time, so let's go. Massie can catch some rest when we get back." Mr. Ashley rubbed a heavy thumb on an overall strap and allowed, in his sombre way, that concealed a warm heart and a wry wit, that he would live through the day. So we piled into his 1965 Dodge and started up for Smock Prairie.

The road, first paved and then graveled, scissored through meadows that stretched like seaweed lakes to a low chain of hills stealing down from the north and to the mantled Cascade slopes westward. Across the open prairie a shawl of cloud was draped about the shoulders of Mt. Hood but the head of the mountain was clear and I tried to imagine myself driving a covered wagon, about 120 years ago, and looking at Mt. Hood, that last great beacon to the Oregon homeland. How it must have seemed not to come an inch closer after hours and even days of plodding westward.

One of the meadow washes swept around a log cabin that excited our attention, there being so few log cabins still standing in the state. But the Ashleys didn't think any of the covered wagon pioneers on their way to the Willamette Valley had built the structure. It was put up much later, most likely by a homesteader, they reasoned, and was probably erected to serve as a potato or storage shed.

"A storage shed," concluded Mr. Ashley, after some pondering. He said it twice, which meant the subject was closed.

We stopped again in front of Smock Prairie No. 44 School, probably the first built in these parts. It's no longer used as a school, hasn't been for a long time, but every now and then the old building, looking like something that flew in out of Halloween, serves as a community hall.

"Mrs. Walters went to school here for eight grades and

after college returned here as a teacher," Mrs. Ashley informed us. Mrs. Walters, then, I would judge, must have started school more than 50 years ago, and she was not in the first class.

Massie Ashley drove his '65 Dodge with the passion of a dare-devil. Somewhere inside that stoic-looking ex-farmer the fire of a test pilot burned brightly. He zipped over chuckholes and bumps as though they were painted spots on a velvet rug and when he turned onto a dirt road he seemed to gather abandon. But he was at his boldest when he approached streams of rocks, some of them fierce enough to make me weep silently for his tires. Massie Ashley, though, charged straight on, showing them who was boss. If it had been my car, with me driving, I would have halted at the edge of some of those rock fields and requested my wife to dismount and push the larger and sharper rocks off the road. But Ashley sailed ahead, his eyes glowing, without a single curse and without a word of caution from his wife, who took his onslaught upon the rocks with sweet equanimity.

Eventually, on a dry plain, we came to a cattle guard and a sign reading: Barlow Road. Beyond the cattle guard the road entered timber. The initial look is deceiving, because the dirt road appears in good shape. Actually, the first 10 or 12 miles now constitute the roughest part of the road, too difficult for most late-model passenger cars to negotiate.

It was at this point that the wagons on the Barlow Cutoff began their agonizing snakedance to the shoulder of Mt. Hood.

You know about the Barlow Road, of course. It was scratched out late in 1845 under the leadership of iron-willed Samuel Kimbrough Barlow, who asserted that "God never made a mountain that He had not made a place for some man to go over it or under."

Captain Barlow, as he was called, because he captained a wagon train, was responding to the cry of history. The time had come when a more practical route to the Williamette Valley not only was desirable but was a critical necessity. The Dalles had become a bottleneck, choked with wagons and hungry people. The only way to the Williamette Valley was down the unpredictable and sometimes maniacal Columbia River, as costly in money as it was vexing and dangerous. Many a wagon was left behind or burned for firewood at The Dalles because it couldn't be taken downstream (though other wagons were partially dismantled and placed on rafts); many a draw animal lost its balance on the river cliffs, as the stock were being driven separately, and killed in the fall; and many an emigrant, who had survived all kinds of near-misses in the 2000 miles of overland travel from the Big Muddy, was drowned when the flimsy craft on the Columbia capsized.

By 1852 there was already a white settlement at Tygh Valley, right next to an Indian village, and at the East Barlow Gate, which must have been not too far from the cattle guard in front of us. E. W. Conyers, one of the more lucid diarists of the trail, reported that he met an emigrant who had arrived in the Williamette Valley two weeks earlier, sold his outfit, purchased "a supply of the necessaries of life," returned to East Barlow Gate, and set up a small trading post. The new merchant told Conyers, evidently with relish, "All those traders that we met out here skinned us emigrants for all we were worth, and now I have come back here to skin all the balance of the emigrants." And, added Conyers, somewhat philosophically, "I rather think that he made good his word."

"I wonder which way the wagons came to this road," drawled Massie Ashley. He pointed to what looked like a faded rut lane that swung across the plain, in the shape of a scythe, and reckoned that might be it. His wife spotted what appeared to be a wheel track emerging from timber to the north. My wife found another way the wagons might have approached the place where the sign read: Barlow Road. When you think about it, they may all have been right, for in open country the wagons cut a wide swath, keeping apart so they could dodge some dust and avoid the areas where all the grass had been eaten. Beyond the sign and cattle guard was the first heavy timber the emigrants encountered and they could not have gotten through any other way except by the narrow road hacked out of the forest.

When we were ready to start back Mr. Ashley asked if we'd be interested in meeting an old hermit, Ed Disbrow by name.

Fine, we said, but Ashley didn't know how much we'd get out of the visit. "He's shy around strangers. He's pretty close-mouthed, too. You'll have to be awful tactful to get him to talk." I replied nonchalantly that I got along fine with hermits. Ashley tossed me a glance of dubious merit and hustled up a set of tire prints toward Disbrow's home.

A small, thin, bent man, who quickly brought to my mind the image of a hunched sparrow, was bent over a pile of odds and ends in front of his house. The yard, with all kinds of bits and pieces strewn here and there, recalled the farms I had seen and worked on more than 30 years ago. Almost all the farms you see today are a lot neater, and a little less colorful.

As soon as I noticed that Disbrow was wearing long johns, the top of which showed under the open neck of his shirt, I felt at home. I never have failed to get along with an old farmer who wears full-length underwear in summer. So, easily attuning myself to Disbrow, whom I liked right off the bat, I squatted a few feet from him until he had worked through the scent of me and hadn't found any skunk in my makeup.

After a bit I told him that I had written a couple of books on Oregon and was gathering material for another. "Friedman?" he mused, arising. "Ralph Friedman. That's it, isn't it? You bet! One of the neighbors loaned me your book to read. Say, that was all right! I liked it."

Massie Ashley had said that Ed Disbrow spoke sparingly and wouldn't give us much time. But after he remembered my book there was no stopping him. If we had listened all night he would still have been going strong by morning. It got so I was afraid to ask a question and cast an evil eye at anybody in our party who did because Disbrow answered every question in encyclopedic detail. Even when we gave up asking questions he continued talking, putting a query to us and then providing a long explanation in reply. Once, as we were ready to step into the car, he came up with, "Say Massie, you know that young fella who was here a few years ago? Well, I got a letter from him a while ago." And he scampered into the house and returned with a six-page document, reading each word (and very fluently, too), and interjecting voluminous footnotes at places he thought might not be readily explicable to Ashley.

Again: "Do you remember those two men who slept in my barn one night?" And he was on the run again.

I do not mean to cast fun at Ed Disbrow. I came away with respect and affection for the man, only wishing we weren't so cramped for time.

In his talking Disbrow revealed something about himself. He was born in Hood River in 1900 and came here with his homesteading folks in 1911. Now he lived alone, as he had for years, on his 440 acres, most of it in pasture.

"I make an existence of it, that's all," he said. "I got 22 acres water right. Irrigate a little hay and grow some fruit. That's it."

He built his two-story house, on which he started in 1940, trading timber for lumber and doing all the work himself. It cost him $67.50 "for windows and doors and ceilings and hinges and things I had to buy" and another $8 for used bricks, which were made on the site of the present Wamic schoolhouse. He had the roof on by the winter of 1940 but it took him the better part of two years to complete the building.

Disbrow didn't consider himself a hermit. He had good neighbors and he saw them as often as he wished, which was, I gathered, not too rarely. "I bring my neighbors fruit and eggs and berries and they bring me cakes and jams and jellies and pies. We get along fine."

He looked up from shooing off a busybody chicken and added: "I don't have time to get lonesome. There's always something to do. Someone comes every day or two."

He was proud of his sons, who lived elsewhere, and spoke of them at great length. His eyes glowed when he said, "My youngest boy, who works over at Zigzag, gave me a deep freezer and then he filled it up for me." He repeated that statement, in various forms, three or four more times before we departed.

I told Disbrow that the Ashleys regarded him as an authority on the history of these parts. He acknowledged the honor, as a fact beyond speculation, and promptly launched into a discourse on Smock Prairie which Disbrow said was named after a man who was really named Smock. He thought that was a piece of incredible information.

Then he pointed toward Gate Creek, where he said toll was once taken. "In the early years the Barlow Road wagons came over that ridge, and if you go up there you can find their tracks. Later, they came across Smock Prairie."

We didn't have time to search the ridge, but that's not saying I'll never try it. Just as we started to leave his ranch, Disbrow made another statement, this one directed at me. Briefly, it went something like this:

"You ought to come back here and we'll write a book together on this country. I've been here a long time and I know this country like the back of my hand. I know all its history, a lot of it that's never been told. We could write a book, based on truth, of what really happened. So much of that stuff you read about Smock Prairie is just made up. I could spend weeks telling you about this country. You wouldn't believe it, would you?"

I said I believed it, and I was never more sincere.

A reason for Maupin

It had always been hard for me to figure out why Maupin stood where it did, on a naked plateau that slides down into the cavernous gorge of the Deschutes River.

Every time I came through the town I wondered what would keep a soul there, on that wind-scarred ridge, but somebody must have liked it; the population numbered about 500.

Years back Maupin survived because it was a market place for a lot of homesteaders in that part of central Wasco County. Then, when the homesteaders departed, like tumbleweeds bouncing out of sight, and there weren't enough folks around Tygh Valley, Wapinitia, Boyd and Wamic to keep the business blood circulating strongly, Maupin kept alive as a sort of communications hub, being the eastern anchor of State 216 and sitting astride US 197, the shortest road from Madras to The Dalles.

There was also a saw mill now, a few yards from the motel where we always seemed to find ourselves when night overtook us in Maupin. My daughter thought the motel was creepy, being without television, but it was for that that I liked it.

About the only time the motels (three, including a covey of Model A-vintage cabins we used to call a tourist court) and the barn-like hotel—which the locals referred to as a roadhouse, perhaps because of its stagecoach flavor —were filled to capacity before the sun went down, was when the All-Indian Rodeo was held near Tygh Valley. Then you couldn't buy a spot to roost for love or money. Everything was spoken for a year in advance.

We tried to reserve a motel unit seven days prior to one rodeo and didn't have a speck of luck, even when I confided to the proprietors that I was a newspaperman who had been assigned to cover the big doings by the New York *Times*, *Playboy*, *Christian Science Monitor*, London *Express*, the Japanese wire service and *Pravda*.

All these motel operators were just then riding so high they weren't a bit impressed by my phoney credentials.

"I think it's a crying shame," I told a lady who answered the phone at one motel, "that a journalist as famous as I am can't find a single place in town to stay."

"Sorry," she chirped. "Try the week after the rodeo."

The wheel of life turns and the location of Maupin, which had always bewildered me, might prove a boon to its future. Opening of the 25-mile-long Deschutes River Access Road from Maupin, at the bottom of the grade, to Mack's Canyon, had put the town on the map for thousands of fishermen, campers, rockhounds, bird lovers and just plain old sightseers.

The real beauty of Maupin was the river at its door, the Deschutes, an eddying stream, deep and dark, that at times, like a normally placid man pouring out his pent-up emotions, explodes into bursts of fury.

The river was made for fishermen, said fishermen, but non-anglers would not be denied its intrinsic or peripheral loveliness, whether that beauty rested in the craggy-faced canyon walls brooding down upon the trail of intruders, or mountain jays and blue herons skimming in silky hum over the fluttery water, or a deer bounding in shivers through a clay-bellied draw, or a breeze come to loaf by your fire at eventide.

Yes, the Deschutes was still a fair, unpolluted river and its banks yet uncrowded. There were no factories here to debase it, the cities that could foul it were a hundred miles distant. (Was that far enough? At Bend there was already strong concern.) For miles and miles the Deschutes touched no community; on some stretches of the river the mileage between houses could span a county in western Oregon. At points, half-hidden in a crook of the canyon, a cow hockdeep in rushes was all that reminded us of the presence of men somewhere in the area.

But now the Deschutes was being opened, and in 10 years or less, probably less, there would be little of the primitive landscape untouched, or unsullied. Here and there, even where the sight of man was for the moment absent, we saw a cardboard beer can container flabby in a rush, a beer can floating on a ripple, an empty cigarette pack on the bank, broken soda pop bottles sprayed around a rock, and dirty paper napkins scudding across a tramped bush, the discarded battle flags of spoil. And we can't wait until we colonize the moon! Why? To see if we can pollute that luckless star quicker and more thoroughly than we have debauched Earth. We who have not solved our minimal difficulties here would send our major problems a quarter of a million miles into space. Shall we cry now before the ludicrousness of the situation dawns upon us?

We wound down the Access Road, raising dust on the gravel and wading through the choking gray clouds churned up by those who passed us. Four miles from Maupin we halted and climbed down a slope to the Handicapped Fishing Ramp, which we were told was the only such facility in the entire United States. It was built by the Western Rod and Reel Club and maintained by the Bureau of Land Management.

An old gentleman from Arkansas was sunning in his wheel chair on the ramp, his line out for steelhead or salmon. His daughter, a competent-looking woman of about 40, stood by, ready to assist if needed.

"How'd you hear about this place?" we asked.

"Oh," he replied, 'it's known all over the country."

We asked his daughter some questions about their self-propelled mobile camper, one of the biggest we had seen on the roads of Oregon. She knew all about it. "I'm the driver and mechanic," she said. She was also cook, maid and nurse. "I just do the fishing," her father laughed.

Another four or five miles up the road brought us to the heights above Sherar's Falls. The Deschutes, squeezed here by the walls of a low, rocky canyon, went berserk like a wild horse frantically trying to throw its rider. It spumed and fumed and kicked up a rampant fuss as it flailed and stormed and bull-lathered its way through a narrow trough formed by cinder-colored ledges extending from the cliff.

The falls, near Sherar's Bridge (more comfortably reached by paved road from Tygh Valley), was the historic fishing property of the Warm Springs Indians. Only a Warm Springs could occupy one of the rickety wooden platforms perched on the rocky headlands thrust into the boiling trough. Plenty of whites were around, maybe 100 yards farther north, toward Mack's Canyon, but mainly they were just looking on. With all the publicity, Indian fishing at the falls had become a tourist attraction.

Three Indians were on the platforms, slouching on beat-up chairs or boxes. They weren't talking to one another; separated as they were they probably couldn't hear each other if they shouted, what with the angry and wounded river bellowing its lungs out. Actually, none of the three seemed to pay any attention to the other two, and in the hour we were there not one of the fishermen showed the slightest interest in the spectators on the paved road across the stream on the bank downriver. Once you've seen a crow of whites you've seen them all. The Indians didn't look at the Deschutes either. One of them chain-smoked and when he ran out of cigarettes he plodded off, over the slippery rocks under a film of spillwater, to rustle up another pack; a second had his head down, maybe wondering if this was the kind of work he really was born to do; and the third, the youngest man, was absorbed in a paperback book. Their lines didn't seem to need watching; after so much experience on the platforms they could tell if they had a nibble. In the 60 minutes of our stay not a single fish was hauled in. Some days, I understand, the catch per platform was as high as a fish per minute. But when you've got a lucky fellow like me around, what can you expect?

Just below the road, at the bottom of the bumpy slope, a Hooverville-type shanty had been slapped together. Outside, a wizened elder, his ancient face a wrinkly patch of scrolled papyrus, dozed in a dust-coated rocking chair facing the river. Perhaps, in the vigor of his manhood, he had stood above the steaming spray, the eye of an eagle sharp for salmon. The turn now belonged to those two or three generations younger. A century had turned and six decades gone by since he had first mounted the rocks. The salmon still ran. But where had so much else of the woods and rivers gone?

A breeze flapped the old man's collar and he slowly raised a gnarled hand to the back of his neck. Gently he closed his palm, as one holds a small bird. Then his arm fell to his side and dangled there a moment before climbing stiffly on his lap. He would not reach for the wind much longer. He nodded on, preparing for the long sleep.

We completed the run to Mack's Canyon and turned around. At Beavertail Campground about a dozen campers and trailers were already there, and it was still mid-morning. More were on the way, license plates from five or six states. Even a few from Oregon.

"If we come back this way," my wife said, "let's make it soon. Five years from now may be too late."

"I reckon," I muttered, and drove back to Maupin.

Just for the heck of it I stopped at a motel and asked the manager if we could reserve a unit for the All-Indian Rodeo weekend two years ahead.

"I'd sure like to," he smiled, "but we're all taken for then. People from back east are coming out here."

"Maupin is getting mighty popular," I groaned.

"You bet," he replied. "Would you be interested in a place for tonight?"

Prineville and parts east

Tongue-in-cheek I cautioned Jim Watson, the young city administrator, that Prineville was practicing socialism and might someday be investigated for such subversive activities.

"Socialism?" mused Watson. "Hmm. Never thought of it that way."

Watson looked mildly perplexed. "Socialism. Hmm. Well, what's a label? The railroad is good for the community; that's all that matters."

We had been talking about the City of Prineville Railway, which was the only rail line in the U.S.A. that had been continuously operated by a municipal government from the time of construction, which in this case dates back to 1918. It was possibly also the only city in the country then owning and operating a railroad.

For a long time Prineville boasted that it was the only city in Oregon that didn't levy property taxes. This was because of the railroad, which had poured millions of dollars into the city treasury. But in 1967, to keep up services, a small property tax was enacted. If you lived in Prineville in 1969 and had a $15,000 home, your property tax would have come to $21, which would still be lower than most anywhere else in the state.

Prineville was an up-to-date city. All its streets were paved, it had 50 acres of parks, a municipal swimming pool, two ambulances and well-equipped police and fire departments. No wonder that any suggestion the city sell its railroad to private enterprise was regarded as arch heresy.

Howard Wilson, the very genial CPR agent, filled us in on some details. The 19-mile line ran from Prineville to Prineville Junction where it connected with the Oregon Trunk and the Union Pacific. Outbound, it hauled lumber products and, to a lesser amount, potatoes. Inbound it mainly carried grain, oil and gasoline. Two freight trips were made daily, six times a week, with an average train length of 20 to 25 cars. Gross revenue in recent years had been $450,000 annually. Most of the money was plowed back into the CPR but a good chunk of the earnings were turned over to the city. "It's like having a gold mine in your back yard," a banker told us.

The CPR inventory included three diesel locomotives. I could take that in stride. But a passenger coach? That was something else—and to learn that the coach was purchased not for profit but for pleasure!

In its early years the CPR did a lively passenger business, but better roads and automobiles pared volume to the point where passenger service was discontinued. That was in 1939. About 20 years later a lot of people worked up a strong nostalgia for riding the line. Since they wouldn't go by boxcar, the CPR shelled out $5,400 to buy a coach from the Union Pacific. A veteran of the Portland-Seattle run, the coach was now used for excursion groups and special trips, usually on Friday nights during the summer. No fare was charged and nobody asked if you lived in Prineville.

The town had something else going for it: a million dollar annual intake from rockhounds. Under the leadership of chamber of commerce manager Ivan Chappell, rockhounding had been developed from zero to 85,000 visitors a year. Chappell, always thinking, was promoting Prineville as "Rockhound Capital of the U.S.A."

You didn't have to part with a cent to search for plume, moss agates, obsidians, thunder eggs and other beauties in the chamber-owned claims. "It's a steady business," said Chappell, "and we're not exhausting our resources because the rockhounds don't take enough out to deplete the area."

Some day, of course, at the rate the hobbyists were coming in, the claims would be exhausted, but all Ivan could see in his crystal ball was more and more rockhound money spent in Prineville.

There was still another distinction to this Ochoco community of some 4,000 population. Every presidential election a swarm of pollsters flitted into town, armed with clipboards, forms, notebooks, pencils and ball point pens.

If they had been locusts they would have devoured the city, crunching and crackling until everything in sight had been rendered lifeless.

Crook County, of which Prineville was the administrative seat, was one of several—I think the exact number is four—"bellwether" counties in the nation. Each of these counties had since its inception voted for the winner, no matter how close some of the presidential contests were.

It seemed to me that the good citizens would tire of being treated as prime guinea pigs. But I didn't stop with this hypothesis. Being a scientifically-minded fellow I put my formulation to the test, knocking at doors. "I'm taking a poll as to how you like being polled," I said, half-expecting doors to be slammed in my face. But everybody was right pleasant and they all replied they didn't in the least mind expressing their views.

Some of the people went a step farther, which showed how sophisticated they had become. Like, for instance, the lady who wanted to spruce up first if she was going to be on television. "The last time I was on camera I looked like a wreck," she explained.

The most enlightening statement came from a perky 70-year-old widow. "Why," she bubbled, inviting us inside, "it's a lot of fun giving our opinions. Makes us feel pretty important. And we see a lot of new faces that way. I'll tell you one thing: it's more interesting than some of those daytime soap operas."

My hypothesis shattered, we drove to the Crook County Fairgrounds, which was practically across the street from a broad-lawned residential district. There we found Ivan Chappell, working like all getout to prepare the fair for its opening.

Every time I came into Crook County I half-way expected to bump into the peripatetic Ivan, a bustling beaver honeybear of a man. He was manager of the Prineville Chamber of Commerce, manager of the Crook County Fair, secretary-treasurer of Prineville Economic Promotions and chief cook and bottle washer at every civic clambake.

"A fellow has got to do a lot of things in a small town to make a living," Ivan said. "You've got to be a moonlighter."

We asked Ivan to tell us something about the fair. He

was off and running, whip to the flank. One or two of the things he said might have been exaggerated some, but that didn't bother us a bit, Ivan being such a likeable cuss.

"This was just a little 4-H, FFA county fair but we've made it into one of the most outstanding small fairs in the whole United States," Ivan began. "But we've kept it old-fashioned, and therein lies its charm.

"It's the only county fair I know of that has no rodeo or carnival. We feel that carnivals divert the attention of children from what is really useful. So we've banned the hoopla and put up a lot of exhibits aimed at the curiosity of youngsters."

Ivan came to Prineville from the Virgin Islands, where he had been a chamber manager. "We got tired of looking at trees not losing their leaves," he said. "I wanted deciduous trees and a frostline—not too cold or too hot. We searched all over the United States—covered the country doggone good. There was no place that struck our fancy until we came to Prineville. It has every type of recreation a person could ask for except skiing; you have to go 50 miles for that. When we retire we'll make this our home. I don't know where else I'd want to live."

The mayors of Prineville came and departed; county commissioners were elected, defeated and retired. The people forgot them quickly but Ivan Chappell, who had been around about a quarter of a century, was a name everyone knew. He must have shaken hands with every man, woman and child in Crook County, including a lot of people who didn't belong to anything except Blue Cross.

An hour after we left Ivan we met Cecil Sly, a former superintendent of schools, and rode with him up an excellent paved county road to Paulina, 55 miles east and slightly south of Prineville. The scenery was generally pleasant: a few striking rock formations; several low canyons; now and then, far off the road, a ranch house; here and there a deserted homesteader's cabin or barn; wastelands and grasslands. For some distance we paralleled the Maury Mountains, a small range of rumpled hills where homesteaders in the area went for wood to build their dwellings. For many miles we followed the Crooked River, much of it disappointingly narrow and shallow. In its upper stretches irrigation had reduced it to a rustling dribble. And we whizzed through Post. Had I blinked at the wrong second I would have missed it.

Cecil Sly remembered that as late as 1950 the road was a twisty dirt pike, one-way where the hills closed in, and, depending upon the season, muddy, choked with dust, piled with rocks, and a mosaic of craters.

Not too many years ago, he said, there were one and two-room schoolhouses along the Crooked River and he showed us those that were still standing, though no longer in use. Now the kids are bussed, and sometimes long distances. For instance, a bus carries high school students from Paulina to Prineville—a 110 mile round trip every school day.

A few miles before we reached Paulina we paused at a homespun, dung-caked, rickety rodeo arena. In all my years of wandering around the West this was surely as crude a piece of rodeo construction as I had ever seen. Still, that's what gave it an air of Western authenticity. No great names came here—only unknowns from the hamlets and ranches of eastern Crook and western Grant counties, to compete in the amateur contests. That's how rodeos started—cowboys entertaining themselves. Something, I suppose, like musicians at a jam session.

There was one ingenious touch. The bluff on the north side of the arena had been terraced into strips wide enough to hold cars, and that's how most people watched the salty gladiators strut, swagger, ride, wrestle calves and bite the dust. A separate trail led to each terrace, making parking arrangements very simple.

Some spectators, women as well as men, preferred viewing the action from atop the fences. Such practice is strictly prohibited at every professional rodeo. But this, being for amateurs, the rules were different. It had the mood of an impromptu rodeo in the days of the open range, when the buckeroos straddled the corral fences and roared, "Powder River, let 'er buck!"

Paulina itself was as rustic and unvarnished as the rodeo grounds. You had to go a long way to find anything like it. Chances were, in a few years it wouldn't be around. But while it still had breath it made a mighty interesting scene.

First off, there was the white-painted community church

planted on a bald-pated knoll. It had once been a school-house at Beaver Creek, northeast of Paulina.

This was typical of backcountry improvisation, changing the use of structures to meet the needs of the people. Why build a church when there's a schoolhouse standing idle only ten miles away?

The Paulina school, with a large quonset hut for a gym, stood across the street. Two teachers comprised the faculty. One lived in a house, the other in a trailer. The children came from farms within a 40-mile radius, bussed from the hems of the Maury Mountains, the North Fork of the Crooked River, the G.I. Ranch, Twelvemile Creek, Suplee and places even more remote. I did some hasty figuring and concluded that a kid who lived 40 miles away would log 115,000 miles on the bus during his eight years of school here. If he went on to four years of high school at Prineville he would ride a bus for another 80,000 miles. All told, about 200,000 miles—a distance equal to eight times around the world.

Fascinated with my statistics, I did a little more calculating and estimated that the same youngster, during his 12 years of education at Paulina and Prineville, would spend about 9,500 hours on school buses. I wonder how the hours are used. Might make an interesting sociological study.

Well, then there was the dance hall, sometimes called the Pau-Mau Club, after the organization which ran the monthly shindigs. They were gingery stomps and some of them, especially at rodeo time, lasted all through the night. Generally the music was provided by a four-piece combo playing country music like they had invented it. The sound waves, generated by electrified instruments and amplified full blast, shook the hall and were murder on eardrums. But nobody complained. Came dance night, almost everybody in that vast and sparsely settled region showed up. The hall was packed so tight some of the patrons jokingly referred to themselves as sardines, especially when they started sweating.

The hall was also used for other community functions —everything from town meetings to box socials. It was the gathering place for the residents of a 2,500-square-mile area.

Paulina was pretty young in its experience with modern gadgets but it was learning fast. Electricity didn't arrive until 1950. Now most of the homes had television and trying to get the kids to bed had become a problem, as everywhere else.

We were told this while talking to a few people in the general store. Enlightened, we took our soft drinks out to the porch where we met Jack Banta, a lean, straight-talking workingstiff who had been around Paulina since 1924, except when he wandered off to labor in the woods or drive log trucks. Now he hired out to farms, whoever could use him.

"Damn if I know why I came to Paulina," Banta said. "That's something you never know. But that was a long time ago, wasn't it, when I was young and feeling my oats. You know where the years went? I don't.

"When I come first there was three stores, all general, and a barber shop, and a blacksmith shop, and a two-story hotel. Late as 1945 there was a restaurant here. The town went downhill because when the road was made good people started shopping in Prineville.

"Not many cars when I first got here," Banta continued, in the honed, impersonal tone of a man who had warmed himself at few intimate fires. "Car wasn't any good unless you had a team of horses ahead of you. Took all day for a car to get down to Prineville. Round trip took two or three days if you planned to stay overnight. The mail stage was sometimes hauled by horse. If the stage driver came in late he just stayed for the night.

"There was more folks around. One fella didn't have the whole operation. All these places had a family on them. Now one outfit has half the valley."

Banta looked up to see a station wagon crunch by the old Charlie Congleton place, about 50 yards east, and stop at the gas pumps outside the store.

The Charlie Congleton place, with its old buildings and fences, was just about the purest picture of a pioneer homestead in all central Oregon. It really belonged far away from any town, and here it was, just a loud whisper from the store. Well, Paulina wasn't an ordinary town; it was an outpost, and before the road was paved it was really in the way-out country. At that, the blacktop ran out just a few miles east of town, so that the folks from Suplee had to bite hard into gravel before they reached asphalt.

Jack Banta squinted toward the Charlie Congleton place, which he had known when Charlie had the spread, and remarked laconically, "When you grow up with a country you don't see much change. You have to look back and see all that's happened."

Neither Banta nor a couple of other men on the porch had any clear notion of what Paulina's population might be. They pondered on it awhile and Banta said, "Oh, from 20 to 25, counting kids and maybe dogs."

What the town could have used, said Cecil Sly, who was no stranger to Paulina, was a good fire engine. He pointed to strews and rubble that had been buildings the last time he had been there. "They won't be rebuilt," he muttered dourly. "Just more of the town gone."

But Paulina did have an ambulance, donated by the Elks Club of Prineville. Operated by volunteers, it had saved several lives. The Prineville hospital was only an hour away and the speed at which the drivers flew could reduce the time to 45 minutes. Everybody in these parts had a heavy foot on the pedal; car and hunting accidents made the most business for the ambulance.

We thought we'd mail a postal card from Paulina. So we returned to the store and found the post office inside. There was a tavern on the other side of the store but it was deserted except for a red-faced stockman brooding over a beer. We asked when the store closed and the lady then in charge shook her head. "When we run out of business," she said. "During the hunting season we're open day and night."

Eight miles west of Paulina, now bound for Prineville, we crossed the South Fork of the Crooked River. It was down this stream, coming up from Buck Creek and the vicinity of the G.I. Ranch, that a section of the ill-fated "Lost Emigrant Party," originally led by Stephen Meek, limped toward the Deschutes River, which would lead them to the safety of The Dalles. So we were at an historic juncture and I walked around a bit, trying to set the scene in my mind.

The South Fork, intaking Beaver Creek, which slants past Paulina, turns west where we stopped to look around. After my imagination had run its course we continued, wheeling over practically the same ground the battered covered wagons had as they creaked up and down choppy sagebrush hills or squeezed through a rock-jumbled defile into a lea along the stream. For all reconstructing purposes, the road to Prineville follows the trace of the lost emigrants.

Old timers say that all this country along the Crooked River was once thick and high in grass. Now, except in green patches, the land is sage and juniper. The common belief is that the climate turned dry. Without sufficient rain, the grass died.

Our last stop was at Post, which consisted of a weathered Grange hall and a small store. The entire population was Mrs. Patricia Wells, unless you counted her two Chihuahuas, one of which was snippily curious and the other very shy.

Yellow-haired, loose-limbed Pat Wells, a divorcee and a grandmother, was a jack-of-all-trades. We saw one customer test her talents. First, he ordered some groceries. Pat sacked them. Then he reckoned that he'd like to buy some stamps. Pat strolled back of the cage, in the rear of the store, that was the post office. When that big transaction was completed he allowed as to how he'd like a beer. Pat trailed him through an interior door into her small saloon and served him his brand. "Anything else?" she asked. "Yeah," he said, without gruffness, "I need some gas. Fill 'er up. You don't have to check the oil. It's OK." So Pat sauntered outside, to the pumps, and took care of his car.

Pat Wells arrived here in 1951. Like Jack Banta in Paulina, she didn't know why she came. But she did, became acquainted with the couple who had the store, and bought it from them. That automatically made her the postmaster. There were six people in Post then but they had all moved away, leaving the town to Pat and her dogs.

"I feel like I'm living with the ghosts of the pioneers," Pat said in good humor. Her lips looked like they were always ready to smile. "This store was built in 1889, the same year the post office was put in. When I have to retire from the post office, in 1977, I might leave. But I might keep the store. It's a good living and I'm in no hurry to go anywhere."

She was quite proud of her store. "People come all the way from Prineville to buy my cheese," she bragged.

"They say nobody's Tillamook cheese in town is as good as mine." She bought cheese in 25-pound wheels. Some people think that when cheese is made in larger units it has a chance to develop zestier flavor.

Life was never lonely for her, she said, and I believed her. She seemed very contented. "Someone is in and out all the time," she declared. "I have TV on all day and once in a while I get to look at it but I'm generally pretty busy. If I wasn't happy here I wouldn't have stayed all these years."

She opened the store at 8 a.m. and had no idea each morning when she would close. "Sometimes they'll drink until past midnight, up until one o'clock. As long as there's somebody here I'm open." She said she didn't mind working 17 hours a day. "Keeps me out of mischief," she laughed.

You might get the impression, running your eyes over this ghostly plain, that social activities would be almost nil. But Pat Wells didn't see it that way. "Oh, there are a lot of things to do," and her smile was complete, her whole face was smiling. "Someone in the area has a pinochle game or something. I join them if I can. There's a potluck at the Grange hall every three months—and we'll dance a little after we eat. No sir, you don't get bored around here."

Her biggest excitement since 1951 came when she was robbed by three boys, who broke into the store while she was asleep. She must have been a sound sleeper because the boys cleaned out the cash registers and took about five cases of beer. They were apprehended, returned the money, and were placed on probation.

"One of them comes in all the time now," said Pat. "No hard feelings. He was just a kid."

As we prepared to leave, Pat followed us outside and called: "By the way, I don't know if you realize it or not, but this is the geographical center of Oregon."

If we hadn't been told, I would never have guessed it.

No place like Bend

Phil Brogan's living room, from which you could look out to Mirror Pond, that liquid sapphire of Bend, was a testimonial to Phil's long career as an outdoor and science writer. Framed citations, books long out of print, old maps and Western relics tastefully filled the beautiful room, which was also Phil's writing workshop, but nowhere could we see a fish or game trophy.

The simple truth was, the man who knew Central Oregon's mountains, woods, rivers and lakes better than anyone in the state didn't hunt or fish.

"I killed a deer once, 45 years ago, and after looking the poor creature in the eye I wondered why I ever killed the poor thing, and I haven't shot a deer since," Phil said. "I'm sorry I killed the animal. I'm a poor hunter. If I was over in the Ochoco, a young fellow over there in the mountains, and had to live on deer meat, well, maybe. . ."

He stared at the floor and shook his head. "Why should I kill an animal like that? Didn't he have as much right to live on this earth as I did?"

Phil had looked the deer in the eye as it was dying but he didn't want to go into detail about his feelings.

"Make you weep!" exclaimed his wife, a sparkling silver-haired woman who had been Phil's sidekick for about half a century.

"I get too romantic about this," Phil chuckled self-consciously. "I just looked at his face you might say."

Way back in 1923 a man from the Bend Chamber of Commerce had taken Phil out fishing on the Metolius River. "He promised me a lot of fish. I didn't even get a strike! So, I gave up fishing. I'm easily discouraged." And he laughed, as though it was just another good anecdote in his full and active life.

Phil Brogan was a native son of the land East of the Cascades, the title, incidentally, of his popular folk-history of this immense area. He was born in The Dalles in the early spring of 1896, the son of Irish immigrants. When he was a year old the family settled on the highlands of eastern Jefferson County, where Phil's father built up a stock ranch. Although the post office was named Kilts, after a Johnny-come-lately homesteader, the old timers fiercely persisted in referring to the rural community as Donnybrook. "I wish there had been a post office called Donnybrook," Phil mused. "It was a good old Irish name that should be on a map of Oregon, some manner, some way." But even in Phil's youth the post office had become Ashwood, which it still was, 60 years after he left the Donnybrook plateau.

Phil grew up working on ranches and hayfields around Ashwood and Antelope and for two seasons was a camp tender for flocks of sheep grazed beyond McKenzie Pass, in the Cascades. Then came World War I and Phil joined the Navy. He became a signalman and never forgot the semaphore system he learned. He doodled in dots and dashes and would later try to figure out what he had written. "It may take some time but I can do it," and he beamed. Phil took more delight in such little accomplishments than in those which had made him famous. He was that kind of a modest guy.

With the war over, Phil returned to his Uncle Tom's sheep and cattle ranch at Antelope, but by now he had his sights set on college. He'd stay awake nights wondering how he could enter some eastern university—he'd read articles about people working their way through schools back there—but had just about given up the hope of higher education when he heard that Oregon had started a program which would give a veteran $25 a month to attend a state institution.

"Imagine trying to go to college in this year on that sum," Phil declared. "But I went to the University of Oregon. I went down in a funny way, a strange way. I'd been up at the top of the Cascades, over the west side, one summer, with our band of sheep, and a man was killed on our range, a bullet through his back. Well, the prosecutor in Lane County figured some of my marksmanship up in the mountains might have been responsible for the man's death. It wasn't; anyhow, another chap was convicted. My way was paid from Antelope to Eugene, and being over there and without any money, I decided I should enter the University."

Not having completed high school, Phil was required to take a special examination. But he had read a lot of books by that time, in 1919, when he was 23, and easily passed the test.

"Out in the range country I carried a dictionary in my pocket," Phil said. "My wife'll vouch for that. That's the way I learned to write to her."

Phil entered the U of O as a journalism student. Up to then all his writing experience, apart from letters to the girl he married, had been a column of local tidbits in the now long-defunct weekly Antelope *Herald*. Four academic years and two summer sessions later he left the university without a degree, being short of credits in algebra and military training. "I simply didn't have time to take them," he explained. "I didn't graduate for 30 years." Then, at a commencement exercise, two of his old classmates, the governors of Idaho and Oregon, took part in a ceremony which gave Phil Brogan his B.A. "I didn't get to wear the cap and gown and all that stuff, but I got my diploma anyhow. Many years later the administration called me back and they presented me with a very formal citation; I've forgotten what it is now." He turned to his wife. "Where is that thing?"

"Right there," his wife replied, pointing to one of the framed scrolls on a wall. "It's the 'University of Oregon Award for Distinguished Services.' It was given that year to only two other people. One of them was Senator Morse."

The citation stated that Philip Francis Brogan was "an enthusiastic journalist with unusual ability to portray accurately but simply the important advances in the fields of geology, meteorology, astronomy and anthropology" and that he was "pre-eminent as an authority who is not only proud of the State of Oregon but is also eager to share its treasures with others."

Phil's interest in geology, for which he gained a national reputation as a feature writer, had been only incidental before college. "I remember riding in the Ashwood hills and finding a fossil in a creek side once when I was a kid, and I wondered about that, and all like that, but I'd never gone into it in any great detail. I didn't learn the story of Oregon geology until I went to the University and heard about Dr. Condon and his exploits, in the very country where I was raised, practically."

His first writing on geology was for the Eugene *Register-Guard*, where he found a job to help pay his way through school and to gain reporting experience.

"I was assigned to cover the Geology department," Phil recalled, adjusting his spectacles and running the tip of a finger across the gray stubble of his naked dome, "and I used to go out on field trips with them and talk to the professors and I got a pretty good background through that. I remember going down into old mines on field trips and the first feature about geology I ever wrote was about an old mine."

That feature was the first of several thousand articles of interpretive science he was to pen in the next 50 years.

In his last week at the University Phil was called into the office of the dean of the Journalism school, Eric W. Allen, Sr., and asked if he wanted a job. Phil did. Well, said Dean Allen, up in Bend there's an opening. But—.

The "but" was that the owner of the Bend *Bulletin*, Robert W. Sawyer, a wide-read scholar with more than amateur scientific interest, expected his staff to know something about the universe. One evening he had taken a young reporter, who had studied under Dean Allen, out front and asked, "Do you know the name of that bright star up in the West?" The reporter didn't and was sent packing.

"If you go up to Bend you'll have to know about astronomy and all that because Mr. Sawyer is very, very exacting," Dean Allen told Brogan. Phil promised to try. He traveled to Bend, landed the job, and got along fine with Sawyer, who never criticized anything Phil wrote. When he retired, in 1967, Phil Brogan had, in essence, spent his full-time journalistic life on one paper.

Phil considered that his most significant contribution to the Bend *Bulletin*, and to all the other publications which used his material, was his willingness and ability to interpret the science of the region to newspaper readers. He had worked with many eminent scientists whose field studies had taken them to Central Oregon and some of them had come to him. "I feel honored that they should ask me to interpret what they've found," he said. "Darn it! so many reporters don't understand, they misinterpret and they can't get the story, and those professors clam up. But they've been very nice to me and with all the background I've acquired I've been able to write the stories."

Of all his many articles on science Phil regarded the "astronaut stories" as the most important. "They're something different for me and for that reason, I think, I call my astronaut coverage my primary stories here." All other articles were, by comparison, "routine, virtually on the same level."

Before the first lunar landings, groups of astronauts came to the volcanic fields of Central Oregon to acclimate themselves to surfaces similar to what was expected they would find on the moon, and Phil Brogan accompanied the parties as, he humbly put it, "a sort of guide."

Several years after his association with the astronauts Phil was still thrilled by his mingling with them. "I think it's quite a jump for a fellow with my background to rub shoulders with the men who were going to land on the moon."

But jubilant as Phil was for having had close contact with the space men, he was skeptical of manned moon landings and what had been discovered. "They didn't find anything we didn't expect them to find. We knew everything." And he was disappointed in the reports which had come from the astronauts regarding the geology and volcanology of the moon. "We know it is a meteor impact surface but when these meteors hit, did the lava come up and spread out? You'd think those guys could have looked out and tell about a lava flow."

He shook his head grimly, a rare gesture for the generally ebullient Brogan. "I think, frankly, we could have gotten all this information without landing on the moon. It was a great achievement and all that, and they brought back some rocks, but we could send down dippers and things like that to take up samples and bring them back to earth without risking a man's life. And what good is the moon going to do us? Man will never be able to live on the moon."

On clear nights Phil and his wife would carry their three-inch reflector telescope outdoors to scan the heavens. "That's another one of my hobbies," he said. "The 'scope is a type used by amateurs but it's very nice. Picks up the moons of Jupiter and the rings of Saturn. It's not very good on a moon-lit night. A full moon is beautiful but not good to observe. Too bright. You can't see the stars and when you look at the face of the moon its glare blinds you. You don't have the contrast, or the craters and rills and mountains which show up otherwise."

Hearing Phil talk about the telescope his wife lifted another citation off a wall. "It's the Thomas Jefferson Award," she announced, with a toss of her chin. "Phil was one of seven in the United States that received it. He got the first one. Would you like me to read it? It reads:

" 'For having voluntarily taken daily climatological observations at Bend, Oregon since 1923, recorded them accurately and reported them properly without missing a single day, and for valuable assistance given to the bureau in the dissemination and publication of local weather data.' "

Phil explained that when he joined the *Bulletin* the paper was recording maximum and minimum temperatures and precipitation. The low man on the staff totem pole was assigned observational chores and Phil, being at the bottom of the pecking order, was quickly chosen to relieve the man who up to then had the least seniority.

Well, 47 years later he was still at it and by then had long been the weather man with the most years of service in Oregon.

When he was out of town his wife marched into the back yard to check the battery of instruments for the information to transmit to the weather bureau in Portland. High school students Phil had trained carried on when both Brogans were absent.

During World War II the Brogan home had been a full-time weather station, with a staff of five—Phil, his wife, and three students—and detailed readings were taken every three hours, night and day. "It was a pretty active place," Phil grinned. "There was no time to get lonesome."

Phil glanced about the room and remarked that he was

a member of a lot of state and county groups. He beamed at us and said, chuckling, "I have to look on the walls to see what they are."

One of the groups had honored Phil for his exploration of caves and he told us about an experience which he later deeply regretted. "Many years ago we found Indian writings out in Dry River Gorge near Mexican Hole, a whole wall covered with paintings, and I thought in my ignorant way I'd let the public in on that. Well, I got the highway commission to put a road in there, from the road down to the gorge, and show the people. Fine. But in a couple of years there was hardly anything left. They even chipped those off with chisels, the paintings. If I ever again find anything like that I'll never publicize it. So help me. I'll never publicize the place. I'll write the story but I'm not going to give the exact location. If they come to me, and I think the people are O.K., I'll tell them, but to let the vandals in on it too, no!"

I asked him what assurance he would have that the people who he thought were O.K. would talk only to other people who were O.K.

"Well, that's a problem," Phil agreed.

"I don't think you ought to write about it at all," I advised.

"You're probably right," Phil said.

I told Phil I was offering him this counsel because some places which had appeared in my *Oregon for the Curious* had been desecrated and since then I had not written about several precious sites I had found.

He nodded. "It isn't worth the few bucks you get for the story. It's terrible you have to keep information from people but that's the only way you can save some places. Nobody else seems to want to protect them."

We asked Phil one more question: Is there any place but Bend you'd like to live in?

He looked puzzled. "I can't imagine where it would be."

Right then, with the moon shining bright on Mirror Pond and the sky a blaze of stars and off in the nearby woods pine musk seeding the wind, it did seem that the best place in the world was where Phil Brogan had said to the publisher of the *Bulletin:* "That bright star up in the West? It's the planet Venus, sir."

The sage of Fort Rock

My wife was having trouble with the tape recorder, which was malfunctioning as though it had a grudge against us, and she was ready to spit nails.

"If it makes you feel better to swear, go right ahead," Reub Long said sweetly. "Wouldn't bother me a bit. Don't guess there's any word you could use that I haven't heard."

That was Reub Long for you: the stumpy, baldheaded, courtly, twinkle-eyed sage of Fort Rock.

You remember Reub, of course, as co-author of *The Oregon Desert*, that classic about the blowed-out homesteader country east of the Cascades.

Reub didn't really pen the chapters attributed to him; he just dictated them to the late Russell Jackman, the other author.

"I was 50-odd years gathering material and we were, I suppose, a couple of years getting it wrote," he said in that off-hand modest way of his.

Reub could tell stories from supper to breakfast without repeating the same yarn twice but he'd rather talk than scribble. Fortunately, Russ Jackman recognized this trait so he didn't prod Reub to set the tales down on paper; Russ just encouraged his old pard Reub to talk, and by quoting Reub verbatim Russ performed a great literary and historic service for the state.

Since Reub became famous he had received heaps of letters from all parts of the U.S.A. but replying promptly was not one of his stronger points. "I let them pile up," he worried. "I think it must be kind of a form of insanity to hate to write letters. Writing letters is kind of like taking your weekly bath—you hate to get at it but it feels mighty good afterward."

The Oregon Desert had mushroomed Reub into a statewide celebrity but his neighbors around Fort Rock treated him as they always had, which was fine with Reub. "I'm just one of them. They don't think I'm better than they are, which I'm not, and I don't see that I am either."

But life had changed. He had been interviewed hundreds of times, he supposed, and had been invited to address groups up and down and across the state.

"One thing that I'm particularly interested in now is the history of our Northwest country and I feel pretty well qualified to talk about it because I've studied it considerable and my people on both sides of my family are pioneers," he told us as he crossed his cowboy-booted legs. "My father brought the first cattle I guess that I know of in southern Oregon—I guess about a hundred years ago—and my mother's people came across the plains by wagon train in 1845. They were in the lost wagon train that found and lost the Blue Bucket mine. They were lost on the desert for some time and suffered great hardships and privations and some people died but my great-grandfather with 11 children made it through without a loss in the family."

Reub Long was born in Lakeview early in 1898 and grew up in the northern part of Lake County, where he gained renown as stockman, conservationist, cowboy, local historian and grassroots philosopher. By and by he was appointed to "quite a few boards and commissions statewide and I'm traveling in that connection."

He mixed in, or up, his official traveling with "autographing books along the route and talking to service clubs and pioneer associations and that sort of thing." He didn't speak for hire, he said, but once in a while he did get travel expenses, which was about par for home-grown writers in Oregon.

He'd talk about Oregon history or livestock raising or conservation or mountain camping or wilderness survival but he never had a speech prepared. "I start out to talk and I wander into several fields," he said with that smile of sagebrush innocence.

"And you might tell different stories to different audiences," he explained. "If you're talking to a bunch of older people you might talk about pioneer things; if you're talking to a bunch of young people, then you might talk about whatever they're interested in in the outdoors. Of any of those kind of stories I think my Indian stories are the best accepted and I tell quite a lot of them. About, oh, most of them are telling about some incident, and I try to mimic the Indian way of saying things, and those stories seem to go over best, I think. Sometimes they're legends, or experiences, or something an Indian has said, and always ending up with a punch line."

Reub wasn't reluctant to tell us one of his Indian presentations but figured it might take too long. Nonsense, we said, so he started:

"An Indian was setting with his back to a tree one day, just settin' there gazing off into space as only an Indian can, and a friend rode by and saw this Indian settin' there and he knew something about the way Indians were so he didn't bother him and he just rode by. And he came back in the middle of the day and the old Indian was in the same place and in the same position and so he rode by again without saying much, but he came back in the evening and there was the Indian still settin' there, and so he thought maybe his friend was sick, and he spoke to him and said, 'What's the matter with you, John? What are you doin'? Are you sick?' And he said, 'Me no sick.' And he said, 'Why are you settin' there? Are you thinkin' about somethin'?' And the old Indian said to him: 'All the time, long time, me see black horse, white face; never see white horse, black face.'

"Well," Reub remarked, "there isn't much point to that story except you have to draw your own conclusion: was the old Indian telling him just to mind his own business or was he really telling him about the wonders of nature? And that's the kind of story I tell, many times."

Many of his yarns came from his own experiences and he had discovered, he observed, that people enjoy listening to tales that have some foundation in fact.

For some reason I declared that nature is a pretty wise old mother and we could learn a lot from her. Reub responded immediately, with a child-like intensity that made him so endearing. "Well, I've often said that I'm a pretty fair veterinarian—I take pretty good care of my livestock and I have two of the very best veterinarians on my side helping me all the time, and one of them is Mother Nature and the other is Father Time."

That turned the subject to horses. Reub said he still rode a lot, even though his sister and some of his closest friends wanted him to quit. Maybe they were afraid he'd get tossed once too often.

"I don't suppose there's a man living that has been

bucked off, or run over, or fell down with more than I have," he said without bragging. "Anyone that tells you they've never been bucked off never rode very many horses. There isn't a fella riding that hasn't been bucked off."

He said it with his ever-quiet conviction and straight-forward look that made you feel Reub Long would be the last man in the world to speak untruth.

"You learn to fall," he continued, "and if there isn't anything in the way to throw you up against, you can manage to roll. You learn to fall off a horse just like a wrestler or anybody else learns to take a fall.

"You usually have a little bit of notice," he went on. "Of course, if your horse steps into a badger hole or stumbles and falls with you, you get *some* notice. You endeavor, when a horse falls, to let him throw you away from him. The main chance of getting badly hurt when a horse falls is to have the horse fall on you."

As suggested, Reub had done a lot of things in life. "I've worked around the desert at almost every job there is, handling horses, or cattle. I've trapped. I've been a trader. Done everything there was to do in the early days to try to make a living and accumulate some things." He had packed into the High Cascades for 20 years, with a dude string to Diamond Lake, starting in 1926, before there were so many trails in the mountains. And because he knew the mountains he was often called upon to search for people lost in the woods.

He had been in a couple of movies, too, both of them made in Oregon, and was associated with a third, "The Way West," as a contact man. The livestock were quartered on his ranch and he helped find locations for the film makers.

Reub liked working in movies. "You bet! You get a chance to talk with interesting folks. One of the local people that was working in one of the shows that I was in felt that the pay wasn't quite good enough and my reaction to that was that if they'd cut off my pay I wouldn't quit, I was having too much fun." And he smiled again. "But they do pay real well."

He had also been a sheepherder but in a burst of laughter requested that we didn't emphasize that part. "Most people would think that a sheepherder was a low individual, which isn't really true," he added seriously.

I don't think I ever knew anyone in the state who got along better with his fellow humans than Reub. Like Will Rogers, he hadn't met anybody he didn't like.

"I enjoy some people more than others," he declared, "but I've got quite a lot of tolerance for pretty near everybody; there isn't anybody that bothers me much. And I like to visit with sometimes the strangest people, or what you'd think are the strangest people, and when you get to talking to them you find out there's something they know or something they can do that you'd like to be able to know or be able to do. Maybe the tramp you see on the road can wiggle his ears or do something you can't, so every individual, you'll find them interesting if you just take the time and effort to find out what they know or what they can do."

In his younger years he sometimes rode deep into the desert to spend a night there, just his horse to keep him company. But of late he used a camper and pickup. "There was a time when I didn't need those comforts so bad, but I do now." Whether by horse or motor, the purpose was the same: "to kinda get acquainted with my soul." He believed it would also be good for others to every once in a while go out under the big sky and listen to the silence. "I enjoy doing that and I think it would do each and every individual good," he said. For him the healing solitude of the desert was the best medicine he knew.

In his wisdom Reub Long had learned the importance of luck. He could talk about it at length, and to us he said: "I've been a lucky individual in that I've always, with no particular effort of my own, seemed to be in the right place at the right time where things were happening, so that I've become part of things. And the only thing you can attribute it to is luck.

"There's probably a couple of things that are necessary for success in pretty near any endeavor. One of them is to have some real good judgment and some good know-how —about what you're gonna do—and another one is luck. And of the two, I believe I'd rather have the luck. The fortunate man has all of those and if he's smart enough to combine them perhaps he can achieve this thing called success."

Reub was absolutely sure his life had been successful.

He didn't know anyone who had lived a more interesting life than he had.

In recent years he had sold the main and largest part of his ranch to Dr. Warren Wegert, who lived in Portland. Reub retained a section and a half in the Devil's Garden area and 160 acres near Hole in the Ground. "I guess I got too lazy to run the whole ranch," he said mildly. "That's kind of a tragedy, when you build something up and have a real nice plant and all at once you find out you're too lazy to run it."

Chances are, we guessed, Reub was more tired of ranching than he was lazy and he agreed that might be. But he wasn't too tired to enjoy life; he had that boundless curiosity of all young people, whatever their age. "Like I mentioned just a little bit ago," he declared with happy earnestness, "there's no one in this world that's had more wonderful experiences than I had, and I'm still having them, every day."

The rainbow bird of Lakeview

Bob Ogle's Kiowa Indian name was Running Bird and it was most appropriate.

Every time I think of Bob I have the vision of a gorgeous rainbow-colored bird, elegantly poised, with quicksilver wings and tremulous eyes.

He was adopted by a Kiowa family for his work with Indian arts and crafts, but there was much more to him. I can't remember anyone I have met in recent years who had so many irons in the fire and who seemed to be carrying on through sheer nerve.

Bob owned and operated the Indian Village, Lakeview's largest restaurant. He did all the bookkeeping, personally managed the gift shop, the largest in Eastern Oregon, and did the purchasing. At home, where he lived with his mother and teen-age son (he was a widower), he cooked, attended to house and yard chores and, on the side, raised quails. His Indian artifacts collection was one of the largest in the West, he lectured widely on Indian culture, and read extensively on the Indians.

Everything about Ogle was intriguing. His grandparents were pioneers in Northern California's Surprise Valley and, except for college, he had all his life resided in Lakeview. But he wasn't born there. "My mother lived in Lakeview and then moved to San Francisco to have me and then came back," he laughed. "She wanted a son of the Golden State."

That was in 1929. I had the impression, from reading so much about his work with the Indians, that he was born much earlier. I expected to encounter a craggy, drawling Westerner, the kind you associate with the range and desert country. But the Ogle we met was handsome, swift-talking, debonair and dressed like an avant-garde swinger. Who could have imagined a Lake County native in plum-colored shirt and suit to match its flair?

Bob and I talked until the tape ran out and then, together with my wife, we chatted for another two hours. He was heady with ideas and refreshingly frank, a combination that made for most provocative views.

"I think 150 years ago or 250 years ago probably I was an Indian," he said ingenuously, with an off-hand gesture of turning a palm up. "That's what old Chief Tommy Thompson told me. My skin's white but my heart's red."

Suppose you were an Indian addressing the white men crossing the plains, I put to him. What would you say to them?

"Well," he replied spiritedly, "what would *we* say if the Russians started marching across the United States? I would probably have said, What are you doing here and get the devil out! If I could I'd push 'em out."

A while later, somewhat wistful, he declared: "I was born a hundred years too late. I'm not interested in going to the moon but I'd have given anything to be in the westward movement. If I had lived then I'd probably be mixed up with the Indians in some way, probably fighting on their side. Or at least for fair treatment. My Lord! the more I study into what happened the more sick I get of being a descendant of it. It's disgusting."

Ever since boyhood I've heard that Indians can't hold liquor. I've never believed it and expected Ogle to demolish the statement but, to my surprise, he supported it.

"I'm not saying they're *all* this way but I believe there's a basic weakness in the Indian's physiological makeup that makes him intolerant to liquor," he argued. "I know lots of white people who can't tolerate it either, myself being one, but I don't believe that there's any Indian that I know of who can drink to moderation without being brought down by it."

Not even an Indian completely raised in the Caucasian world? I asked.

"Even an Indian that goes to Harvard, the liquor will bring him down," Bob persisted. "There's a physiological weakness there that will hit them some day. I'm probably crazy as the devil but that's my own theory because I've never seen it any different. Liquor probably was the biggest downfall of the Indians."

We had heard that Ogle had sometimes been asked to teach Indian groups about their own culture, and I asked him how.

"Well, specifically, with the Klamath Indians, particularly

with the younger ones, to upgrade their thought," he replied. "The white man has tried to get them to forget this. They tried to teach them to be ashamed they were Indian. Their Indian culture was beat out of them for so many years. Lord, until the thirties most of the Indian dancing was forbidden. The Sun Dance, on the Great Plains, wasn't even allowed to be held, it was an illegal function. Then the government saw what a wonderful background and ethnic culture they were repressing, so they tried to revive it, but they tried too late, everybody's dying."

Bob was loaded with challenging statements. For instance, his notions regarding Chinese influence upon some Indian art:

"I do know—well, I think—that the Chinese were here much earlier than the white man because there's too many lotus designs and things like this that you find in your primitive art of your North American Indians, particularly on the Pacific north coast. And where would they ever see a lotus? I'm sticking my neck out, but these are things I'm working on, Chinese designs in American Indian art."

There was nothing halfway about him and when he was stirred he could sometimes be poetic. Listen:

"The Indian has always been attracted by the esthetic values of art. They had art in everything they did. Everything that was used, practically, had to be decorated. They found beauty in everything. It was their belief that everything has its spirit. The rock has a spirit, the tree has a spirit. So you don't want to offend the spirit, you want to learn to live with it. I sort of believe in it myself. If you can adopt this idea—you can't anymore because of our society that's forced on us now—but if you could go back to thinking about some of these things, I think the world might be a better place to live in. I don't know. My beliefs usually tend to be more Indian than white. I get into arguments all the time on this."

Almost all whites who have studied the Indians have been moved by the strength of the Indians' spiritual medicine. Bob Ogle was no exception.

"When we say medicine," he explained, "we think of aspirin and stuff like that but there's also the Indian medicine, the power feeling they have, that every inanimate object possesses. I have several medicine bundles of the Plains Indians and I have never opened one. These things make every hair on my body stand up and vibrate. I don't know why. Speak of the Holy of Holies, the Ark of the Covenant: to the Indians these things were their most personal possessions."

For 20 years Bob had been consummately involved with Indian arts and crafts but he was beginning to feel it was a lost cause. "The Indian isn't interested in revitalizing his culture because he can't see any benefit to it. They have to pay the same price for groceries as you and I. Well, they're not going to sit around and weave a basket and sell it for three dollars, and maybe it takes them 25 hours to weave, when they can earn two dollars an hour doing something else. You wouldn't either. They can't get anything for their craft." He added that he was aware of only two people in the Klamath tribe who knew the basics of Indian basket making.

Language, too, was fading. Bob remarked that there was not a Klamath under 65 who spoke the tongue and only half-a-dozen of the elders who did.

"The old people are all gone," he lamented. "It just makes me sick. There's so much I wanted to glean from them and before I get it down it's gone. And what gets me is the experience I've had with them during the past years. I'll say, 'So long, we'll see you in the spring, or next year when we come back.' and they'll say, 'I won't be here, I'll be dying this year, I'll be dying in the spring.' It's amazing. They seem to know the time. It gives me the willies."

Bob had trenchant opinions about the characterization of Indians in the movies and television. "I detest them," he fumed. "They rarely portray them correctly. If you have Arapaho Indians, or Pueblo Indians, or Northern Cree, they usually all have the same thing on. No one ever goes to the bother of getting the right costume and so forth, except like in 'Cheyenne Autumn'."

It is a pity, a shame and a tragedy that even to this day the role of the Indians in our history has been neglected, aborted and distorted. Some day I would like to write a book on the settling of the West as witnessed through Indian eyes. It would include the Modoc War, which is seen by almost all white historians as provoked by a "treacherous and renegade savage," Captain Jack, who had the arrogance to defy the mandate of white bureaucrats. Bob Ogle was one of the few paleskins I have known who took the side of Captain Jack— and he did it with passion.

"All Captain Jack was doing was fighting for something which was his own to begin with. The stupid Americans! They fought a war—they could have given him what he wanted, which was the Lost River Valley, at a cost of not more than $20,000. So instead of doing this, and maybe making six or eight families mad by relocating them on some other land, they forced a war. The land of the Lost River was the ancestral home of the Modocs. And rather than let him have his ancestral home they fought a war which cost more than any of the other Indian wars ever fought. This poor little band of Modocs were moved onto a reservation with their linguistic cousins, the Klamaths, who dominated them and beat them down and practically drove them out, and they couldn't take it, so they pulled out and left. So the government sent troops after Captain Jack and his little band and then called the Indians warlike."

I asked Bob, who had spent more time studying about Indians than running his business, what he thought was the solution to the Indian situation.

"They can't be wards of the government forever," he began. "They're human beings. The young people have to be educated and assimilated and they have to be built up with a pride in their past so that they'll carry it on as just a hobby or something, because they can't depend on it any more. I don't know if doing away with all the reservations is the answer but I know the way they did it with the Klamaths isn't the answer. The government gave each one who wanted to terminate the reservation $40,000. You can't imagine what it did. One girl bought seven Cadillacs with her money."

There had been a lot of wild stories about what the Klamaths did with their money and I asked Bob if most of these accounts weren't fabricated or exaggerated.

"Oh, they *are* wild," he retorted. "Not all of them did this. There are some very fine Klamath Indians in Portland who invested their money and are coming out fine on it. But the great majority of them, it was just sad.

"They should have first been educated what to do with this money. An elder of the Klamath tribe sat right in the bank as these people came in and he advised them to put this money—it was tax-free and in government checks—in the bank and draw interest on it, and think of what they wanted to do, but they were like so many children, a lot of them."

But if white people found themselves in the same circumstances, wouldn't many of them do the same, I wondered.

"Probably," Bob said. "You and I would to a certain extent, but we'd keep some of it. They didn't keep any of it. One time a gal came into the lounge of the Village and I thought she had a bottle of wine in a grocery bag, and I took it away from her. She never said anything when I asked whether I could keep the sack for her. When I picked it up I realized it wasn't heavy. I got it in the office and there was nothing but full of hundred-dollar and fifty-dollar bills, all wadded up in little balls. I nearly died because I didn't know what to do with them. It wasn't wine as I had anticipated. So I kept it until she left and I gave it to her and I said, 'Why don't you put it in the bank?' She didn't trust banks!

"And then the unscrupulous merchants in various areas—I mean, they really descended upon these people. It was awfully sad. I believe the ones that maintained their tribal interests, that is administered by the United States Bank, I think they're the smart ones. They can still terminate any time they want to but they were wise enough not to take this one-grab deal and I think they will probably end up with the best situation."

Bob Ogle has spoken before scores of childrens' groups on Indian lore and I asked him to tell his favorite legend.

"This one," he proceeded, "is from the Teton Sioux and it's how the rainbows came about.

"The fall was approaching and flowers were talking to each other. They said that it didn't seem fair that when the Indian died he went to the Happy Hunting Grounds. And the other flowers said, 'We just live for a short time and die and we're gone.' And the Great Spirit heard them and didn't think it was fair, either, so he created a place for the flowers to go when they die. And when they go up in the sky they form the rainbow that you see after all of the storms."

That was lovely, I said. How about one more?

Bob smiled agreement and recited the Sun Flower legend of the Sioux.

"This little boy was fascinated by the sun. Every day he went up on the hill and he would sit there and he would watch as the sun came up, follow it all the way across the heavens with his face, and watched it go down in the west. And day after day he would do this, and he was totally fascinated by this, and he watched the sun so long that he went blind. Still he could feel the warmth on his face, and he could still follow the sun day by day, and they called him Sun Boy. And one day someone went up on the hill and found him dead. So they buried him. And later, when his friends came back on the hill where he was buried they saw a flower grow out of his grave, and it faced the sun as it came up and followed it all the way across the heavens, and watched it go down in the west, and that's what our sun flowers do, you know?"

Bob Ogle left with us a flurry of thoughts, an image of a comet ready to explode into a hundred iridescent fragments and a jar of pickled quail eggs.

We put the jar in the refrigerator and it stood unopened for many months. My wife and friends wanted no part of the eggs. Finally I gathered enough courage to test them. They were delicious. And every time I think of them I am reminded of that zany, many-sided, pyrotechnic man of Lakeview.

A maverick sheriff

Everybody in Klamath County knew Sheriff James Murray Britton. Nobody called him Jim. It was either Sheriff or Red. If you wanted to be formal you'd call him Red Britton.

There wasn't a sheriff in the state more colorful, earthy, unorthodox or controversial than the big, burly, rawboned, red-haired, square-jawed, breezy Britton, who had come to Klamath Falls in 1930, at the age of 17, and had been sheriff since 1952.

Nobody in the county, especially in Klamath Falls, was neutral about Britton. They either loved him or despised him. His friends thought he was about the best thing that ever happened to the county; his enemies were hoping he would wind up in prison for a very long term.

He had been arrested by at least one district attorney, indicted by at least one grand jury, chastised as "inefficient" by the Klamath County board of commissioners, and sued four or five times, but on every occasion he had been vindicated, he said. When we saw him he was in more hot water, having recently been sued for no less a sum than $300,000.

"I was just doing my duty," Big Red explained, talking about his latest legal headache. "My deputy and I were performing an act where we had to execute a writ of execution from Multnomah County and it happened to be on the chairman of our board of commissioners. We had to go out and attach his car. That's just exactly what we done according to statute. I had instructions to the sheriff, I was directed to go to a certain address and get a certain license number, which we did, and for doing my duty I have been sued."

He suspected the commissioner was a member of the "Get Britton" crowd but insisted he wasn't worried about the suit.

"Not the least bit," he declared with a tremor of bravado. "I done my duty, I was directed to do this certain thing, and so I haven't worried one minute about it."

But the way he spoke, his words charged up and swift,

and his frowning, and his sudden shift to a carefree mood, indicated to us that maybe he was a little concerned.

His most memorable brush with the law involved a man who had been accused of horse stealing. Red recalled the story:

"Well, this was an ex-marine, from an old-time family that came here in 1884, and it happens that I worked with all of his in-laws the first winter I came here. So I knew the family real well. And I got the man in here, and of course somehow or other the district attorney thought that I had got him in jail and had let him out, but I never had him *in* jail. I got ahold of him and we appeared in court, and so that was what the trail was about. They found out they had made a mistake in indicting him, the case was dismissed, and then several months later some of this 'Get Britton' group found out that he hadn't been in jail and got me indicted. We had the trail, and of course I was exonerated. But I had to get my own attorney and that of course is one of the things I been trying to get back from the county because they are supposed to represent me with an attorney and they did not! I am trying to be reimbursed by the county court and I feel that I finally will be."

Britton readily agreed that the way he went about being sheriff was much different in style than all the other lawmen in Oregon. "There's no question about that, and I get criticized sometimes until they find out what I'm trying to do. I follow the statutes very closely. I always am right. But I sometimes have a special way of doing things.

"Just last week," he exampled, "there was an Indian in here, and he came in to see about a piece of land that had been sold, and I advised him that he still had a year to redeem it, and he's going to redeem it. And while he was here I remembered that we had a warrant for his boy, who had just returned from Vietnam, and so I advised him that we had this warrant that's from a county up in the north end of the state. It's a driving violation, and I said, 'Tell Robert' —that's his son—'to be in and bring 30 dollars and that way we won't have to arrest him.' He advised me that he would be in Friday. Now that's all I have to look forward to. I know the boy will be in Friday, we'll send the 30 dollars to the north county, and I do a lot of things that way. I know that other sheriffs would have the warrant served, but the way I look at it, give people respect. If they say they're coming in I tell my deputies not to bother them."

The Indian veteran was not an isolated case, Britton went on. "We get many calls, wanting to know if there's a warrant for them, and I'll say, 'Yes, you might as well bring a few clothes because you're going to have to stay a few days.' So they'll meet me at the jail with a few clothes and prepare to stay a few days because I had told them that. Now I know that's not exactly the right way, but I haven't lost anybody, and that's the way I work."

Every day a host of people, mostly those who couldn't afford an attorney, trooped into the sheriff's office to lay their troubles before Britton. He greeted each with a hearty handshake, a radiant smile that encouraged: trust me, and an attentive ear. "Lots of police develop a suspicious attitude," he said, "but not me. I figure we're all humans. So I treat them just as though they're good friends, and I have this miserable job of getting papers out and doing these things, taking things away from people, but I always explain it to 'em why, and of course they're at fault, 99 per cent of the time, and many times I'll tell 'em, 'Well, we'll take this and hold it a few days, and give you an opportunity, maybe you can recover it some way.' So I'm always trying to help."

He talked a good deal about helping people—that was his motto, he emphasized—and we wondered aloud how he helped.

"Well, if they ask me," he replied, drumming his blunt fingers on his homespun desk, "I will maybe tell them what happened to a former case similar to theirs. I never tell 'em what to do, and when they ask me, almost daily I get phone calls by different people and they were—'I was recommended by so-and-so' and they should talk to me. It might be over a little deal on renting a house or getting some renters out or recoverin' some kind of equipment or something they want to do, and of course I always tell 'em the first thing they should do is get an attorney and be advised right. Well, they always want to know what I would do. Well, then I always advise them that this is the way I would do it but it would really be better for them to get an attorney but," he chuckled, "I think they do what I said I would do lots o' times.

"Like this morning," he went on, in the warm conversational tone of intimates, "I had a fella in here and he hung around all morning before I had time to talk to him. He's a Western type of fella, has a big hat, and I had his gun permit and he came in to see why I was holding it. And of course he's in a little difficulty and I told him I was going to hold it until we got it straightened out, and then I said I would hold it for a little while after that. And I advised him that I was trying to help him, and told him what he should do, and he said he was going to do it, so you see, instead of trying to hurt the man, why, I have reason to believe he'll pay attention to what I said and, in a little while, we'll be reissuing his gun permit, and everything's all right."

Red had the feeling that too many people came to him with their personal problems. "Really, I shouldn't do so much," he half-lamented, "but you can't help but help those people, that's why they've come to you, because they want to know, and I do my best to help them."

I remarked to Britton that when he shook my hand he didn't know whether I was a bank robber or a forger or what, and that he treated me like a long-lost cousin.

He nodded in affirmation. "I have lots of murderers that's from out-of-state, and that's the first thing they do is come in, and they'll sit right where you do, and they want to tell me, and they'll say, 'I'm in trouble, here's what I'd like to do, I'd like to tell you about it.' If I'm real busy I'll have 'em sit out there for a while, put 'em strictly at ease, and of course they come in and I advise, well, maybe they shouldn't, and they insist on it, and I've had that happen several times, and fellas that's come from out of their way to talk to me."

We could see where some very real legal problems could arise from such situations and where the sheriff might even be accused of entrapment but Red held that he was acting as a friend, "because these people don't have anyone else to talk to and they know I'm square-shooting."

A little later, in talking about the apprehension of law breakers, he said, freezing his eyes in brightness, as he often did to emphasize a point, "Of course I always advise them nowadays not to do it, but they'd burst right out and confess to me, and showed me how they had done this and done that, but that doesn't work very well nowadays, you have to advise them, and not let them tell you. You want to get them back here and get ahold of the district attorney and, it's possible, after he's advised them and taken it down in writing, that he may permit them to confess."

In all his years as a lawman, deputy and sheriff, he had never drawn a gun. Now, pointing to his holsters across the room, he did not even carry a revolver. It was a nice feeling, he agreed, not to have resorted to firearms, and smiled through an incident he described.

"I've went out when we've had some real, you might say, bad boys that had escaped from the penitentiary several times. I got out there and we happened to run face into each other, and I've remembered I didn't have my gun, so I just started talking and everything turned out all right."

It would take a desperate, half-mad man or a total cynic to be oblivious to Red's infectious grin, his disarming lingo and his cozy equalitarian manner. His critics in Klamath County—and they comprised a significant minority—regarded all these traits as hammier than B-Class film on late late television. But most of the citizens were fond of Red's flair and continued to keep him in office term after term.

Red was friends with anybody who gave him half-a-chance, including prisoners and ex-prisoners. The disenchanted charged him with being too personal with the incarcerated but Red didn't see it that way and for-instanced us about one man in his custody.

"He's been over here around 28 months, and he doesn't get outside but he helps inside. He's trying to get an appeal, get a new case. He's been in the penitentiary 27 years for murder and he thinks that they made a mistake years ago, so we're very friendly, and he's very helpful at the jail. I never think a thing about him getting away because I just have that feeling. He isn't locked up. He helps with the kitchen and helps clean the jail, and he just doesn't go outside, is all.

"You know," he added, "I don't believe in looking down on people who have been to jail because there's some time in everybody's life that if a lawman had been there, why, it's very possible that most all of us would be subject to some violation of some kind."

Big Red waved off the conjecture that he, like so many other sheriffs, might have problems with young people. "We haven't had a lick of trouble with the juvenile crowd; we get along with them real well," and a grin lit up all the freckles on his open face. "Why, I can go down the street and any number will wave at me, and I was surprised the night before last when I was going through the neighborhood a real small boy, and I don't know how he knew me, but he hollered, 'Hello Sheriff Murray!' It kind of tickled me, that's my middle name, and of course, I waved back and said, 'Hello sonny, how are ya?' and kept going. But it's a very good feeling."

Cattle rustling had been a fierce bother to Britton a few years ago but now he felt the situation was coming under control. "Course," he conceded, "naturally there'll be a few. They've been one or two cases this year and we're right hot on the trail. Whether we'll catch 'em or not I don't know. They're very difficult because there wasn't much left so we would have the matter of evidence that you'd have to produce to courts, but we're working on a couple now."

Few sheriffs enjoy serving papers; some leave those chores entirely to their deputies. But not the gregarious Red Britton. "I do it every day," he said. "I like it because it gives you an opportunity to stay close to the people and to find out the problems and they seem to be very happy when I come out."

Red figured on being sheriff as long as the electorate wanted him. "I enjoy the job and seem to keep getting along better with the majority of the people, so I haven't thought of anything else. I probably work 15-16 hours a day, seven days a week."

His schedule wouldn't seem to leave him much time with his family, but Red said they understood. He pointed to a picture. "I have a wonderful wife and there's my children. Five." They ranged in age from nine to 30.

Red beamed and we commented that he looked like a most happy fella.

"Oh, I am!" he exclaimed. "Nothin' bothers me, I'm clean as a whistle. But what do you think about that commissioner suing me for three hundred thousand dollars? Isn't that a mean way to treat a man who was just doin' his duty?"

A time for remembering

We paused at Collier State Park, in the ponderosa pine country near Chiloquin, to show our daughter the great display of old-time logging equipment.

There was quite a bit for her to see in this collection of vehicles, machines, implements and other relics that comprised a hundred years of logging.

After a bit my daughter and wife drifted off to take pictures and I walked at random until I came to the replica of an old-fashioned logging camp. It looked something like the camps of northern Washington I had known in my youth.

Three others came by to stand in front of the bunkhouse. Two were the portraits of young newlyweds, their arms twined around each other. The third was a tall, slightly bent, whitehaired man with a square, furrowed face.

"Those must have been colorful days," the young man said.

"I'll bet it was exciting," she said.

"The days of the individualist," he told her. "It's all mechanized now. All the romance has gone out of logging. Power machinery, big rigs, walkie talkies—just factory work."

"I'll bet they had a lot of fun in the bunkhouse," she said, and they tripped on in love.

"Colorful! Romance! Fun!" the whitehaired man snorted. "Listen to them!"

I turned slowly and looked up into his eyes, thin blue and heavy lidded. Were you there? I asked.

"I was there," he said, pounding a fish into a gnarled hand.

Then it must be different for you, I said sympathetically.

"These people, the tourists, they see machinery and cardboard loggers," he replied intently. "I see real people; I see struggle."

I nodded: It wasn't the carefree life, was it?

127

He puffed out a laugh of bitterness. "It wasn't. Never was as I knew it. That was 60 years ago, when I started. I was a kid then, a big strapping kid, 15, but I could pass for 18 or 19, and I went to work in the woods with two older brothers. One was killed and the other was crippled. You don't see things like that told here, do you?"

If you've got a minute, I said, tell me about it.

His broad mouth parted into a dental plate smile. But it was not a happy smile. "I've got all day. I'm just gonna make Klamath tonight. At my age I don't try to push myself. I got plenty o' time to get to my niece's, in Sacramento. When she sees me she'll know I'm there."

The afternoon was warm and he removed his jacket. He pulled a blue bandana from a jacket pocket and blotted his brow. Instead of returning the bandana to the pocket he balled it in his fist.

"I started in the short log country—northern Idaho and western Montana," he began. "It was drive country—you know, drive logs by water. You could only work part of the year and there were no roads into camp. We walked 30 miles over trail to camp and when the logging was done for the year we walked 30 miles out. That's how I started.

"Later I logged in Washington and Oregon. It didn't make no difference where you were: the conditions were the same until we forced them to be better. We had to strike for everything—better chuck, clean blankets, wash house, better bunkhouse. I was in camps where 100 men had two wash basins, which meant a lot of guys had to go in to eat without washing. We had to strike for the eight-hour day, better wages—the bosses don't give anything away.

"We were crowded in a steamy bunkhouse, two men in a bunk, sleeping in wet clothes. No bath. I was in a dozen camps in a single year and only one had a bath. One, by God, and that's the God's truth! We didn't get nothing without fighting for it."

Were you a Wobbly, I asked.

"I was. Industrial Workers of the World. I.W.W." He stood proudly. "I carried the red card. It was the Wobblies that won the fight for decent bunks, decent food, decent everything. We were roasted in hell for it: vigilantes, stockades, blacklists."

You've heard of Joe Hill, of course, I said. Did you ever meet him?

"I don't know," the old man said slowly, doubtfully. "I can't say as such. Once, when I was a kid, a tall, thin, blonde, quiet fella come to our house in Spokane and was introduced as Joe Hill. Dad didn't take kindly to Wobblies but when he heard that fella was a Swede he warmed up to him, Dad coming from the old country. Now, that's all I remember, and that's a long, long time back."

But the old man remembered Joe Hill's songs. "Oh yes," he laughed. "You betcha! God, I've sung 'em a thousand times, and I still do once in a while. You know any?"

"The Preacher and the Slave," I said.

" 'You will eat, bye and bye, In that glorious land above the sky,' " my friend sang in a husky voice that cracked and cackled. " 'Work and pray, live on hay. You'll get pie in the sky when you die.' "

"Where the Fraser River Flows," I said.

"Yes, yes, and 'Casey Jones—the Union Scab,' and 'Mr. Block,' and 'The Rebel Girl' and 'It's a Long Way Down to the Soupline' and 'There is Power in a Union.' Yes, all of them, and the songs by Ralph Chaplin and Dublin Dan and Jim Connell and all the rest of them. Every place we went we sang 'Solidarity Forever.' I carried the little red songbook all over the country, Maine to Californ-i-ay. We were a singin' army, full of poets and songwriters. Joe Hill and T-Bone Slim and Haywire Mac. You know 'Hallelujah, I'm a Bum?' Mac wrote that, and 'Big Rock Candy Mountain' and a lot of other things."

The happiness dried on the old man's lips. "Maine to Californ-i-ay," he began again, with a cut in his voice. "I got blacklisted by the bosses and couldn't rustle a job in the woods to save my soul so I packed the balloon— was a bindle stiff, you know. Rode the rattlers, homed up in the jungles, and organized all the way. Organized for the Wobblies, organized for the One Big Union. We didn't have no paid organizers, we was all organizers, by God, like the disciples of Jesus. I useta tell those black frock ministers who'd holler atheist and subversive at us that if Jesus come back to life he'd be a Wobbly. Hell, what else could he be?"

When I was a young fellow, I told him, I had been a migratory worker and had met a lot of Wobblies.

"Oh yes," he said, "we had to move around, the home guard had all the jobs. There was nothin' else for us to do but be boomers. Christ, I done everything! gandy dancer, puncher, ground hog, mucker, fruit tramp, biscuit-shooter, harvest stiff. The employment sharks made a mint out of the transient. I guess you heard the one about the slave market had discovered perpetual motion. They had one work crew on the job, one crew going to the job, and one leaving it, and collecting from all of us."

They were hungry days, I recalled.

"I been on skid road many a day without a cent," he said. "That should break a man—the hunger, the crummy flophouses, hassled by the cops. But if you had the faith you stayed strong. I've seen the worst of times and places but I never turned tin horn or stew bum or rummy. I never scabbed and I never finked. And where there was other Wobblies around they shared. One for all and all for one. Them wasn't just words, we lived it. If I had a snipe and you had none I'd give you as many puffs as I took. If I had a piece of bread I divided it with you. We lived brotherhood.

"We never got too hungry to keep on fighting," he went on. "We fought 'em all—the scissorbills, the railroad bulls, the town clowns, the vigilantes, the bosses. The young folks today have no idea how rough it was 50 years ago. You come to town and you had to stay off the main stem or the town clowns would frisk you. You wanted to go into a good store or to a town dance or even a church, mind you, you'd be told, No calks allowed in here. Well, that was all we had, those kind of shoes. Couldn't afford one pair of shoes for work and one for dress.

"Like I said, we rode the rattlers. The shacks threw us off and the cops picked us up as vags and the judge barked: 'Thirty days!' They was just like parrots: 'Thirty days!' " He blew out a remembrance. "I done my 30 days once or twice," he said tightly. "And I done time for organizing. The only friend we had was our own strength. Solidarity Forever. But it didn't go far enough."

The old man sighed, looked down, and nudged a pebble with his toe. "That was a million years ago and it was yesterday, depending how you look at it. There ain't many around who remember."

What happened to all you fellows who had the red card and the burning dream, I asked. What happened?

He shook his head wearily. "A lot of guys got burnt out in the struggle or got old and discouraged and dropped out. And one by one they died, those that didn't get killed or rot in jails."

And you, friend?

"I got tired too. I got a job in a sawmill and married the schoolteacher. I retired ten years ago. She died five years ago. The biggest regret was not having children, wasn't able to. Should have adopted a couple, I guess. I don't know why we didn't. Maybe we kept thinkin' we'd have our own, and then it was too late for anything. I useta lay in bed and imagine me talking to my kids, telling 'em what the struggle was all about, telling 'em the truth, makin' 'em understand, giving them the knowledge to carry on the fight. You don't learn nothing true about the I.W.W. in the schoolbooks. By God, somebody should tell the truth. We gave the best part of our life for the brotherhood of man."

Suddenly he was silent again. He put his blue bandana to his nose and blew awkwardly.

"When we were working for unionism," he said slowly, sadly, bitterly, "who would have thought that unionism would come to what it is—just a two-bit piece in front of your eyes? I think if we'd a-known we'd a-got discouraged and quit."

My daughter, who I saw peeking in at the cookshack and then in the cabin of the bull of the woods, the camp foreman, lazied over to us and I put my arm around her. The old man nodded hello and continued:

"When I was 20 I was sure we'd see the One Big Union in America and the brotherhood of man all over the world in my lifetime.

"I won't see it," he said. "You won't see. Maybe she will."

Maybe, I said.

Last of the stone-grind millers

The only mill in Oregon that still stone-ground flour was Putnam Brothers, at Eagle Point, in the Rogue River Valley.

We heard about the mill from Marjorie O'Harra, the regional editor of the Medford *Mail-Tribune*, whose boundless curiosity in her home country led her to all the odd and charming people and places in Southern Oregon. So we took her suggestion, drove to Eagle Point, looked the mill over, and said: Thank you, Marjorie; this is worth seeing.

The building, put up in 1872, the same year a post office was opened in the hamlet, had a weathered pioneer character which immediately summoned images of buckboards and steaming roans and farmers swapping barnyard stories before they began the slow haul home. Only the sheet metal roof and the window panes were not of original vintage.

The loading dock was there when covered wagons were still creaking into the valley and was in use for almost four decades before the first horseless buggy pulled up to it.

Francis Putnam, who was born in 1902, had been with the mill since 1930 and was, he said, the last surviving Putnam associated with the enterprise.

A sombre-faced man with a slightly harried appearance, Putnam looked blankly at me when I asked questions, but he was surprisingly keen-minded and patient. Nothing went by him and though people were coming and going he handled all their needs with ease, never showing irritation and never free of that hollow and worrisome demeanor.

The only difference in his flour, he explained, is that he left all the wheat in it and the other millers took out the bran and hearts.

"The hearts is good flavoring," he said. "It's to the grain what the seed is to apple."

"Stone-grind flour is tastier," he went on. "Stone-grind is coarser, and I think that's better. But," he conceded with a trickle of a smile, "it's still a matter of choice."

Putman milled 200 to 300 pounds of stone-ground flour a week, which he sold for 10 cents a pound. His customers came not only from Jackson County and the rest of Southern Oregon but "clear from the East Coast. They hear about it and when they come out this way they buy some."

He did little wholesaling. "The flour won't stay on the store shelves. The moths get into it."

It was a slow milling operation, grinding only four sacks of wheat per hour. But Putman Brothers had other interests. Putman stone-ground corn meal, operated a cold storage room, sold feed and he butchered, being well-known in the valley for his custom cutting of beef, pork, deer, elk and bear.

"You got to be a millwright and a refrigeration man, right along with business, to operate the mill," he pointed out so you'd appreciate the load he was carrying. "There's a lot to attend to."

Putman didn't know what he liked most about the mill. "It's just something," he said with a flat backcountry twang. "You got to have something to do." He was no romanticist. About the only people who are, I've observed, are those who have the freedom to do something else.

The mill was for sale but thus far there had been no takers. "I wouldn't mind running it for another six, seven, ten years," Putman reckoned, "but you might as well start planning now."

He sounded then like the portrait of him that was developing in my mind: a thrifty, hard-working, sparse-worded New Englander, one of Robert Frost's Hampshiremen. I didn't ask where he was raised; it was probably a long way from New England.

My wife bought two pounds of stone-ground flour, which he advised her to put in the freezer when we reached home. While he was measuring it out I commented that the floor was probably the original, since it was put on with square nails.

"Yes," he replied, "there has been some changes but there hasn't been many."

My daughter prodded me to ask Putman if there were

a couple of square nails around she could have. He was pretty occupied then, with several people standing around to buy one thing or another. But I made the request anyway, adding that we would wait until he was free. He looked blankly at me and nodded at someone else talking.

A few minutes later he trotted up a flight of ancient stairs and when he jogged down again he handed my daughter four square nails. She was delighted and I asked Putman if I could pay for them. "Oh, no," he replied. "They don't use those kind any more."

Each of us comes away from a scene with a different impression. When my wife thinks of the Putman Brothers mill it is to remind her of the very delicious bread she baked with the stone-ground flour. My daughter recalls the square nails, which are among her most precious souvenirs, and which she associates, rightly, with Oregon pioneers. And I rue the day when Francis Putman will someday close the doors of that old building for the last time. (You see, not having to work in the mill, I am a romanticist.)

"If you can't get a buyer who will continue what you're doing," I observed, "there won't be a mill in the state stone-grinding flour."

"I suppose," he said, and clacked across the planked floor, rubbed by almost 100 years of wear, to pick up a sack of feed a lady from Shady Cove wanted put into her station wagon.

Jacksonville voice of the past

George Wendt, a bouncy man with a boyish grin, had lived in the same house in Jacksonville since 1923, which was getting on close to 50 years. But his ties with the famous old mining town ran even deeper. His father had come here as a farmer in 1888, George was born here, in 1893, and he had been reared on a ranch about a mile from the porch of his house, where he talked to us on a fair summer day.

As a young man George Wendt had left Jacksonville for six years, trying his hand at various occupations, mostly in Eastern Oregon. He was also away from the town for a year during World War 1. Altogether, then, he had spent about seven decades in Jacksonville, which made him an authentic old timer.

He remembered the Jacksonville of his boyhood as "a pretty rough town. Rough characters, in other words. Older characters—tobacco chewers, hard workers, rough." He met some of them close up when, as a grade school lad, he drove a milk cart around town, pouring out milk into customers' containers at five cents a quart.

His father was a stagecoach driver between Jacksonville and Applegate for 20 years and George went along on many of the runs. He was still a youth when he took the route himself.

From 1923 to 1929 he was in the dairy business. But prices were too low and there was a surplus of milk so he turned some of his good meadow land over to the gold dredgers, receiving a 10 percent cut of all gold mined. The dredges, biting down 35 feet, tore up about three acres.

Wendt didn't have any regret about the land being chewed up for gold. "I needed the money," he said simply.

When the depression struck, the people of Jacksonville who didn't have acreage to lease to the dredgers dug shafts in their back yards and pulled out the buckets with a hand windlass.

"One fellow was down there and the other was on top," explained Wendt. "When they got down there they tunneled and if they struck a paying streak they kept going until they got too far. They made a living at it; they was all eating."

The dredging activity was halted in 1941, when the federal government set about building military camps and decided it had more need of men and equipment than of gold. So Wendt became an electrician. In 1967 he retired and when we saw him he was having a ball, visiting folks, entertaining, and doing all the enjoyable things he didn't have time to do in full measure, like just plain loafing, when he was a dairyman and wage worker.

Wendt was having company the day we barged in on him but he consented to reel off a few tales about the Jacksonville of his youth. His most zestful tellings were his experiences with and commentaries on the Chinese. Not too much has been written about them and their life in this historic gold camp and we were anxious to gather whatever information we could, even though Wendt obviously could not tell us about the very early days of the Chinese here.

An irritable note for us was his name-slurring of the Chinese. When he started with "Chinamen" and "Chinee" I interjected with "Chinese" but he paid me no heed and rolled on with his story spinning. It became apparent that, though he hadn't really gotten close enough to the Chinese to understand them as individuals, he had no animosity toward them as a people. The terms he used were the common language of mining Jacksonville. He had never changed the terms, partly because of ingrained habit and partly because he connoted no derisive association with the names. In attitude he was kinder to the Chinese than the fate they suffered from the miners.

"I remember the Chinytown," he began. "We had quite a Chinytown. Most of them were miners. Very good sociable people. I had a lot of passengers on the stage who were Chinamen. I was about 16 years old when I was first allowed to drive and I'd bring all the gold from the Chinee mines. I'd sell it to Beekman, at his bank. Old Beek—we called him Old Beek—he'd take those leather pouches and pour the gold on the scale and he'd pay me off in 20 dollar gold pieces, 10 dollar gold pieces, 5 dollar gold pieces, and silver, down to 25 cents. Sometimes it would amount to 225 dollars—around there. He only paid 7 dollars an ounce for gold, when gold was selling for 16 dollars an ounce elsewhere—but there was no place to go. There was a lot of gold—there had to be a lot of Chinee digging for all that gold.

"There wasn't a scrap of paper in all those transactions. I didn't give the Chinee a slip; Beekman didn't give me a slip; no paper.

"After I came out of the bank I threw the gold and silver pieces—each Chinaman had a different pouch—on the front seat of the stagecoach. Then I'd drive down to the ranch, leave it there all night, and forget about it. Nothing was ever taken.

"Each Chinaman gave me 25 cents when I gave him his pouch. He didn't count the gold, didn't ask me no questions."

Cornelius C. Beekman was the wealthiest and most powerful banker in Southern Oregon and modern-day Jacksonville has resurrected him as a sympathetic legend. But George Wendt was not in the chorus of praisers. "I don't know why they make such a fit over him," he said, after first declaring he'd rather be silent on the subject. "Beekman, he was just a hog for money. Peter Britt, the photographer, he accomplished much more for the good of Jacksonville."

Having dismissed Beekman, Wendt returned to the Chinese:

"We got along very well with the Chinamens. My Dad favored them a lot. When they had the Chinese New Year, every kid in town would line up in front of the different Chinamen doors and we'd always get invited in and they'd fill our pockets with Chinese candies and Chinese nuts. My brother and I, we'd always get a little extra treat, because my Dad favored them. They'd give us a China lily and glass bracelets. All that stuff come from China.

"There's a Chinese tunnel—the Chinee built—that runs right under Jacksonville. Nobody knows where it started or where it ended. Nobody knows how they got the water out. Years later a white miner found an old wooden pump and he figured that's how they kept the water out. The Chinee tunnel was there many years before it was discovered. All the cribbing was in perfect shape, sound as a rock.

"The Chinee mined about 12 miles out from Jacksonville. They left this country in about 1915. I heared they went to San Francisco. There was quite a resentment against them around this town. The people thought the Chinee were shipping the gold to China. The resentment got to be pretty nasty and the Chinee left."

We asked Wendt how he would react if a Chinese family moved next door to him. He grinned with the pleasure of a man who long ago had put all pettiness aside. "Wouldn't bother me a bit," he replied heartily. "I always got along well with the Chinamen."

Soul music on a rocky ridge

The one-handed fiddler split time with his music, opening it wide enough for memory to come through. He was on *Redwing* now, flying high with eyes aglow, and I was back in Kansas, hearing another fiddler slipping, sliding down the long sour-string grass notes . . .

Could I forget that night: the girls, cheeks red as polished pippins, and the boys, pounding the haymoss floor hard enough to churn up a twister?

Whirl and circle and hold me fast while the music coils inside our arms and itches up our limbs. Oh fiddler man, with your bow dipped in cider and your strings drawn from the throat of a mockingbird, tell me the truth: does my love love me?

Old man, Old man, tell it to me straight. Don't lie to me now, I'm feeling too good.

Redwing, O pretty *Redwing* . . .

The one-handed fiddler was Ed Forsha, a stocky, craggy, straight-tongued man of 75. He and his wife, Jean, 85, lived four miles out of Murphy. Their house sat on a ridge a mile up a rocky, humpbacked trail off the Gray's Creek Road. Part of the house looked sunlit suburban and the other part pioneer homestead. The toilet was outside, 50 yards down a well-worn path. "I told you we were building," Jean Forsha laughed.

In this house the Forshas made music, Ed on his fiddle and Jean working the chords of an old piano. On a glorious August afternoon they played for us, much as they entertained themselves evenings.

"Give 'em *Old Maggie,*" Ed gruffed, and he bent into the fiddle, pumping away like he was hacking at a tree, and in a minute I was more than 30 years back, an aimless wanderer in Cimarron County, Oklahoma . . .

Oil lanterns, slung from the rafters of the pungent-odored barn, stenciled a crosshatch of lemon-colored light on a grayhaired fiddler with a Buffalo Bill beard. Sweat

139

splotching his fringed deerskin jacket, his arms soared and dived like a nighthawk, the notes flying to the far corners of the barn and spilling into every crevice. A starling, roosted on a rafter, accompanied Buffalo Bill with squeaks that filled in when the fiddler paused. He winked at the starling with a gold-toothed grin and rode on to the races.

I see it all again: the unlimbered farmers rigidly furrowing the planked floor as they moved the ladies around, the men making labor of it and the ladies resilient, the men waxing into a springy plod and the ductile ladies smiling as they remembered with eyes liquid as April rain the romantic swains of their courting years.

Outside, chickens scurried in a lather, bowing and sashaying, hot in their own Virginia Reel. All except one feisty old rooster who spread his wings and minced in a straight line, like a tight rope walker.

Ah, *Old Maggie*. Where have those days fled? . . .

Ed Forsha lost his right hand and forearm helping a neighbor raise a house. "The jack let go and the spike went through my hand. Tore my hand all to pieces."

That was in mid-October of 1936. He fashioned himself a violin bow holder to fit over the stump and two weeks later started playing again. His doctor told him, he said, "You'll live, Ed, when the rest are all gone."

So he hadn't let the loss of his hand slow him down, especially when it came to fiddle playing. The Forshas blew up spumes of music, Ed wrestling with the fiddle and Jean, erect on the piano bench, belting out the chords as her head snapped up and down to the rhythm, like a robin pecking at a worm, or tilting her chin and tossing her head from shoulder to shoulder. Whatever she did, she always beamed love at her man and life as their hearts sang through their instruments on a dim ridge 12 miles from Grants Pass.

"What'll we give 'em now?" Ed muttered, in a voice that was handsaw biting a dry log, or sandpaper rubbing at rust. *"Money Must,* that's what we'll give 'em. You ready?"

"Ready," Jean trilled.

The music sinuated through the cabin and filtered out the door, where it set the Forsha pooch, a fluffy facelicker, into spasms of enigmatic barking. I couldn't figure out whether he was pleading for the concert to halt or to be allowed inside to join the revelers.

Ed charged with zest, stroking all his soul into his art, thrumming with every drop of blood pumping through his vibrant heart. And I was once more turned around, now to that Grange hall in Eastern Oregon, up in the grazing pine country . . .

The low-pitched hoot of a flammulated owl introduced the fiddler, an ancient stubble-cheeked scrag who spread his legs to keep his balance. Lord, how that man labored! The catgut groaned and wheezed; it mumbled pain and screamed in agony; but he slapped on, roughing over it; and then the strings and the bow took to his bidding and the air pined with nostalgia. The honeyburr tunes whiffled down the gully of stealthy night all the aches of the immutable weariness. Tomorrow would be another callusing round of chores but tonight was a gorge sheltered from care. Keep this night fresh, old fiddler man, we've toiled a week of Sundays in waiting . . .

"I never took a lesson," Ed boasted, and we believed him. But self-taught, his music spoke for him. It was strong, rugged, perservering, uncomplaining. Years of laughter, years of struggle were in the strains of the Forshas. The music was the beat of their hearts, joyous and indomitable.

"Hell, I learned to fiddle when I was 14 years old, in Vermont," Ed said with a put-on brusqueness. He had an air of being gruff and aggressive but his sentimentality and unselfishness gleamed through every chink of his rough facade.

"I played Rhode Island, New Hampshire, Massachusetts for the Elks, the Painters Union; played my way across the country and up to Canada and down to Oregon. I played pretty much all over Oregon—Newport, Corvallis, Waldport, Depoe Bay, Oceanlake, Yachats; I played all over the state. I was all the time having a good time, playing. Here we played at Jacksonville and Grants Pass and at Medford and White City.

"Never read music in my life," he boasted in a gravelly, twangy growl, "but I played with those who did."

He had come to Oregon in 1926 and had been a roustabout, like thousands of his day. "I done everything. Firing boilers, running trucks, flagged and surveyed for the State, felled timber, bucked timber, I'd done all kinds of work, everything, I've done it all. Most money I've made in my life was picking ferns; I made six and seven dollars a day and as high as twelve. Now, if I was back on the Coast picking ferns, I'd make $25 a day."

Ed's fingers were pawing at the strings. He slung the fiddle into place and swung into *Hornpipes*. Jean's hands bounced on the keyboard as her face lit up again, star syrup on her lips, sapphire in her eyes . . .

I looked away and it was late summer in Idaho. Another barn, another dance. They had traveled from miles around, by flivver and flatbed truck and pickup and even on horse; come from all those no-place villages that had corrals right off the main street and stock animals on it; come from towns so big they had a filling station; come from the crossroads of cow trails, from the murky folds of sheepranch hills; from cabins so deep in woods the coyotes got lost, from the brambly banks of rivers that ran cold silent all year.

So they came, each with refreshments and ready to swap samples. The ladies bussing and the men slapping each other on the back, the ladies inquiring about kids and the men about crops and stock. But when the fiddler appeared all was forgotten for the dance.

He was a bald-headed oak stump with ham hock hands who picked up moonlight money playing at the country stomps. Otherwise he was a schoolteacher, a principal, in fact, of a two-room schoolhouse. The folks loved him. He was a local boy who had gone off to the university, plodded on to a degree, and returned to his people. He was still one of the boys; education hadn't changed his hat size, and here he was, a boiler full of steam.

His happy pumpkin face glowing, he stood before them, and when they had quieted a bit he cheerfully teased, "Are y'all in good shape tonight? I wouldn't want to exert yuh."

The crowd laughed, a yipee rang from a corner, and someone hollered, "Let 'er rip, Knute!" The fiddler turned to his task, his arm muscles bubbling with verve. He smiled merrily at everyone and everything: man, woman, child, dog and cat. The music reared and plunged and roared and wailed and cougar-called through the night, loosening the juices of life.

A stockman's double-chinned wife, round as a partridge and frisky as a colt, looked good for at least until dawn. All she needed were handkerchiefs and she had brought an abundant supply. By the time the fiddler rasped into *Hornpipes* she had worn out three men: her husband, her brother and her brother-in-law. Now, in partner with a man from the other side of the county, she hit her peak. Toe and head in perfect timing, she beat a staccato spin around the floor, her open mouth sucking in the excitement and her coal black eyes far-away hungry.

Beyond the barn a shaft of lunar glow impaled on amber hayrick, behind which a slouching couple stole away. A star shivered and a doodlesack note born in the shed fluttered to the dungcrust at the forehoof of a sorrel, who shuffled it aside . . .

Jean patted the piano affectionately. It was the first household article she and Ed acquired after they were married, in 1964. They bought it from a second-hand roadside store at Foote's Creek for $125.

It was hard to describe Jean Forsha. Here she was, 85 years old, young and wise and gritty. You could say, in a detached way, that she was a delightful, unpretentious little woman with a voice of silk; out of character, at first glance, for a woman who had farmed and mined and been so closely bound to grime and toil. I ran her through my mind again and again until an expression, or definition of her, sieved through the hundreds of words: a blushing twig of velvet flint. That, I thought, most appropriately summarized her modesty, gentleness, tenacity and pluck.

Kansas-born, Jean was early married. "Seventy years ago," she said, with a wide-eyed pinch of wonderment. "How do you like that?" But she had been divorced many years before meeting Ed Forsha in the Senior Citizens Club at Grants Pass. She was 10 years older than Ed but no one could tell it. Not that Ed looked his 75 years; it was just that Jean was so refreshingly youthful. Who could believe on sight that she was a great-great-grandmother?

Ed's left hand fingers pawed at the catgut and the taut strings hissed back. He frowned impatiently at the rest of us and announced that since we wanted *Casey Jones* it was coming up next . . .

Man, that was a sweaty night in the West Virginia hollow, inside that soot-streaked hall where the lodge brothers had met before the depression drove most of them out of town. There was this tall, skeletal, wide-shouldered, long-legged, beak-nosed fella in fresh overalls, with a red kerchief at his throat, scraping toward the pie-sized stage with bustard awkwardness. He opened his violin case and removed his instrument with a strange daintiness, scowling off a bottle pushed at him. Then he swayed there, this odd-framed Ichabod Crane, strands of hair at the fringes of his temples reeding across his bumpy pate, otherwise bald as an egg. An eerie pillar of a man, darkly glowering at the jabbering mass. But once he set bow to fiddle he was an alchemist brewing magic. God awmighty, he could squeeze sugar out of a snipe and set a horned frog doe-si-doeing. He lit up that dank, smelly hall with all the rainbow colors of string sound and when he tore into *Casey Jones* the hard-whiskey miners and railroaders went wild. "Hit 'er, Jeff!" they shouted. "Blow that whistle!" "Whee-Wheeee!" "Thar she comes!" "Come onnn, Ca-sey!"

That was a moment to mark for all time in one single, simple span of existence . . .

Jean Forsha arrived from California in 1930. "We had to get away—we would have starved to death."

She had heard Southern Oregon was gold country but "it was the fascination of the minerals" that made her want to become a miner. She started sluice-panning on the Applegate River but didn't scoop up enough color to trade in for a pot of beans. Then the Applegate flooded "and it throwed some of the gold up on top of the ground, along in the grass, and I was able to pick that up and that's all I needed."

From there she began a search for a lode of rich paydirt. "I found some little pieces of quartz and I traced them along up the hill from yonder along the road, up over this hill, and down over to here, and here's where my mining claim is."

She had two claims, the Keystone and the Greenstone, had had them since 1936, but had worked only the Keystone. In all those years she had gone down no more than 37 feet. The mine hadn't produced enough to feed a sparrow, she admitted with a chime of laughter, "but I never put much cash into it. I've had a bulldozer to move some of the dirt away a time or two, is all."

Now she mined only two or three hours a day, "all I can take at one time." She used only a shovel, not touching a pick, even though "the formation is very, very rough.

'Course," she added, "a miner would have had some powder in there." But powder would destroy the pink and green sapphire she had found and while she was disappointed to learn that the sapphire wasn't quartz, it was better than nothing.

When the Forshas married one of the first things Ed told her was, You're not going down in that mine any more. As he might have expected, she lovingly ignored him. So he built her a stout ladder, and with her power light she felt safe in the cavern. Ed didn't go with her but after a couple of hours he'd start to peer uneasily toward the mine. Jean had never failed to return after a three hour absence but if she had Ed would have hiked across the ridge to see what was wrong. She thought his solicitude for her touching but amusing. Long before she met him she was in the mine alone, with no one close by to fret about her.

Jean still had hopes of striking it rich but if she didn't, well, at least she had given it a go. She summed up her feelings in a lengthy poem to her sister. The close, which I have set in prose style, goes like this: "That pot o' gold at rainbow's end is ever, always beckoning/ But I am getting along in years, there comes that time of reckoning/ So, should I fail to reach that goal, till on my deathbed lyin'/ I want the waitin' world to know I've had some great fun tryin'."

Ed scratched a few notes, like a turkey snagging for corn under a tin can, and allowed that he'd now meet our request of half-an-hour ago for *Bicycle Built For Two* . . .

Up in the New Mexico highlands spring comes late and it was only early April. The ranchers and cowpokes booted in, blowing steam and clapping their hands together. After they had helped their ladies out of their coats and hung the wraps on the wall hooks of the old school gym they removed their wool mackinaws and cowhide jackets.

There were two fiddlers that night, a small graying man and his larger wife, her hair tinted red. They played separately or together. They joshed through *Bicycle Built For Two* facing sideways, she behind him, in tandem style. Once or twice he put his fiddle between his knees and pretended to be leaning over the handle bars while his wife sawed on, laughing and nudging his ankle with her gloss-slippered foot. On the planked benches against the wall the folks who were sitting the number out swayed airily from side to side while the lighthearted couples on the floor lilted on their toes as though they were pedaling down lover's lane . . .

Jean owned 40 acres. For a long time she lived alone in a log cabin about three-quarters of a mile down the trace that led to Gray's Creek Road. In 1961 friends and relatives gathered for a house-raising bee on the ridge and put up another cabin. Again, as in the past, she was the only occupant. After she and Ed married they began improvements upon the home. A few more years and they'd be living in style. "Next time you come we might even have an indoor toilet," Jean twinkled.

The house, on the open brow of the hill, overlooked Missouri Flats, a serene green-drenched vale that was the picture of an early Oregon setting, a smoke-whisp portrait of an idyllic scene unbruised by man. I could have gazed at it all day and told Jean so, but she was unimpressed. She thought more beauty had come out of her labors on the scraggly ridge than nature had bestowed upon the churn of emerald below. She had dug two ponds for fish, planted rows of flowers, freed the earth of stones and turned and watered and tended the soil to produce a vegetable patch. "I'm a normal, natural-born pioneer, I guess, at heart, because to get out here and make something grow where there never was anything before," she said.

Ed nagged at the catgut, loosening up for another pulsation. "Now I'm givin' ya *Take Me To Saint Looie, Louie*," and Jean was in stride with him . . .

The aroma of oysters and wood chips filled the tangy breezes in that rambling house on the far shore of Puget Sound. All furniture had been pushed into smaller rooms or stacked on the porches. Came now the maestros by boat from their cove home at the lip of the soggy forest. The girl was young and tall and lissome, with long-braided hair blond as wheat and eyes blue as Hood Canal under the sun. Her father, a rangy man with a lantern jaw, was the stereotype of the stolid Swede until you caught his mouth, which was curled for smiling, or his eyes, a frolic of orbs, or saw him greet old friends with jocose exaggeration.

They played together until that song Ed Forsha had his soul into now; then the girl lay her violin down, tapped the shoulder of a brooding dark-haired young man, and they waltzed off together, she so stately, so supple, so pure . . .

"Do you like to dance?" I asked Jean Forsha.

Her head flew up and her eyes ignited. Sparks crackled around the room. At that moment she was 16 years old.

"You're very feminine, you know that?" I called to her.

Her chin twitched up, as a bird surprised. She stared at me until the surprise wore away. Then she laughed in a warm whirlpool of giggle. When she regained her composure she replied, with a touch of coquetry, "I'm supposed to be the world's worst old tomboy."

"No," I protested, "you're very feminine. I noticed that right away. You have a beautiful voice."

"And a beautiful smile," my wife added.

"You have a voice of rustling silk," I said. "And that's today's love story."

"I love it," Jean said.

Before the afternoon was out Ed showered us with other numbers, some I had heard before but could not immediately identify. As the unhoned notes flew through the kitchen, like chips from a blade-struck tree, there continued to flash before me, as on a screen, snatches of other dances and fiddling contests and old men bowing away on their mail order beauties in shacks that turned to tombs when the music ceased.

Mostly the Forshas played by themselves but sometimes there was company—relatives and friends. (She had enough family around Grants Pass to fill the house.) As many as 30 or 40 people might be involved in a gusty jam session on the ridge, the youth bringing guitars and the elders carting their younger years to crank up again.

"We have a time," Jean winked.

"Sometimes I think they'll push the walls down," Ed grumbled good-naturedly.

We asked Ed and Jean to dance. "I don't know," Jean demurred. "I've been a bit under the weather." But she agreed anyway. Ed set aside his fiddle, shoved a mouthharp between his lips, and the shindig erupted.

They were true country stompers, driving their bodies into the rhythm of the music until their faces were tight with the ecstasy-agony of the wound-up intentness. All of them was in motion: their arms, heads, hips, thighs. They thrust, ricocheted, gyrated, lowered, popped up, bent, straightened, twisted, curved—and all the time their feet were flying: clicking, drumming, thudding, slapping, beating a stout and furious tatoo on the old kitchen floor.

Alabama, Carolina, Dakota, Colorado, Texas; the California Mother Lode and the Arizona desert; Essex Junction, Vermont and Kennebec County, Maine; Mississippi cotton-pickers and Montana wranglers; Kentucky schoolmarms and Oregon stump ranchers; the whole country came alive, my youth reborn, in the dancing. Cumberland nights and a mountain plover downcurving over Jackson Hole; a hobo jig around the sassy fire of a ditchbank jungle after the last mulligan had been scraped from the coffeecan; the first autumn breath of Rocky Mountain wind on the streets of Laramie; the feral whistle of a lonely train echoing through a far-off tunnel of starless mist in the sand hills of Nebraska; a cajun song on a Louisiana shrimpboat: the folk-root of the nation was in the dancing here on the hill above Missouri Flats, and all the wondering and wandering frontier years of my life were gathered together in the home of the Forshas, the gypsy native returned to his American womb.

We drove on to Grants Pass.

"They're groovy," said my daughter with rare enthusiasm. She did not enjoy herself at most work sessions. "They're really nice."

"They're precious," my wife said. "Beautiful people. I'd like to come back, just to visit."

And I, silent, was in Arkansas.

A pitcher of moonbeams dripped down a clearing of a hummock and, like molasses, rolled off at the edges to blotch into the long-leaf pine. The moonlight waded across a shallow fen to the porchstep of an angular hall, where it met the lamp light from within. Out of this saffron confluence stepped the fiddler from his buggy, leaving the languid-eyed mule to a tousled bare-foot boy.

The fiddler wore rimless glasses, a flannel shirt and a string tie. That is all I remember of him.

Nor do I recall what tunes he played. Nothing, except that he awakened all the sweet songbirds under Heaven, shook the laughter from out the hills, lifted the moonbeams from the swamps, sounded every love and passion that hid in a hollow or was buried in woodstove shacks rutted on dark bumpy roads.

Oh babe, my bonnie, gentle babe: the air is too close, the heart too full. Glide out with me, out to the secret ground under the long-leaf pine, and if you stay till the moon goes down you'll hold always to this night . . .

Fiddle on, old man on the ridge. Chord on, old girl.

Fill the hill, fill the valley with your music, your testament to life.

Play on, play on . . .

The courage of Grandma Brown

Interstate 5, the great north-south freeway of Oregon, is fast and easy to drive. It is slowest and curviest and hilliest and hardest to drive between Grants Pass and Canyonville.

Before the freeway was built the north-south road through the western valleys, US 99, was far slower and windier than Int. 5 is now. And then, too, the most difficult section lay between Grants Pass and Canyonville.

How well I remember this part of US 99 in the 1930s: a black-smudged lamprey slithering blindly around tightly-curved slopes in a dank corridor of mossy shadows.

The tedious, treacherous road I knew in my youth is recalled every time I drive the freeway over the Umpqua Range. And through my reading I harken beyond those days—90 years beyond—to the sufferings of the first Applegate Trail emigrants and the magnificent courage of Tabitha Brown.

You may place the name of Tabitha Brown as somehow being linked to Pacific University. She was its germ cell, its germinal seed. Without her it may nevertheless have come into being; but then again it may not. There is no absolute assurance that if one seed is not planted, another will be. And sometimes, when the situation dictates, the difference between what is and what is not to be is determined by a factor that at superficial glance may seem insignificant. Tabitha Brown was that factor.

She arrived on the far rim of the Tualatin Plains late in 1846, impoverished in money and health but brimming with plans for a new life. They could be summed up in this simple request: to establish herself "in a comfortable house and receive all poor children and be a mother to them."

Together with the benefactor who made her wishes possible, Reverend Harvey Clark, Mrs. Brown gathered together the children of those emigrants who had passed away and in a log church established the first orphanage in Oregon.

The next step was a boarding school, called Tualatin Academy. Mrs. Brown, the house mother, was turned by affection into "Grandma" Brown and remained so until her death in 1858. By then the settlement of West Tualatin had become Forest Grove and Tualatin Academy was stretching its wings, to fly as Pacific University.

This is the way Tabitha Brown may be fixed in your mind. But to me she is most vivid when I am wheeling down from the summit above Azalea to Canyonville. The canyon road the freeway erased followed the most harrowing stretch of the Applegate Trail Mrs. Brown and her fellow pioneers endured in that brutal first crossing.

She had come a long way to Oregon: her full hazardous journey took nine months. It would have been very much easier on her and the others if they had adhered to the Old Oregon Trail.

There were in the mid-1840s a sufficient number of Oregon-bound travelers to provide any promoter with enough wagons to stir up dust clouds on his fresh cutoff. All along the trail, especially west of South Pass, that rolling passage through the Continental Divide, numerous cutoffs, or short cuts, had been blazed. Most of them were not decisive in settling the fate of a caravan. A few were. The Applegate Trail was one.

It does not require an abnormal supply of imagination to conjecture the feelings of the pilgrims at Fort Hall or Fort Boise or wherever the cutoffs were proposed. The caravaneers are tired, disgusted and anxious to get on to the green fields of Oregon. The trek across the inhospitable plains has been no lark. Runaway stock, fear of Indian attacks, scorching days and bone-chilling nights, thunder storms and heavy rains, choking grime, broken wheels and axles, accidents and sickness and death, endless bickerings, and that most insidious of enemies, monotony.

Some of the pilgrims are in a hurry because the trek is becoming too much for them; others equate mileage with trouble and reckon that by reducing mileage they will cut down on trouble; and still others, viewing from a knoll the long waves of prairie schooners ahead of them, want to beat the front ranks to the best land.

The three Applegate brothers, the most illustrious of whom was Jesse, had reached Oregon as early as 1843. It did not take them long to make their names known. Jesse, in particular, was on his way to becoming a legend before he felled the first tree for a homesite.

On June 22, 1846, Jesse Applegate, leading a party of 14 other men, including his brother Lindsay, started from the La Creole, near present Dallas, to brush out a trail from the Humboldt River in Nevada to the upper Willamette Valley. Charles, the third brother, stayed on in Polk County, tending the Applegate farms and watching over the Applegate families.

There have been several motives attributed to the Applegates and their cohorts and supporters for their zealousness in promoting the cutoff. The most frequently cited is an obsession that war between the United States and Great Britain for possession of the Oregon Country was inevitable and that the safest route for U.S. troops to the Columbia River would be via a southern route.

On August 9, Jesse Applegate wrote from Fort Hall, on the Snake River, to another brother, Lisbon, residing in St. Clair County, Missouri:

"I arrived here alone and on foot from the Willamette Valley at the head of a party to meet the emigrants. We left our homes . . . to explore a southern route into that valley from the U.S. After much trouble and suffering we succeeded in our object, but it occupied us so long that a part of the emigration had passed our place of intersection before we could possibly reach it."

Most of the comers at Fort Hall paid little attention to Applegate, ignoring the alluring pictures of the cutoff his compelling tongue painted. They were too cautious, too conservative and too skeptical to bet their all on an untried route. Stay with the true and tested way and reach Oregon safely was their motto, and they stuck with it.

But, as said, there were always the impatient ones, the gamblers certain they had a sure thing, and they gave close heed to Applegate. They listened raptly to his rosy descriptions of the new route he had but recently surveyed on horseback. They were moved by his stark accounts of the Columbia River gorge; they shuddered as he enumerated the dangers of crafting down the Columbia; and eyes were damp when he told of a boat capsizing in 1843, with the drowning of his son and nephew. (They had not yet heard of another cutoff, the Barlow, which would carry them beyond the Cascades without having to chance the fearful Columbia.) And they were sold when Jesse Applegate, a name already gaining renown in the jumpoff towns, promised them not only a shorter and safer route but a more comfortable one.

Tabitha Moffat Brown was one of those charmed by Jesse Applegate, that man of such noble bearing only a scoundrel could suspect him of dipping his tongue in snake oil. She had every reason thereafter to regret her judgment.

On the day Jesse wrote to his brother Lisbon, the first wagons to test the southern route rolled out of Fort Hall, waving goodbye to the larger contingents poised to take up the march again on the older, well-marked trail.

One of the wagons belonged to Mrs. Brown's son, Orus. Another held the family of the Virgil Pringles, Mrs. Brown's son-in-law and daughter. A third ox team she herself drove.

Her only companion, her inseparable companion, was her brother-in-law, Captain John Brown, closer to 80 than 75. He was very precious to her, being the brother of her deceased husband, Reverend Clark Brown, who had passed away when she was 37, leaving her with three children to support.

Here is Tabitha Brown on the scurfy, jolting grind. A frail figure, with delicately shaped face, blue gray eyes and gray hair that never whitened. She is crippled by paralysis of one leg and much of the time she is in pain. She is as stout-hearted, generous, self-sacrificing and resourceful in this strange and violent land as she was back home and as she will be on the Tualatin plain.

"Move on," cries Virgil Pringle, the wagon train pilot, and Mrs. Brown moves the oxen on, reassuring her brother-in-law with a spunky smile that they will make it to Oregon. She is 66 but her mind is young. On the seat beside her he nods wanly.

Little does she know then the trials that will measure her capacity to survive. She was to document them later in one agonizing sentence: "We had sixty miles of desert without grass or water, mountains to climb, cattle giving out, wagons breaking, emigrants sick and dying, hostile

Indians to guard against by night and day, if we would save ourselves and our horses and cattle from being arrowed and stole."

Four days after departure a young man named Robey, burned by consumption, is dead. He was going West to regain his health. No one knows his grave will be the first of many to be dug before the Willamette Valley is reached.

About the middle of August the wagons churned into a vale of multitudinous hot springs, appropriately named, by someone who counted in round figures, Thousand Springs. A week later the caravan creaked to the banks of the sluggish Humboldt River and followed its meanderings westward for more than 200 miles. They left it at a point where the California Trail followed the river south.

Up to now the Applegate party had done nothing inventive. They had merely followed the California road. But beyond where the Humboldt arched south they bore the sole responsibility for the new route. The critics, and there were many, lambasted Jesse Applegate, the prime mover of the cutoff, for a grossly irresponsible blunder.

Death became more common along the Humboldt. Sutton Burns left a wife and three children to fend for themselves. Two men were mortally felled by Indian arrows poisoned with rattler venom. Two young women perished of typhoid, which the emigrants called mountain fever.

At the last bend of the Humboldt River all possible containers were filled with water and the caravan broke up into small companies, each traveling on its own. Now the emigrants faced the hellish prospect of the forbidding Black Rock Desert. They met it, flinched, and pushed forward. You can hear Tabitha Brown encouraging John, weary and feeble, "It has to end somewhere."

There were some men in the caravan whose names would later shine in the annals of Oregon history. One was J. Quigg Thornton, who to his dying day never really forgave Jesse Applegate for having induced him to travel the southern route. He wrote of the Nevada desert: "Nothing presents itself to the eye but a broad expanse of uniform dead-level plain which conveyed to the mind the idea that it had been the muddy and sandy bottom of a former lake . . . It seemed to be the River of Death dried up. Even the winds had died."

And he spoke of the desert at another place: "No object presented itself to the blood-shot eyes but hot, yellow sand, and here and there a low rock just rising above the plains. A strange curse seemed to brood over the whole scene."

At last the wagons inched into Surprise Valley, in the northeastern corner of California, and found grass, and at Goose Lake drew all the water they needed.

The deserts were behind them but now mountains had to be conquered. It was tough pulling across the Cascade Range and a great relief when the emigrants sighted the Rogue River Valley. They had been three months and five days traveling from Thousand Springs to the lowland vale of the Rogue. Applegate's surveying party, moving the other way in early summer, had covered the same distance in 37 days.

There was little time or reason for rejoicing, however. The chill, wet winds of Autumn were riding swift, cutting flesh with their sharp spurs. Provisions were consumed at a far faster rate than they were being replaced. The weak were growing weaker, the sick sicker.

Two more ranges to cross: the Umpqua and the Calapooya. After the Umpqua the Calapooya appeared small and pliable.

The Umpqua Range. What terrors it stored. How innocent looked the southern slope of the last summit. All the agonies pressed upon the emigrants up to now were to be multiplied.

There was only one way off the summit: down a narrow funnel through which the icy waters of a mountain stream ran swiftly.

The pioneers called the defile Umpqua Canyon. To those who came later it was Canyon Creek or Coldstream Canyon. And there was some confusion as to its length—12 miles or 15 miles. But all agreed that the gorge, which ended where the creek opened into the valley of the South Umpqua River, where Canyonville now stands, was without even momentary doubt the most disastrous stretch of the entire route of tears.

Tabitha Brown remembered to her grave the grim

spectacle: "I rode through in three days at the risk of my life, on horseback, having lost my wagon and all that I had but the horse I was on. Our families were the first that started through the canyon, so that we got through the mud and rocks much better than those that followed. . . . Only one [wagon] came through without breaking. The canyon was strewn with dead cattle, broken wagons, beds, clothing, and everything but provisions, of which latter we were nearly destitute. Some people were in the canyon two or three weeks before they could get through. Some died without warning, from fatigue and starvation. Others ate the flesh of cattle that were lying dead by the wayside."

She and Captain John Brown found themselves alone, a dazed man nearing 80 and a crippled woman four years from 70. Two gaunt, aching pilgrims in a new world wilderness, slogging numbly on near-exhausted horses. They were hungry, pelted by rain, attacked by freezing winds, and fever-ridden. His days were doomed but she would hold him fast to the end.

The old man became delirious and would have fallen from the saddle if Mrs. Brown had not held onto him. Once, when he had dismounted, he was too weak to lift himself up again and mumbled sounds about dying. But he reckoned without his sister-in-law. She had not braved the crossing of a continent to watch either of them perish short of their goal. Death would have to wait its fragile plunder. Somehow, using her two canes as props, she lifted him back into the saddle.

It was a triumph of spirit.

A corner of history at Eagle Creek

At Sandy we turned south to follow the Barlow Road to Eagle Creek, where the Oregon Trail emigrants made camp at Philip Foster's farm before continuing on to Oregon City, regarded in the early years as the unofficial end of the Trail.

The covered wagons had ground west from the toll-gate at the foot of Laurel Hill. Before stores were established at The Dalles the nearest place to purchase supplies had been at Fort Boise, on the Snake River. That was a long way back and by the time the emigrants left the Sandy River to find Foster's place they were very tired and very low on foodstuffs.

Below Sandy the terrain was a long roll of low hills, looking like smooth waves blown up by a lazy wind. On one of these hills, two miles south of Sandy, we found the old Sandy Ridge School, which the children of the pioneers had built for their children.

Another four miles and we were at Eagle Creek, whatever remained of it. It was only a wide place in the road now, at an intersection of two state highways. But a century ago it was a very important small community, and in the prime of the Barlow Road it was filled with covered wagons and freighters.

On the left side of the road to Estacada, standing in front of a barbed wire fence enclosing a pasture, a large boulder bore a plaque that read: FOSTER'S PLACE and THE BARLOW ROAD.

Foster's large, well-furnished log house, which was located about 150 feet back of the marker, was the first dwelling many early emigrants saw in western Oregon, and it must have been a rewarding sight. Here was proof positive that civilization had again been reached. And when the comers took in Foster's outbuildings, fruit trees, stacks of hay and land under plow they had all the convincing evidence they needed that they had not come to

Oregon in vain—for what Foster had done, so could any enterprising man.

Few men, of course, were as enterprising and shrewd and had been as lucky as Philip Foster had been but ambitious men—and most emigrants began with more ambition than anything else—pay little heed to the success factors of others which are absent in themselves.

Philip Foster was a man who took pride in his past and present and, until history outdistanced him so that he was no more than a general storekeeper in an outcountry hamlet, he had confidence that he was preparing the way for a proud future.

He could trace his genealogy back to a ninth century Great Forester of Flanders and his American ancestors to two Fosters from Ipswich, England, who landed in Boston in 1634.

One branch of the Fosters moved to Maine. Philip was born in Augusta in 1805. His second wife—his first died —was the sister of Francis W. Pettygrove, who lived far fewer years in Oregon than Foster but got more mileage out of historians.

In a real sense Pettygrove was the founder of Portland and gave the city its name, winning that right by the toss of a coin with a Massachusetts man named Lovejoy, who would have called the town Boston. Why Pettygrove did not choose Calais, the Maine city where he was born, or Bangor, where he was a merchant, is a question Pettygrove should have been asked while he was around. (Maybe he had a premonition about his new "city" and was thinking big.)

Calais, Oregon. Doesn't that sound grand? Or does Bangor, Oregon sound better? What's in a name? Would the Willamette be less polluted today if it were called Jasmine River?

Not content with founding one town, Pettygrove moved north in 1851 and started another, Port Townsend, Wash. There he remained until his death in 1887, outliving the older Philip Foster by three years.

In 1842, having resolved to venture to Oregon, the Maine brothers-in-law, lumber merchants and storekeepers, sold out their property and in New York purchased supplies to set up a general store on the far side of the continent. It took them and their families seven months to sail to Honolulu, where additional goods for resale were bought.

Foster and Pettygrove arrived on the lower Columbia in April, 1843, 13 months after they boarded the *Victoria* in New York for the long voyage around Cape Horn. At St. Helens they hired Indians to transport them by canoe to Oregon City. Less than six weeks after they reached their destination they had constructed a three-story building, with the ground floor used as a store. Maine men were always in a hurry. They were not in business to let their tills gather dust.

Philip Foster was optimistic. On Dec. 1, 1843, he wrote from "Willamette Falls" to his suppliers and agents in Honolulu:

"Quite a city has been built up here within one year. We have something like seventy five buildings in this place; and people are still going ahead, we shall in a short time go ahead of Honolulu."

Before another year had passed Foster was to regard his days in Oregon City as a closed chapter in his life and he could not have cared less whether that settlement would supplant Honolulu or anywhere else. But while he was in Oregon City he seemed to have a hand in everything.

He was one of the builders of Oregon's first flour mill, erected homes for other budding merchant princes, served as agent of the Willamette Cattle Company, was the first Oregonian to process and ship salt salmon and peas in barrels, was the biggest shake shingles shipper on the river, ran a flourishing general store, and found time to father the first white girl born in Oregon City. She was his sixth child. Four more were born later. (The first white boy born in Portland was Pettygrove's son.)

While Foster was building the flour mill a friendly Indian told him of rich land about 14 miles east of Oregon City. Foster found the area, staked out 800 acres, returned to the falls to complete the mill, and the next year, with the help of some hired men, put up the big log house that had stood 50 yards from today's marker at the junction.

Yankee entrepeneurs had large dreams. But Philip Foster could not have foreseen that cold late autumn day in 1845 when two men, holding each other up as they stumbled on and cried for help, would mark his greatest stroke of luck. The haggard strangers were the advance guard of the thousands of emigrants who would choose the Barlow Cutoff, providing Foster with hordes of customers.

The newcomers had been in the party which, following an old Indian footpath, had sought to blaze a wagon trail around the south end of Mt. Hood. Snow had stranded the party and the two men had churned ahead for aid. Foster's place was the first they had found, as later it was the first Willamette Valley settlement caravan after caravan was to reach.

If Foster had designed the whole scheme of things he could not have blueprinted anything better than what the logic and quirk of history and topography provided him. For it was certain that somewhere a crossing of the Cascade range would be hacked out, the river voyage from The Dalles to Fort Vancouver being too expensive and impractical. Foster had not bet on location; he had not even thought of it. His aim in moving out of Oregon City was rather simple: he wanted a lot of fertile land near an urban market; he would become a key supplier for Oregon City. He also had a feeling that Eagle Creek Valley would be settled, giving him a first line of customers. He was right on the second consideration, wrong on the first. As the emigrants poured in he became a fat account for Oregon City and, later, Portland distributors. The wheel he spun had turned in the other direction, to his good fortune.

It did not take Philip Foster long to see the immense possibilities of a pay pike which would lead the emigrants to his farm. He could profit two ways. So he and Samuel Barlow, who had engineered the cutoff, formed a company to build the Barlow Toll Road. Foster had the money and Barlow the construction experience. The road was completed in time for 152 wagons to use it in 1846.

The venture, however, was not as successful as anticipated and posed more problems than had been expected. Not in business to lose money, Foster and Barlow sold their road company. But the covered wagons continued to halt at Eagle Creek.

Before Foster was established there, in the summer of 1844, he had been elected Treasurer of the Provisional

Government of Oregon—the first treasurer elected by the people. At that time the Provisional Governemtnt administered, theoretically, all of present Oregon, Washington, Idaho, and part of Montana and Wyoming. In practice, its jurisdiction was limited to a small strip of the Willamette Valley. Foster served a year and was succeeded by Francis Ermatinger, who had fought the Americans tooth and nail when he was employed by Hudson's Bay Company.

At Eagle Creek, Foster was the mogul of the hinterland. He was elected clerk and treasurer of the Philip Foster School District, appointed by Governor Curry to organize a company of "Rangers" to defend the settlers against "hostile Indians from the Deshutes or elsewhere in that direction," was named first postmaster, built the first grist mill, co-owned the first saw mill, opened the first general store, and planted the first orchard and tree nursery in the area with seeds carried from Maine.

Still, if he is remembered—and few Oregonians have even the vaguest notion of what Philip Foster is supposed to have done for or to the state—it is for his role as keeper of the portico to the end of the Oregon Trail.

Here at Eagle Creek the emigrants could turn their cattle into his pasture and buy a "cut of hay" for them. The fatigued caravancers could rest on his campground. They could purchase grain at his grist mill and, starting in 1848, medicines and hardware and other supplies at his general store. And they could buy the first good indoor meal since leaving the Missouri River.

Meals at the Foster House were 50 cents each. Dinner consisted of fresh beefsteak, boiled potatoes, cole slaw and hot biscuits, served with hot tea or coffee. Some of the famished comers stuffed themselves so injudiciously they paid with stomach aches; more than a few threw up everything they had shoveled down, thus parting with a precious 50 cents for nothing more comforting than a bad case of nausea.

Departing Foster's place, the wagons forded the Clackamas River, which Enoch Conyers, a diarist of 1852, described as "a beautiful, clear cold stream of water, about one hundred yards wide and about three or four feet deep," and then pushed on to Oregon City, the great dispersal point in the early years.

We inquired if any Fosters still remained in the Eagle

Creek area. None of the six persons we asked knew of anyone around who was named Foster or who had descended from a Foster. "There's Foster Road in Portland," quipped a man who had lived in Eagle Creek for several years. It surprised him a bit to learn that it was named after Philip Foster.

While were were snooping we discovered that the first house on the right side of the road leading to Oregon City had been built in 1860, by J. A. Burnett, a compatriot of Foster, and was still known as the Burnett House, even after half-a-dozen owners.

Invited inside, it seemed to us that the interior hadn't been altered very much. "I believe it is just about the way it was built," said the lady of the house. "It would cost too much to really fix it up."

She directed our attention to a huge lilac bush fronting a frame house across the road. "It's the oldest in the state," she said. "And the biggest, too."

From the lifestalk of purple lilac brought here by Mrs. Philip Foster had grown this spreading, twined and ancient beauty, which in its more than 125 years had never failed to bloom. It stood more than 35 feet high, had a width greater than 40 feet, and in circumference measured better than 100 feet.

While we were admiring it, the man who lived in the frame house pointed to the right hand corner of the road leading to Estacada and said: "See those steps? That's all that remains of the store Foster built."

We asked where Foster was buried. The replies were simple enough: "In a small cemetery up the hill." None of the several people with whom we were now chatting had ever been there and each had a separate idea of how to reach the burial ground. Finally it was agreed that the most feasible way was to start back toward Sandy and, about 100 yards up the slope, turn right onto a gravel road.

"It's private proterty," we were told, "but nobody will bother you."

So we drove up the hill looking for the turnoff. I saw nothing and neither did my wife and daughter.

We gave it another try. No luck. The third time my wife thought she spotted an opening that looked like it might be wide enough for a car to negotiate. I asked a girl who lived in a big house on top of the hill about the cemetery.

She said it was halfway down the hill, across the road from the schoolhouse, and I crept downhill, until we glimpsed a half-concealed narrow pebbly trace. We followed it, driving about three miles an hour, until we reached a wooden gate, on the right, held fast by a wire. We opened the gate and hiked up a clearing about 60 yards to a V-shaped ladder on the left. Up four steps, down four steps, and we were inside the shrouded, tangled Foster Private Cemetery.

According to E. L. Meyers, the venerable chronicler of Eagle Creek, the first two bodies to be placed in the cemetery were nine-year-olds Nancy Black and Mary Conditt, members of an 1853 wagon train.

Nancy's mother passed away on the Sweetwater River, in Wyoming. The burial service was performed by Rev. Conditt, Mary's father. A few weeks later Nancy's father died, leaving the girl an orphan. Rev. Conditt "took her in as one of the family."

By the time the emigrants reached Foster's farm they were weary of the lean and monotonous fare they had had to endure. The children scrambled into the orchard and gorged themselves on the thick, fleshy peaches, hot under the burning sun of that late summer afternoon. That night several youngsters writhed in pain. The nearest doctor was a day's travel off, in the summoning and arriving. By morning all the children but two were feeling better. Nancy Black and Mary Conditt had died. They were wrapped in blankets and laid to rest on the hill overlooking the campground. Their graves lay under a wild apple tree that each spring opened in full bloom, like a great rainbow bird spreading its gorgeously colored wings in tribute to innocence.

Philip Foster slept a few yards away, surrounded by his wife and children and other members of his family. Scarcely a stranger came looking for the cemetery. The grave of the man whose face thousands of pioneers had seen had all but been forgotten.

We paused at the plaque on the boulder facing the junction, and lifting my eyes beyond the barbed wire fence to deep in the pasture I tried to imagine the big log house, the outbuildings, the stacks of hay, the fruit trees, the oxen and horses in the fields, and the campground gray with dusty wagons and teeming with emigrants who had come so far and now had to choose where home would be. They were close to the completion of the beginning of the beginning. Ahead of them awaited the selection of land; the construction of a cabin, to last the winter through, and maybe a roof for the stock; the chopping of firewood; the search for food; and, when spring came, the breaking of earth. In time, roads would be snagged out, a cordwood bridge laid across the stream, sturdier houses and ampler barns built, a store opened, and a schoolhouse put up by everybody pitching in. There would be a community, then, and a man would know where he belonged.

But, in truth, I could not imagine the scene at Foster's place very well. Not with all the cars and trucks going by and the air full of exhaust fumes and the roadside littered and the pasture so drab. Only the wooded slope leading up to the cemetery in the thicket possessed a touch of historical magic.

After a few moments a man who lived in Eagle Creek, and with whom we had spoken earlier, came by and asked how things were going.

I swept my hand in a broad arc. "Right where we're looking there were hundreds of prairie schooners."

"In a few years," he replied with laconic good humor, "all that land will probably be covered by automobile junk yards."

I shuddered. "Suppose Philip Foster awoke from the dead and saw those acres of his just one big junkpile of maimed cars. What do you think he would say?"

"If the junkyard was pretty profitable," the man from Eagle Creek said, "Foster might figure he had been born ahead of his time."

"That wasn't a nice thing to say," I declared.

The man grinned. "No, it wasn't. But Foster came out here to make money, didn't he?"

A wayward marker on Sauvie Island

The sign off Sauvie Island Road, two miles beyond the Bybee House junction, on Sauvie Island, read:

"600 yards southwest on the east bank of the Multnomah Channel was the site of Fort William. Nathaniel J. Wyeth, Massachusetts trader and founder of Fort Hall, established Ft. William near Warrior Point in 1834. In the spring of 1835 he moved the establishment to this site. Neither salmon fishing nor trading was as successful as Wyeth hoped and he abandoned Ft. William in the spring of 1836."

The sign stood at the edge of the gravel driveway leading up to the home of Mr. and Mrs. James D. Lyons. We commented to Mrs. Lyons that the sign seemed to be pointing the wrong way, and she agreed. "It's been turned around," she declared. "People are always doing things like that."

Somehow there was an appropriateness to the sign facing the wrong direction. History turned Nathaniel Wyeth around, setting him against every current, so that in the end he was lucky to leave the West in one piece.

Nathaniel Jarvis Wyeth, a Cambridge, Mass. ice merchant, with a mechanical bent (he spent a lot of time inventing contraptions to boost his business) dreamt of developing a commercial empire in the Oregon Country.

He had already solved one problem of trade and distance, shipping ice to the West Indies for consumption. Maintaining the ice in its frozen state was a process he had developed and the feat still brings his name occasional publicity, but if he had not ventured from his Fresh Pond business no history of the West would carry his name.

Wyeth's eyes were turned to the West by several persons, particularly Hall Jackson Kelley, the stuttering, weak-eyed, exceedingly brilliant, disputatious Boston schoolteacher, who spent so many years agitating for American sovereignty of the Oregon Country that he came to be heralded as the "Apostle of Oregon."

Wyeth was too pragmatic for Hall Kelley, with whom he

broke, and he lacked the flexibility to fit snugly in the wilderness, but he was adaptable enough to leave Cambridge as Nathaniel J. Wyeth, ice merchant of Fresh Pond, and return, in the eyes of knowledgeable writers, as Nat Wyeth, a part of Western history.

In February, 1832, when he was 30 years old, and eight years married, to his cousin, Elizabeth Jarvis, Wyeth organized a party of adventurers, whom he took to an island in Boston Harbor for 10 days of military discipline, conditioning, and simulated frontier living.

Before Wyeth was through with the West he must have recalled those 10 days as a bad joke. And looking back, after he had acquired the know-how of a mountain man, he must have grimaced at the fancy preparations he had made for his spring expedition. He clad his company in an outlandish uniform, instructed them to master the bugles he purchased, so that there would be lively music to move the expedition on, and had built for the trip three boats on wheels. They resembled a hybrid species—the crossing of a canoe and a gondola—and when Wyeth rolled his odd craft down the streets of Cambridge the Harvard students, loudly expressing their sense of the ridiculous, derided them as "amphibiums." The wheeled boats did not go beyond St. Louis, where Wyeth, acting upon the advice of experienced hands, sold them.

His original party consisted of 24 men, few of whom were cut out for the frontier. More than half left him before he reached Fort Vancouver. One of those who came with him to the end was John Ball, who was shortly, in his own way, to become a pioneer, the first schoolteacher in the Oregon Country.

Wyeth didn't fare well on this first venture into the far West. His proposals for commercial arrangements, first with Dr. John McLoughlin, Chief Factor of the Hudson's Bay Company's Western region, and then with the wary Captain Bonneville, whom he found on the Upper Snake, did not materialize. But he did draw up plans for a salmon packing industry and when he reached Cambridge again, in the autumn of 1833, he organized the Columbia River Fishing and Trading Co.

The spring of 1834 found Wyeth heading West again. He had spent the winter making arrangements, including the chartering of a brig to carry the bulk of his trading supplies and fish equipment to the mouth of the Willamette River. He aimed to go heavy into the fur and salmon business, and he had a strong notion about agricultural investments.

With Wyeth overland came the first missionary party, headed by Jason Lee. A Quebec church school teacher, Lee had been selected by the Board of Missions of the Methodist Episcopal Church to establish the Mission to the Flathead Indians. Seeking first-hand information about the West, Lee had sought Wyeth out and Wyeth seeing the missionaries as propagandists for the waves of emigrants who would become his customers, offered to transport free the church group's supplies on his ship, the *May Dacre*.

At the 1834 rendezvous—that wild and dangerous annual mart, where fur trappers and traders gathered to swap pelts for mountain men supplies—Wyeth learned to his dismay that the Rocky Mountain Fur Company, which had pledged to buy $3,000 worth of trade goods, could not honor its contract.

Jason Lee, too, found disappointment at Ham's Fork, Wyoming, where the rendezvous of 1834 was held. A contingent of Flatheads, together with an even larger representation of Nez Perces, were waiting for the Bible "medicine man" who would preach to them the word of the mysterious White Spirit, that omnipotent force who could make such bad whiskey and strong gunpowder.

Lee did not find the productive scene he had envisaged. Sagebrush and rattlesnake country was no place to turn into a Methodist Garden of Eden. A fertile valley, near a river of commerce that flowed open to the sea, would be much better. The more Jason Lee thought on it the more he was not for going north with the Flatheads, to Montana. He did not even visit their camp. On July Fourth he instructed the rest of his mission party that they would travel with Wyeth to the Columbia.

Later, at Fort Vancouver, John McLoughlin, the all-wise "White-headed Eagle," corroborated what Lee had probably concluded at Ham's Fork: "Teach them first to cultivate the ground and live more comfortably than they do by hunting, and as they do this teach them religion." The Willamette Valley, said McLoughlin, was the likeliest place for such an enterprise, and near Salem, Lee built his mission.

Wyeth had to do something with the trade goods he had been unable to sell to the Rocky Mountain Fur Co. He also wanted a trading post that would give him a geographic edge over the mighty Hudson's Bay Company. Coming to the confluence of the Snake and Portneuf, in Idaho, he built Fort Hall, which he named, not for Hall Kelley, but for Henry Hall, elder partner in the Columbia River Fishing and Trading Co.

In a letter dated October 6, 1834, he described the baptism of the fort: "We manufactured a magnificent flag from some unbleached sheeting, a little red flannel and a few blue patches, saluted it with damaged powder and wet it in vilanous alcohol . . . It makes, I do assure you, a very respectable appearance amid the dry and desolate regions of central America."

But John McLoughlin's stepson, Tom McKay, leading a Hudson's Bay Company brigade, had other ideas. McKay and Wyeth had traveled close to each other for a spell west from Bear River, and McKay had observed the building of Fort Hall. Then, while Wyeth was still congratulating himself for having outwitted the wily McLoughlin, McKay went on to where the Boise River empties into the Snake and built a trading post which came to be known as Fort Boise. It was meant to render Fort Hall ineffectual, and it succeeded, as Wyeth hoped it wouldn't and as McKay knew it would.

On Sept. 14, 1834, Wyeth reached Fort Vancouver, to learn more bad news. The May Dacre had not yet arrived. A day later it did, but it was three months late, having had to lay up in Valparaiso for extensive repairs after having been struck by lightning. So there went Wyeth's hopes for a successful salmon season.

On a tongue of land wetted on one side by the Columbia and on the other by the Willamette, which Wyeth called the Multnomah, he built a post on "this Wappato Island," now Sauvie Island, and named it Fort William, for another member of his Columbia River Fishing and Trading Co.

A salt kettle was removed from the May Dacre and transported to Fort William, where it was to be used for salmon drying. But the salmon business floundered at the start and the metal container stood unused. Then a settler by the name of Ewing Young, who two years later was to lead the first long cattle drive in the present United States, from the San Francisco Bay area to the Willamette Valley, took the kettle to his Chehalem farm, intending to use it as a vat for his distillery, the first in the Oregon Country. After a deluge of protests, chiefly from Jason Lee's hurriedly-organized temperance society, Young abandoned the wide-open whiskey-making field.

Whatever Wyeth tried collapsed or oozed into failure: fur trapping, fishing, farming, trade with the Sandwich (Hawaiian) Islands. His men folded under fever, perished, deserted. He wrote: "Our people are sick and dying off like rotten sheep of bilbous disorders."

Desperate, he beat a path between Fort Hall and Fort William, explored the Deschutes River, probed the Willamette Valley, hurled his energy into every possible opportunity that might turn the tide of his defeats. But bad luck dogged him and no matter which direction he turned, the long hand of McLoughlin was there, to undercut and outflank him.

By June, 1836, Nat Wyeth had enough of Oregon. He made a broad sweep through the Great Plains, from Fort Laramie to Taos, with a last adventuresome look in his merchant's eyes. Nothing excited him and when he put his feet eastward on the Santa Fe Trail he knew his Western days belonged to the past. So he returned to Fresh Pond, resuming the ice business, and dispensing his learning of the West to those who came asking for it. One of those was a bright young man named Francis Parkman. Not too many years later he wrote a book we know as *The Oregon Trail*.

Fort Hall was sold by Wyeth's agents to Hudson's Bay Company in 1837, after it had been rebuilt as an adobe structure. The Company maintained it into the decade that Oregon gained statehood.

As for Fort William, it also passed into the hands of Hudson's Bay Company, probably more by simple take-over of an abandoned site than through payment. Already in bad repair, it was sparsely used, vacated again, and fell to pieces.

On the last day of August, in 1856, Nathaniel Wyeth closed his eyes forever, in the very house in which he had first opened them. But what memories of the Oregon Country he took with him to the grave!

He had known so many people—all of the great names

of the Western fur trade, Indians chiefs, mountain men, explorers. He brought West the first Oregon missionaries, in Oregon he knew the first settlers on French Prairie. Everyone he brushed shoulders with became at least a footnote of history.

There exist only two material reminders of his presence in Oregon—a minor place name off the Columbia River highway and the marker on Sauvie Island.

The place name was once a railroad station, but trains haven't stopped there for years, and the marker on Sauvie Island Road is often turned in the wrong direction.

Meriwether Lewis of Quintana Roo

Robert O. Lee, of Portland, a vice-president of Georgia-Pacific, was pushing 50 when he led his third major expedition into the Territory of Quintana Roo of Yucatan, Mexico in the late autumn of 1968.

An international mountain climber and a veteran jungle explorer, he was still lean, tough-minded, self-disciplined and possessed of outstanding leadership capacities—but his best physical days lay behind him, and if he did not tell himself this openly he knew he was borrowing time to play in a young man's game.

Bob Lee had sought traces of the ancient Maya civilization before, but he was younger then, and even a few years make a difference. But could he know how much of a difference?

I wondered about this when I asked Bob if I could extract passages from his personal journal. He agree, and reading the diary of his ordeal and his triumph in the Quintana Roo I found the touches which, when put together, revealed not only a man under stress, desperately trying to balance the loss of youthful fire and energy with the wisdom and patience of age, but a many-sided person functioning in an ever-present challenging and disagreeable atmosphere.

Lee, as leader of the expedition, was responsible for its success and for the survival of his men. The objectives lay heavily on his mind. His own discomfort plagued him. But he had an eye for beauty, too, and a flair for romanticism and nostalgia. Humor did not escape him; if it were a butterfly he would pursue it with a net. He is stoic, explosive, proud, poignant, flippant, grumbling, arrogant, humble, completely integrated, disintegrated, a moody dreamer and a steely man of action—the middle-aged Meriwether Lewis of Quintana Roo.

Sometimes he seems very old and calculating and sometimes very young and impulsive—and at all times he is very believable.

Elsewhere, Bob Lee has summarized the many accomplishment sof the expedition: archeological, ornithological, botanical, entomological, zoological, medical, and others.

I want to quote very briefly what he has written as a background for the journal: "The Expedition covered 150 miles of Quintana Roo jungle including a 114 mile traverse of completely unexplored jungle. . . . This can be considered one of the worst journeys in the world through semi-arid jungle and rough limestone rock in the heart of the Chiclero territory."

The journal presented here begins with the plunge into the jungle. It is not necessary to know in detail where the expedition traveled or to have any inkling of knowledge about the Mayas. Enough will come through, I think, to make the journey intelligible. What is most important is the man himself, and you will find him here, big as life, in this exceedingly human document.

Monday, November 18—Up at 6 AM and the humidity is laying a blanket of mist over Piste . . . One hour drive to Chemax . . . We hit the trail at 9 AM. My back is so-so—and my pack seems to weigh a ton. We head out at 2.5 miles per hour and in 10 minutes are absolutely wringing, soaking wet with sweat. God it is hot! Can I do it? What in hell am I doing here? What a masochist! . . . After several rests we hit Chan Dzitnap—what a relief! Feet are sore, we are pooped and soaking wet. We covered 9 miles in 4.5 hours including 4 rest stops—very good time . . . Feels mighty good to lay down in my hammock . . . We go to a "casa" and, of all things, have a very warm Coca Cola—in Chan Dzitnap . . . I am dumbfounded to find Coca Cola here. Cost 1 peso—8¢.

Tuesday, Nov. 19—Rain has stopped. Have quick breakfast of orange juice, zoom and canned bacon. Then at 7:30 AM I start out again with Murph, Stodd, Kerr, Carlos and Bashor. The trail of rock is slick as glass and we have to go very carefully with heavy packs—and boy, the damned packs *really* feel heavy today! . . . We chop a wide place in the jungle for camp around the deep natural well at Menturo. Looks like an excellent campsite—all rocks . . . Domingo shoes the mules—trimming their feet with a machete—amazing . . . Already I have many tick heads in my lower legs and also on the inside of my arms at the elbow. Rum call at 4 PM and a long discussion between Lee, Hector Bravo, Domingo, Avilino, our arriero and a miscellaneous collection of Indians as to the direction to Ixil—whether we can get there—whether the mules can get there—what is there—etc. Finally I give up in despair because everybody has a different opinion. The only way to find out is to try—I don't think any of them really know!

Wednesday, Nov. 29—Up at 6 AM and feeling lousy—my mouth is dry—veritably full of cotton . . . We are at Coba at 11:05 and take a 20 minute break—we are tired and glad to be at the lake. I have a bad blister on my left toe but to hell with it—I just keep plugging along. We visit Domingo's casa and finally arrive at Macanxoc at 12 noon. Lake beautiful. We are camped exactly where we were in 1965 and Raul and Juan had cleaned the site so it looked exactly like it did in 1965! Strange feeling to be back . . . I find it hard to believe we made it all the way from Chan Dzitnap to Coba in 1 day in 1965—it was long enough doing it in two days! . . . After we get our hammocks up 75 people show up in camp—mostly women with small children—for medical care, and Russ and Bill are busy for over an hour—one man completely blind—one woman with both eardrums perforated and almost deaf—children with hook worm—several children with the "chicle" disease (leishmaniasis) and great wartlike growths on their arms and hands. The docs treat the worst cases and send the rest away for tomorrow's clinic . . . The ruins of Coba are still magnificent—I had forgotten over the 3 year period . . .

Thursday, Nov. 21—At 3:15 PM Jack makes radio contact with a "Blue Bird" station in the U. S. who makes a telephone call to Hood River!! . . . We are amazed—and elated—to get radio word out to the outside world from Coba—good God!! Hope Ginny Baldwin calls other families . . . Our beards are getting long and we are not the cleanest gang . . . Rum call at 3 PM with lemonade and good dinner of corned beef, mashed potatoes and thick vegetable soup—I mixed mine all together! Then bad news. Avilino and Ambrozio gathered around as Domingo rode in to camp in the dark from his hard ride toward Ixil—he reports it is 3 days march to Ixil . . . The big problem is the 10 days to the coast—evidently the trail goes South from Ixil—then turns East—then North to

Tulum—a great deep curve of about 100 miles and with water problems . . . This is too much for us—particularly with 3 twelve mile marches between water. We have several men who would not make it.

From Ixil to Chemax there is a trail—27 miles. A 12 mile—a 12 mile—and a 3 mile. That triangle (Chemax—Coba—Ixil—Chemax) would be possible but again 2 twelve mile marches between water—too much.

From Coba to Ixil is 1 nine mile—1 seven mile—1 seven mile—between water (total 23 miles)—so what to do? I am very discouraged. Everybody talking at same time and suggesting all kinds of unworkable alternatives. I finally decide to sleep on it over night before making the "decision." So, I reverse direction in my hammock so my feet will be downhill rather than uphill tonight, and go to bed. . . . At 3 AM am awakened by Avilino screaming and yelling at top of his lungs—either a terrible nightmare or an animal in camp. I go to sleep again without finding out what the hell the big commotion is all about.

Friday, Nov. 22—I announced that we will do as follows:

1) Go three days march from Coba to Ixil.
2) Spend 1 or 2 days at Ixil.
3) Return 3 days Ixil to Coba.
4) Spend 1 or 2 days at Coba (at our Macanxoc camp).
5) Head 5/6 days from Coba to the Coast.

This is a rough schedule and I am not enthusiastic over it but, if we are to accomplish our purpose of reaching Ixil it is about all we can do. I hate the idea of having to return over a trail we have just covered (Coba—Ixil—Coba). There is nothing to look forward to on such a trip—just sweat and heat and fatigue over the same old ground. However, so be it. All of the men accept the decision . . .

My pack is again full of hundreds of big black ants and I empty it and shake it out and hang it from a tree suspended from a cord—maybe that will keep the damned ants out—they are in every corner of my gear . . .

Saturday, Nov. 23—Leave camp at 7:30 AM for Ixil. Go to Laguna Coba & head south. We hit a ruined mound on the trail at 7:40 AM . . . At 8:05 AM we hit a trail which goes to some small ruins at Ceenacal . . . At 8:52 AM we hit a lovely small temple on Sacbe 14. It is the temple Chacluc. Has a beautiful, caved-in corbelled arch

. . . At 9:45 a trail takes off to the right to Viviende Copoy. We then start climbing up rough rock through an area burned some years ago—no tree canopy and hotter than hell—really miserable going . . . At 11:40 AM we come out at the village of Yonicteh (in Maya "overhead flower"). We call it the village of "Nowhere"! . . . Terrible humidity. Hard to breathe. Yonicteh is a kind of desperate little village of 4 or 5 huts but an excellent well. . . . Our camp is in a sparsely vegetated area about in the center of the village. The young girls make a number of trips to the well—about 75 yards from my hammock—I think as much to see us as to get water. Very handsome girls too! . . . At 3 PM Hector and Raul advise me that there is a trail from Ixil to Tulum only 6 days (rather than 10) and that the trail is an old, much used and good one. This is good news if true. It means we won't have to return to Coba then to the coast. If true we are now 8 days from the coast in any direction . . . At midnight it started to rain and poured—a torrential tropical downpour. It would rain for several hours—then stop—then cloudburst for several hours. My poncho was on top of my hammock but the water was running down the hammock cords, and into my hammock. First down my neck—so I reversed direction in the middle of the night (a very precarious maneuver) then my feet got wet. Then I was wet all down my back and fanny. How a woven net hammock can *fill up* with water is beyond me—and I swear mine did! At 3 AM the whole camp was soaked. Men swearing and wet to the skin. At 4 AM several got up. I gave up emptying pockets of water in my poncho and rolled up in my dripping blanket and dripping down sweater, lit my pipe (I had a dry match) and lay there in the black dismal night in complete despair. At 4:30 AM we all got up, in the black, got a fire going, and stood around it with teeth chattering like castanets. At 5 AM the first light began to show and at 6 AM we could see the shambles—of ourselves and our camp. God what a mess—unbelievable. I made the decision that we would stay here at "Nowhere" and dry out, at least for 1 day.

Sunday, Nov. 24—It was about to pour down rain again so we frantically gathered our gear and moved into 2 thatched huts (moving a family out of one!) I don't know where *they* went but they did it very graciously and hospitably. I think they felt very sorry for us—we were a mess. Baldwin, Mills and I are in a ruined horse hut (horse dung—wet—all over the floor—and most of the roof gone.) We sling our hammocks as best as we can under the palm thatch—which is full of bad scorpions . . . Krantz and Bashor, in ponchos, are fixing dinner. They look like priests in vestments—but their language belies that! . . . Gordon Edwards has gone on to the ruin of Kukincan with the 2 chicleros and found it. He describes it as being 2 storied and very beautiful—on top of a pyramid about 70 feet hibh. He is soaked to the skin but imperturbable . . . Here I am at Yonicteh, a mess—damp with rain and sweat —mud to the knees—covered in festering tick bites—sleeping in a scorpion infested, ruined stable. I think of my clean Glacier Ranch—lonesome and more than a little miserable! Things are not really going too well and we have a long, long way to go. . . .

Monday, Nov. 25—At 12:45 PM come to an abandoned village—after covering about 8 miles—much of it chopping and bad going. This village is full of big ticks but we must stay here—it is 6 or 8 miles on to Ixil— too far for us to go. . . . The mules with my blanket & hammock do not arrive until 3 PM so I stand or sit around for several hours—tired and wanting to lie down . . . One muleteer leaves us here to head back—alone— to Chemax. We pay him 20 pesos a day plus a 20 pesos tip. (160 pesos or $12.00 (Twelve) dollars U.S. for 8 days hard work . . .) We *must* turn East before long— or else we will be back in Merida! . . . A long and "violent" discussion about hippies after dinner. I ask the men to clean up their language and stop the dirty jokes—1 or 2 have a propensity and not liked by the others (the jokes, not the men). So, I am a kill joy, but that is OK . . .

Tuesday, Nov. 26—The "point" leaves at 7:10 AM but I forget my camera and must go back 5 minutes to get it. (Thank goodness no farther!) . . . A little Maya boy of 10 years is guiding and I feel like "a child shall lead them." . . . At 9:25 AM we drop about 100 feet in elevation and break out at a clearing with beautiful big acacia trees and a hut with a radio going! This is a really beautiful spot with some handsome young Maya women

who giggle and hide their faces from us! They have corn
at least 10 to 12 feet high—amazing! . . . At 9:45 AM
we hit the main trail Chemax—Ixil—Tulum and it looks
like a super highway! Obviously much mule traffic . . .
We all smell like vinegar—I call this the "Vinegar Trail."
At 10:30 we hit the Laguna Ixil and it is a beautiful
sight! . . . We are the first white men to ever visit Ixil
and it was tough getting here . . . Baldwin is sacked and
still not well. My back does not feel well at all. Murph
has a bad burn on one hand. Ambrozio Dzib has di-
arrhea. Tomorrow Domingo will ride out east to see what
the trail and water conditions are toward the coast. God,
I hope the trail is good and going east—and I hope
water holes are 6 to 8 miles apart!! . . . There are parrots overhead—the first I have seen on this trip. A dog
and 2 kids have shown up from somewhere—there must
be a village close by . . . Carlos climbed a tree on top of
the Castillo trying to see other lakes but only jungle. There
should be 5 lakes in the Ixil group from my aerial photos
of 1965 . . . I get the boys to work building a dock out
to the edge of the water 150 feet away from the good
water place—where several fellows bathed and washed
clothes—thus ruining the drinking water spot! The water
is amber in color—lots of life in it! However, it's all
the water there is! So drink! . . . This is an eerie place
—beautiful in a remote, desperate way. It is strange to
be the first white men ever to be at this spot. . .

Wednesday, Nov. 27—In thinking over the aerial
photos—and our position—I am convinced we are not
at the lake we thought. So, after breakfast I send Raul
and Juan out into the jungle almost due west to search for
2 lakes and a sacbe—and I send Avilino and Domingo
SE to look for 1 lake and some possible ruins . . . Carlos,
Carlosito, Murphy, Hector, Mills, Baldwin and I go back
to the Castillo behind camp to clean it, measure and
photo . . . It is evident that this is a very important temple and it is very likely the treasure is still buried under
the sacrificial altar in front of the castillo. We will not
dig into it—it is probably in a chamber 3 feet down below
ground level. We will leave instead for future expedition
of Mex. government . . . We decided to move out tomorrow 2 leagues toward the coast for several reasons:

1) There are too many snakes here—we caught 2 coral snakes today right in camp—and we have no anti-venom for the coral snakes.

2) The search teams found only small ruins in the outer-area and no sacbe.

3) The water situation is very bad here.

4) Camp looks like a garbage dump.

. . . There is a simple row of large stones running N along the W edge of the lake to a milpa . . . In the center of the milpa is a great pit—obviously the quarry for the castillo—a large, deep hole, in the middle of a corn, squash and bean field that was abandoned before it came to fruit. Possibly because of malaria—many mosquitos here—morbid. Murphy, Hoss and I visit at 5 PM and return to find camp in an uproar. Where we were gone a "chiclero" came through camp with a story of a lake with ruins. He talked to all of our Indians—all of whom had a *separate* interpretation of direction and distance—then he disappeared. All of the men are enthusiastic—then, as I slowly, painstakingly interrogated 7 Indians individually it became evident that none of them really knew what the situation was. We even offer a 100 peso reward—to be divided equally—if the boys located the lake before noon tomorrow. No takers. For some strange reason they are very reluctant to pursue the search for the "lost" laguna any longer. I am mad as hell—or rather confounded and don't know what kind of a decision to make. Should we poop around here for days trying to find something our boys could not find all day (and a long day)? Should we pick up camp and move in the probable direction (which is the wrong direction exactly away from our line of march)—or should we go on toward the coast? Everybody has a different opinion and all talking at once. *Finally* I get Avilino and Domingo and Hector together and get agreement that "yes, there is a lake 7 or 8 miles West and the ruins there are very small"—but they have never been there. That settles it. I announce that tomorrow we start toward the coast. The men accept the decision in good spirits although I know there are reservations—have reservations myself! Dammit, I hate to make such a decision—maybe we are passing up something very great. Yet, on the other hand, I could drive a whole expedition in the wrong direction for days and never find anything at the end. So the decision is made and I shall live by it. As it is made, a satellite passes overhead, brilliantly, going due east. Maybe this is a good sign—that's the direction we want to go! . . . A half moon shines overhead and a few clouds drift along the horizon. The cicadas are shrilling loudly all around the sparse jungle and the big cats walk. A large snake creates a riffle as he swims across the lake toward our camp. The soft Maya talk of our Indians drones in the background. Domingo sits at my feet in his tatters smoking a cigarette while I pull on my pipe and work on my field notes. Dad should be here, for a few moments anyhow, to have this exotic experience. . .

Thursday, Nov. 28—Thanksgiving—At 7:30 AM we go up to the castillo and take motion pictures but the camera soon jams from the terrific humidity . . . Then we turn east and head for the coast. Lee's march to the sea! We plan to go about 4 miles to a cenote, then make camp and have a big dinner with rum. Disaster! The cenote at Yolanteh was dry as a bone—evidently an arroyo type that only holds water right after a big rain. What can we do? Well, only move on—and the Indians say 3 more miles to good water. As usual, they do not know what the hell they are talking about. The trail is horrible —just rough—really rough, rolling rock. And the sweat just pours off all of us in sheets. We stagger on hour after hour and no water. Finally we run across 5 chicleros loaded with chicle and they say the only real water is at Santa Lucia—7 miles on—and we have already covered 8 miles of terrible going and are very tired. We find a spot where there are some cruddy rain pools and set up camp there—I believe this is enough to keep us alive. Camp not bad except for the lousy, yellow-brown water which we filter through a mosquito net to get the scum and algae out of . . . Here I ruined my mosquito net —I cut a big hole out of the top of the net (thinking it was the *bottom*) to filter the terrible water through . . . What a way to celebrate Thanksgiving! We shall wait and have our big dinner tomorrow . . .

Friday, Nov. 29—At about 11 AM we come to Tres Reyes (Three Kings), an occupied, new ranchero with excellent well—thank God, good water . . . A group of chicleros come through with mules loaded with chicle. The chiclero has a radio going *full* blast—in English—talking about alfalfa! Of course the chiclero doesn't understand a word—he only speaks Maya! . . . At 3 PM a wonderful canned turkey dinner with cranberry sauce. Hoss taking Polaroid photos of all local Indians plus our Indians with me—they love it—what a public relations vehicle a Polaroid camera is! The local Indians brought out a javelina (wild pig) & a small parrot (red-head) for photos . . . To bed about 7 PM and to a terrible night—really bad. The Chiclero kept his damned battery radio on full blast till 10 PM—then tied up all of his 5 or 6 dogs outside his door. They yipped and barked *all* night long just 75 feet from our hammocks. Plus the fact that the rooster crowed mightily every hour on the hour from 2 AM on. No sleep at all and we all got up just pooped to start our longest march . . .

Saturday, Nov. 30—. . . We march until 12:30 PM. We have entered real jungle at last and it is very refreshing and much more interesting . . . We break out at the chiclero encampment of La Central. We are wringing wet and very tired after covering 10 miles southwest—more south than west but I can't really take bearings—the trail winds all around. La Central is a booming place—I would guess 20 chicleros here boiling out their chicle in great pots—like taffy and a brown color . . . Tough looking characters . . . God, I smell terrible—as do all the others . . . Once again the chicleros have a radio going *full* blast . . . Unfortunately our camp site has been the toilet for the chicleros so doesn't smell too good. We visit the Chiclero camp to watch them boiling out the thick sap and putting it into blocks which weigh about 22 pounds. Then they stamp their particular sig into the block . . . There is actually a chiclero restaurant here with a man making tortillas like they were going out of style . . . There is a fine lemon tree in the center of the chiclero camp and we gather hats full of lemons for our canteens . . . Gordon and I sit on rocks talking about climbs we had made—particularly in the Mt. Rainier area —when we were both much younger—terrible to get old! . . . Another long depressing hassle with Avilino on the route to coast. He says 5 days and I know he must be wrong—we are too close. He and I come to a complete impasse and I seek out Domingo to see what he says. He disappears for an hour into the chiclero village and finally I put on a revolver and, in the dark, go into the village to find him. He has a new story of 3 days . . .

Sunday, Dec. 1—. . . The day starts out bad with rain at 5 AM. Doesn't last long but the humidity is at least 100%. Unbelievable—just can't breathe . . . The "point" hits the trail at 7:15 AM for a 10 mile march . . . The trail is impossible—great stretches of large broken rocks covered in slime—slip, twist, stumble, slip again—hour after hour . . . I do not know if I can continue but I do—just plugging along in abject misery . . . We seem to be in purgatory—a wet hell. Finally at 1:45 PM we stagger into Platanar—a village of 6 thatched huts . . . Avilino got here before us and we have a large thatched hut to put our hammocks in . . . To bed about 6:30 PM. . . . A Maya girl is swinging in her hammock with a big candle in her hand—a beautiful sight . . .

Monday, Dec. 2—The trail is bad—and we are running down. After 1 league we come to small clean village of Yopitah—excellent water here and we take a good rest . . . It's a good thing we are nearing our destination. I should really call a rest day but everyone is so anxious to get to the sea that I would have a mutiny. We plod on at a very slow, stumbling, sliding shuffle—again wet clear through. At 11:05 we come out at Kunlum—a sad little clearing of 4 or 5 huts—several women—and the inevitable G-D radio going full blast! . . . As usual Avilino gives me wrong mileages for tomorrow. He says 4 leagues (10 miles) while the "locals" tell me 3 leagues (7½ miles) to Tulum Pueblo. Hell of a difference. I can't figure out this idiocy—why doesn't he ask the locals for right dope? I could kill him! We can make 7½ miles but 10 would finish us off . . . Some of the boys make a night trip and Noble Bashor brings back a wonderful, fragrant white orchid . . . Fortunately the villagers shut off the radio at about 8 PM. But dammit to hell—at 3 AM precisely the radio started again full blast for an hour. These people must be crazy—or else I am losing my mind . . .

Tuesday, Dec. 3—At 11:10 AM—4 hours on the dot —we come into Tulum Pueblo—a great feeling! The place is deserted but as soon as we drop our packs in the thatch roofed, open sided town center, people pop out of all the houses and converge on us . . . As soon as we cool off we buy 5 pesos worth of oranges and grapefruit—about 30 oranges and a dozen grapefruit . . . We save the grapefruit for tomorrow's breakfast—but quickly eat several sweet oranges— they *really* taste good!!! . . . Sick people show up at once and Russ treats several. One woman brings him several dozen sweet lemons (like small oranges) in payment . . . Tulum is a beautiful little pueblo—the ground a blaze of purple phlox and scarlet pentstamen. Orange and lemon trees heavily clustered. And the golden thatched roofs against the stunning blue sky. A number of grunting pigs wandering around. Women in delicately embroidered huipiles . . . At 2:30 PM 4 Mexican Army men show up in the village and we have a friendly talk with them—they are looking for 2 Norte Americanos who are supposedly somewhere along the coast hunting. They want to check their hunting permits. Good looking young men armed to the teeth . . .

Wednesday, Dec. 4—. . . At 8 AM we shouldered packs and headed for Tancah. The trail was good, wide and ankle deep in mud. But we really steamed along because the sea was ahead! . . . The sight of the Caribbean at 9:10 AM was wonderful—the blues, purples, greens etc. At 10:15 Gordon Edwards, Jack Baldwin, Jerry Krantz & R. O. L. walked into Tancah with the others streaming behind us. Great to be here! Soon Don Pepe Gonzales drives up in a jeep from his ranch back in the jungle, unlocks the guest house—and everybody starts the long job of washing skin (in the warm sea!) and washing clothes in aluminum dish pans. Oh God how wonderful it is to get clean—to smell sweet instead of sweat. To get the black mud out of my pants—up to the knees. To swim in the salt water and scour my skin with handfuls of white sand—to grind the sand into my toes and scrape raw the weeping sores of tick infection . . . I send, via Don Pepe, a radio—and cable message as follows:

"On December 4, 1968, at 10 AM the American Quintana Roo Expedition reached Tancah. All well. Difficult trip. Mission accomplished. Notify families."

> Robert O. Lee, Leader
> American Q. R. Expedition.

Pulps to paperbacks

Jess Rich was two years old when his folks came to Portland in 1896, the year his father, Si, and his uncle, B.B., opened a cigar store. Almost three-quarters of a century later the business was still flourishing.

All his life Jess Rich had been associated with the cigar store, which he had operated alone since his father passed away in 1932.

Portland is a fairly young town. When Rich was a boy the city had only one high school and one "college," a business school. He graduated from both.

But the city had other excitements. Jess grew up in a downtown teeming with theaters, penny arcades, a sprawling Farmers Market, and the elegance and dash of the storied Portland Hotel.

"Did you know," said Rich, a sunny man with a chipper voice, "that the people who were in the Farmers Market raised their own products; they didn't buy 'em from the commission merchant, you see what I mean? They raised their own stuff, brought it down, and sold it there. See? That was for years like that."

The great and famous of the day put up at the Portland Hotel when they came to town and Jess Rich saw them, because his father and uncle operated the cigar stand in the hostelry and Jess was often there, even as a boy.

He remembered seeing presidents Teddy Roosevelt and William McKinley, a king of Siam, renowned actors and singers, industrialists and financiers—all the celebrities.

One day H. J. Heinz, the founder of the giant food processing company, saw Jess behind the counter with his father and asked Si Rich to let him have Jess, educate him, put him through college. "I was only a little fellow then," recalled Rich nostalgically. "He says, I'll make him the head officer or something in the H. J. Heinz Company. I'll never forget that. The old man said that. H. J. Heinz."

And there was Mark Twain, about whom Jess had an anecdote:

"Homer Davenport, the great cartoonist, was very well acquainted with my father. Well, one evening at the Portland Hotel stand, he went to one side where he could lay down his paper pad on a flat area, and coming out of the elevator and walking up the lobby was Mark Twain. He was dressed in a white full dress suit with a Chesterfield cape, and Davenport was sketching Mark Twain, unbeknown to him, of course, and when he got through my Dad said, 'I'd like to have that sketch, I'll give you ten dollars for it,' and Davenport said, 'No, I want this one.' That was an incident that happened in the hotel, I remember that."

Some of the headline performers who stayed at the Portland Hotel were not content with their mere stage earnings so they moonlighted by giving lessons to the ambitious and affluent locals.

Jess laughed and laughed, his eyes rolling in merriment, as he told about Herman the Great, whose feats of prestidigitation awed audiences across the nation.

"Herman the Great got hold of a young man who was a member of a prominent family here and he was teaching him a few of these tricks, and there was one trick where you'd put a little stand on one side of the stage and hang a paper bag on it. Then you'd take a canary and put it in the bag on the right side of the stage and you'd shoot this pistol off and the canary would be across the stage in the empty bag, on the other side of the stage. Well, he was showing this trick and he shot the tip of the finger of this student off, and he had one heck of a time gettin' out of town! I remember that . . ."

Although Rich's always advertised itself as a cigar store it was even better known as a publications mart.

No man in Portland had his fingers so directly on the globe, day in and day out, as Jess Rich. He handled newspapers and magazines from all parts of the world: the London *Times* was as close to where he bustled down the aisles of his stores as the Los Angeles *Times;* organs from Africa and Asia were only a few feet from *Playboy* and *Esquire*. Scholarly publications stared stuffily down at heavily-thumbed nudist pictorials across the store.

Jess Rich knew the world through the publications he

received. Name a city in Australia and he would tell you what newspaper came out of there. Bring up Hong Kong and he could spell out the monthlies and quarterlies printed on that febrile isle. Israel? East Germany? Singapore? Toronto? Mexico City? Rio? With a snap of his fingers Jess reeled off the publications he carried from those places, how often they were printed, when they arrived, and how much they cost.

Six days a week he stood in the center of the universe, receiving more foreign printed matter than any other store in Oregon, and perhaps even more than the Portland library. He seldom scanned more than the headlines but even in just touching the periodicals he felt himself a dweller of many lands he would never see and about which he knew next to nothing beyond the brief data that had to do with his bookkeeping. But at least they were there, all around him, and this was his cosmopolitanism.

Because Rich's carried so many out-of-town newspapers and such a wide variety of magazines and paperbacks, some unobtainable elsewhere, the store was patronized by all kinds of people, including some of the great names in Oregon: Portland mayors, governors, U.S. senators and, of course, writers.

Jess remembered the writers best, perhaps because he saw them more often than the others. He recalled a few:

"C. E. S. Wood was a rather tall, bushy bearded, bushy haired man. He was an agnostic, wasn't he? He used to get *The Truthseeker,* that was an agnostic publication that was published in the early days.

"Dick Neuberger used to come in all the time. And he used to say, 'Now, do you think that I ought to run for the legislature? What chances have I got?' You know, things like that; we'd have quite a conversation.

"Ernest Haycox, he was a rather slightly built man. He used to write for the pulp magazines, too, and"—and Rich laughed—"he'd always come in and say, 'Well, I don't know whether my story is going to be in this issue, or next month, or the month after,' you know. We'd always look out for, we'd have to look out for him to see what magazines his stories would be in. They were all western stuff.

"Stewart Holbrook—he was a student. There isn't anything I can think of that that man couldn't talk about or write about. He was fantastic. And he used to come in quite often, and pass the time of day, sure . . ." And his voice trailed off, as memory ebbed away.

Jess Rich had seen a lot of changes in reading matter since he was a boy, more than six decades ago. "In the old days everything was pulp. There was pulp detective stories, pulp love stories and pulp westerns, and those were the biggest sellers. Some came out monthly, some weekly. Today there's only one of those publications printed. It's called *Ranch Romances*. The rest of them died out.

"Well, some of these pulp love story magazines—one was called *Snappy Stories* and there was, oh, *The Yellow Book*, no pictures, but they were considered kind of risque. And one time a policewoman came in and complained that she had complaints about these magazines."

That struck me as rather amusing. I told Rich that old issues of *Snappy Stories* would today make pretty dull reading even in a nursing home for the aged.

"That's right!" he agreed. "Times change.

"This stuff comes in cycles," he added. "I expect one of these days a lot of these publications they print now will pass out of the picture, and something else will take its place. The biggest change is to paperbacks."

He pulled back his head and chuckled. "That's the story of my life. From pulps to paperbacks. That tells a lot, doesn't it?"

The carnival chief of OMSI

When Loren McKinley was asked if he would be interested in the position of director of the Oregon Museum of Science and Industry he candidly replied that in all his life he had been in only two museums, and one of those he had entered because it had the nearest rest room.

But OMSI's board of directors placed greater value on contagious optimism, administrative skill and boundless energy than on scientific know-how, so the man who hadn't the vaguest idea of what happened when he flipped an electric light switch was chosen. Competent scientists could be found without working up a strong sweat but empire builders like Loren McKinley don't come down the pike every day.

You had to see McKinley to believe him—and then you might not have believed your eyes. He was a running dynamo, sprinting inside of himself even when he walked, and he was everywhere and doing everything. The first time I saw him he had his shirtsleeves rolled up to the elbows and was handtrucking part of an exhibit. The second time he was at the admission turnstile and the third time he was selling packaged rocks to a couple of kids. It took us quite a while to corner him in his office at the museum, where the motto of "Science is Fun" is practiced daily in a thousand different ways.

The sheer pleasure of living, of doing, seemed to spill out of McKinley, a rugged, white-haired man with reddish eyebrows, twinkling eyes, an articulate tongue and a wit constantly probing to express itself. "He's the best salesman in the world," said Clint Gruber, the museum's assistant director, and anybody who listened to McKinley wax enthusiastic had to agree there was merit in Gruber's words. Clint had been working with Loren for several years and was still awed by his boss. "He could succeed anywhere, at anything," he declared, and at OMSI Loren McKinley had been a resounding success.

In McKinley's first year, 1960, approximately 85,000

187

persons visited OMSI (no one in the state called it by its official name, Oregon Museum of Science and Industry.) Ten years later the attendance had more than quintupled.

In those 10 years OMSI's budget had increased more than eleven-fold, it had 10 times as many employes, and it had gained a reputation as one of the six most significant science museums in the United States. In 1969 McKinley was named the outstanding science museum director in the nation, the Smithsonian Institute sent him to Korea, Israel and Egypt to lend his assistance in developing OMSI-like educational programs, and in 1970 he was invited to address an eminent conference on science education for pre-college students. OMSI had pioneered the concept of taking science education out of the "staid old classroom," as McKinley said, "and putting it in the open, putting it under shelter halves and tents, putting the action wherever science occurs in the state of Oregon."

It seemed fitting for Loren McKinley to be associated with OMSI, so indigenous to Oregon. His family came to the state in 1878 and one of his ancestors was the first doctor in Tillamook, where Loren was born, in 1920.

"I came out of the land of cheese, trees and ocean breeze," McKinley spieled, never missing a chance for ballyhoo. "My father was a commercial fisherman on Tillamook Bay, and it's my kind of a proud boast that I really didn't live on dry land until I was seven. We lived in a houseboat, and as I look back on it, it was a great, great life."

A journalism major in college, McKinley returned to Tillamook after WW II service and went to reporting for the local *Headlight-Herald*. Eventually he advanced to the post of advertising director and later purchased a half-interest in a shopping guide.

But that was only a small part of Loren McKinley. He was better known as mayor of Tillamook, serving six years in that post, and doing so well at it that he was elected president of the League of Oregon Cities and one year was named First Citizen of Oregon.

Came the day, however, when McKinley had to look for broader horizons. "I had five children and I wanted them to be able to enjoy college, and I could not afford to send them away to college. So I looked around in college communities to find some sort of a job that would support my family and allow the children to go to college. And that's how I ended up as museum director here."

McKinley arrived at an OMSI that was weak in budget but strong on love. The museum had been built in 1958 entirely from contributions, materials and labor. In one day, 400 bricklayers and hodcarriers combined to lay every one of the 103,000 bricks in the building.

"The glaziers," said McKinley, "had their choice of doing picket duty downtown or putting in our windows for free. The floors were laid at a total cost of five cases of you-know-what and I think there might have been one case too many because to this day some of the floor tiles around our building pop up, and I would suspect the mastic was liberally diluted with something called grain alcohol.

"Everyone owns a piece of the museum," he went on, after chuckling about the ingredients of the mastic. "There was a big campaign—Be A Brick, Buy A Brick— and so even now people will come into the building and I'll be talking to them and they'll say, 'You know, I bought a brick,' or 'I was up here and put in your windows' or 'I had something to do with laying the floor' or 'I donated this' or 'I donated that,' and because everyone owns a piece of us, they want to be sure we're successful."

Loren McKinley was too honest a man to take credit for many of the ideas which had made OMSI so unique among museums but without his support the proposals of his imaginative staff members would have died a-borning. Under McKinley's leadership OMSI had been turned into a catalyst for the scientific activities of Oregon. "We put in the science enrichment classes," he explained, "the field trips, and the resident science camps, so we could take the students who were eager, and wanted more science, to where the action is in the scientific world."

OMSI operated for its young enthusiasts a high mountain flora and fauna camp in the Sisters area of the Cascades, a marine biology camp at Coos Bay, a traveling science camp, and Camp Hancock, its famous paleontology and paleobotany research facility on the John Day River.

It is impossible to discuss Camp Hancock without at least rendering tribute to one of the most incredible Oregonians of this century, a Portland postman with a curious mind, a scientific bent, and a life-long devotion to the unearthing and identification of Oregon fossils.

With the cooperation of OMSI, Lon Hancock established the camp named after him. By daylight he supervised the students who had come for two-week sessions; evenings, around a campfire, the geological ages of Central Oregon came alive through his story-telling. Sunday mornings he roused the youths out of their tent beds and led them to the top of a small hummock and delivered what those who were with him still refer to as Lon Hancock's Sermon on the Mount.

The postman and his wife, both passed away, willed to OMSI one of the largest fossil collections in the United States. The Lon Hancock Room of Paleontology, honoring this self-schooled scholar, would be a credit to any museum in the world. But the most precious of his legacies, his field notes and the tapes containing his campfire stories and his Sunday sermons, are seen and heard by only a few people. Some day a writer will use them to pen a biography of this remarkable amateur, who but for lack of academic degrees would have graced the faculty of any major university.

Loren McKinley knew Hancock well. His position at OMSI had enabled him to meet close up some of the truly fascinating people of Oregon and to work with organizations he never even knew existed before he joined the museum.

"One night Reub Long and I sat on the top of Fort Rock," Loren recalled, "and Reub said the only reason he bought all that land around the rock was so that he could come up to the top of it at night and just enjoy the peace there."

That would have been a dialog worth recording on the aerie of Fort Rock, aloof on the lonesome desert: the deeply sensitive, philosophical cowboy and the fisherman's earthy son.

The Oregon Agate and Mineral Society staged its annual show at OMSI. So did the Oregon Archeological Society and the Oregon Geological Society and the Portland Photographic Society. McKinley could anticipate large numbers of people coming for these exhibits but when the Oregon Micological Society asked if it could hold its yearly one-day display at OMSI, Loren first had to ask what micological meant. ("It really means mushroom.")

Maybe 14 or 15 persons would show up, McKinley reasoned. But, believeing that everyone ought to be given a chance to do their thing, he readily consented. "Well, on that day, on that one Sunday, we had something like 4000 visitors come and look at mushrooms, and study them, and I found out to never sell any of these special-interest groups short."

McKinley was especially proud of the exhibits the museum staff had innovated. "I think the finest one," he said, "was the concept that the tiny micro world needn't be restricted to just a few who line up and take 20 seconds to peek through a microscope but rather developing micro-projectors, mirrors on microscopes, so whole classes can stand around and see protozoa, paramecium, all the small things in the micro world without the problems of the slow-down and costly microscopes.

"What we did in this exhibit was to take a microscope, put a mirror on it, use a well-slide so the specimens will stay alive for 24 hours, and the mirror projects the image of these tiny things, swiming in their liquids, on a ground glass projection screen, I guess, is the best way to describe it. The image is enlarged some 200 times and whole classes can see these little wee beasties in their environment of liquid."

There wasn't a school day at OMSI but that a small fleet of buses weren't parked outside. They brought students from all parts of the state, from as far as Lakeview, deep south in central Oregon, and Ontario, on the Idaho border. Children who took the train down from Puget Sound schools were met at the Portland depot by buses.

"The biggest satisfaction I've had in this venture," declared Loren, "is having participated in introducing over a million students to science. We have encouraged them to take one step down the road to science of their own volition because of our science fair. Some of the students who are working now in our research lab, and these are high school students, are turning out true research in areas and in a way that just amazes the professional scientist. We have a sophomore and a junior in high school who spent two years on a project to develop a more nutritious type of algae that will help solve perhaps the world's future food problems, and they are feeding this algae on sewage disposal. This may sound a little bit indelicate but you solve two problems at once, the food problem, and the problem of the solid wastes that are glutting and stifling America."

McKinley said this while we were pacing through the museum corridors, looking for just the right place to photograph him. As we passed a group of youngsters huddled around a guide in front of an exhibit of fluffy chicks, I asked Loren if he would take the guide's place for just a few seconds. He agreed, the guide moved out of camera range, and McKinley stepped into the breach. Holding a chick aloft he started talking vigorously—with simplicity and drama—about his boyhood days when he had chickens to look after. In a moment the children, all eyes upon him, were spellbound. The white-haired man with the buoyant voice was in his true element, relating knowledge to the listener. He seemed a little disappointed when we called him away.

Every day was a carnival of surprises for Loren McKinley. One day a staff scientist would come up with an idea that could stagger a less flexible director, another day a spokesman for a group so obscure in character McKinley wouldn't suspect it existed would ask to hold a show at OMSI. Great scientists came to visit, reporters from national periodicals called upon him, impossible requests were forwarded to his desk. Once, when he felt he could savor a tranquil moment, he heard the tones of a flute. Trailing the notes to their source he found himself in the museum's giant model of a heart. There, seated Indian-fashion on the floor, a bearded young man was making music to the beat of the heart.

"I couldn't see that he was hurting anybody," Loren said, with a quizzical smile, "so I walked away."

Through all the kaleidoscopic carnival of the breezy museum, the man from Tillamook churned on, having the time of his life in the funhouse of science. The air was charged with his outgoing spirit: all the employes were relaxed and responsive. None of them talked down to the visitors or treated questions with contempt. The arrogance of guides I had seen in museums on four continents was absent here. Nor was there a grain of insititutional stuffiness in the building: nobody was asked to talk in whispers or cut out their laughing or throw away the candy bar they were eating. The museum was for the people, all the people, and Loren McKinley wanted them to feel at home. That's why so many returned so often to OMSI: it offered the best entertainment in town.

When Loren McKinley was in school he was frightened to death of science. So he understood what others had gone or were going through. It was his aim to prove that there was nothing to be afraid of, that the pursuit of science could be enjoyable, vastly enjoyable.

At OMSI he had demonstrated his theory to tens of thousands and, in the process, to himself. Now, with the new-found enthusiasm of a middle-aged man who had only recently started to swim, he was standing on the beach shouting, "Come on! It's easy to learn! And the water's fine!"

Sweet were the days of Old Tillamook

There weren't many old timers left around Tillamook. Emma Weiss Ward was one and if her husband, Garret, had still been alive, he would have been even more of an old timer. He had come to Tillamook 19 years before she had.

Garret Ward was born in Ohio in 1875 but had been raised in Kansas. His mother died when he was six and a few bad years, the kind that were always uprooting Kansas farmers and storekeepers, played havoc with his father. By 1892 the family was so poor it had, as Mrs. Ward put it, "just a covered wagon and two horses and little else."

So the horses were hitched to the prairie schooner and the family turned their faces to the Pacific Northwest. They made it all the way from Kansas by covered wagon. Yes, in 1892, years after the railroads linked Kansas to the Northwest, but some families who were bent on westering it then didn't have passenger fare, and if they did, maybe they couldn't afford to ship their household necessities, and if they had the money for that, too, maybe they figured they would need their stock in the new country, and their wagon, too. Worst come to worst, they could sleep in the wagon until they had built themselves a covering.

Or they could sell their wagon and their horses for a better price in the West then they could bargain for in the bottom-dropped-out Plains states, where a wagon and team wouldn't bring enough cash to make it worth your while to find a buyer.

The Wards had set their sights on Chehalis, Washington. (Mrs. Ward didn't say why.) When they reached Portland, however, they lacked enough money for passage on the ferry boat across the Columbia. Just a distance you could walk in a few minutes if it were land but now it was wide as the ocean. No money, no crossing. And no Chehalis.

On such seemingly small things do our lives so often ride. If the Wards had owned a few dollars they would have wound up 150 hard miles from Tillamook and their future might have been altogether different. Certainly, it is extremely doubtful that Garret Ward and Emma Weiss would have met. And the children she would have had by another man would not be the same children she bore Garret Ward.

You can go on like this for pages, but maybe in the end all the bits of luck even out in the stream of humanity.

Anyway, when the Wards found they couldn't cross the Columbia they continued west, trudging a rough dusty road through Willamina and Sheridan and past Dolph to Hebo. That first winter they lived in a lean-to built against a Douglas fir and made shakes for a living.

Come spring they took up a homestead "and were on it quite some years," Mrs. Ward said. By 1908, Garret, already 33, had seen enough of the farm. He buggied up to Tillamook with two suitcases and found a position selling real estate. Three years later he met Emma Weiss.

"I didn't know anything about his early life until shortly before he died, in 1953," Mrs. Ward said as we sat in the sunporch of her comfortable house in Tillamook. "One day, as he lay in bed, he told me all about it."

Emma Weiss was 18 when she reached Tillamook in 1911. She was in the third wave of her Wisconsin family to become Oregonians. Her sister, Ida Zweifel, had arrived first, in 1908, with her husband, on their honeymoon. Zweifel was impressed by the lush meadows, the many streams and the available land. "This is for me," he declared. He sold his Wisconsin dairy business and turned to dairy farming in Tillamook County.

Emma's mother didn't like the Wisconsin climate. The summers were too hot and the winter too cold. She and her husband packed up and took off for California where she found the summer just as uncomfortable as it was in Wisconsin. On their way back, in 1910, they detoured to Tillamook to see Ida. Who knew when daughter and parents would ever meet again, with 2000 miles between them.

Several days of cool weather, with zephyrs blowing in softly from the bay, and Mrs. Weiss was feeling better than she had for years. A few lectures by Ida on the mildness of the winters and Mrs. Weiss was sold. She and her husband settled in Tillamook.

Emma, together with a brother and sister, followed the

next year. They came by train as far as Portland and horseback the rest of the way.

Mrs. Ward told us about her family and herself as she wiggled her toes and fluttered her hands. She was a peppy, brown-eyed, silver-haired woman, good-naturedly volatile and restless.

"Tillamook when I came here?" she replied. "Oh, it was a little town with no paved streets. Planks were laid across the muddy streets, to walk. There were just two nice buildings in town—the Tillamook Building and the one on First Street. They were two-story concrete buildings. The others were pretty modest.

"There were possibly three or four automobiles here then. Everybody else used horse and buggy or bicycle or rode horse—and lots of places where there weren't roads they had to go by boat.

"A few of the old time Indians were still around when I came. I guess most of them just died or intermarried. I think there's one Indian family, that I know, down at Garibaldi."

Emma's first job was domestic for the Fred Beals' household. They had resided in Tillamook longer than most others and were one of the most affluent families in the country. He was a big real estate man and Garret Ward's employer. That's how Emma and Garret met, through their mutual boss.

In 1914 Emma Weiss became Emma Ward. "But I didn't go with him all that time," she noted, with an impish toss of her head. "I don't exactly remember how long."

We asked how young folks went about courting 60 years ago in the small town of Tillamook. Her hands skipped along in a shaft of sunbeams as a freshet of words surged through the sunporch.

"You went buggy riding. Yes, that's what we all did. There were roads around the county but we didn't go to the beach often. That was too far away. That's what we did, just drive around and around the county roads. There wasn't much to do then—go to a movie once in a while. There was a movie house in town and people would sing. There would be a paid singer and she'd lead the singing. They'd flash a picture of what the song was all about."

Mrs. Ward laughed merrily. "Now there aren't any lyrics. Just one line, over and over again."

"And they went to dances," she continued, "but I don't believe Garret and I went to any—guess we didn't have time, mostly; he was a busy guy; and my other boy friend, he didn't believe in dancing."

On Sundays Garret would have the use of Mrs. Beals' team of sorrels—"beautiful, high spirited; they were like Cadillacs to the other horses. They'd prance on their hind feet out of the barn, itching to go, and we'd drive around the county. We did go out quite a ways, as far as Hebo, and that was quite a trip."

It must have been quite a trip—Hebo was at least 20 miles from Tillamook!

Emma Ward had seen a lot of things come and go in the town since 1911. "Just about everything has changed," she said, smoothing her dress at the knees. "We have good roads, good streets. We didn't have electricity in the day time except two days a week, work day and ironing day, Monday and Friday. But the light went on when it got dark.

"From a real estate standpoint, Tillamook has taken on tremendous proportions. It's very hard to rent a satisfactory house these days."

Her husband had been in real estate so long and she had shared this part of their life so intimately that she had a realtor's eye for everything related to property. She asked where we lived in Portland and then we could see her mentally figuring out what our house was worth.

For 10 years she had been deputy treasurer of the county but retirement had not sent her to the rockingchair. She was the kind of person who would invent work if it weren't waiting to be done.

"Now I'm busy with a lot of things—my flower garden, my home, and the Pioneer Society," she dashed off, her smile never fading. "I have charge of keeping the membership records of the society and I'll be busy on it all winter. I don't see idle time ahead. Goodness knows, I could use a few more hours a day!" And she was well past three-quarters of a century. How I envied her her youth.

There is always, it seems, an odd note in every story. In Mrs. Ward's case it had to do with her family. Out of all the Weisses who came to Tillamook, and all their children—there were only four left: Mrs. Ward; Ida Zweifel's son, Karl; Karl's son, Larry; and Larry's son, Karl John. All the others had died or moved away.

"Actually," I said to Mrs. Ward, "there is less Weiss blood here now than when you came, even after all the births."

"I know," she said, arising to answer the telephone, "but that's the way the cookie crumbles."

Well, you think about situations such as this one. After Mrs. Ward passes away, as we all must, and if the remaining Zweifels should leave the area, what would there be to show for all the years the Weisses and their descendants put into the county? Who, a generation from now, will know or care?

The earth turns. Time passes. The scene changes. The Weisses and their offspring who moved on to still undiscovered lands had their day and that, in the summing up, may be all that matters. Whoever departs, humanity remains. I think Mrs. Ward knew this as well as I do.

The glorious fisherman

An architect friend said Astoria had the least-modern business section of any city its size in the West and called the John Jacob Astor Hotel, which was closed years ago, a "festering eyesore."

The Astor, the highest building in Astoria and second tallest on the entire Oregon littoral, was in its prime the most famous coastal inn between San Francisco and Vancouver, B. C. Back in the thirties, when I first looked upon it, it had even in those lean times an air of affluence and great prestige. Before it closed for good, a traveling salesman told me, it had grown seedy and scurfy and its rooms were down to $2 a night.

A lot of people in Astoria thought the hotel should be torn down for a parking lot. (If you can't think of anything else, it's always a parking lot. I envisage a downtown with all parking lots and no buildings. But, so we heard, nobody knew who really owned the Astor and therefore the county wasn't collecting property taxes from the defunct hostelry.

Still, Astoria was more than a frayed and pallid shopping section. Critics forgot the beautiful library, built through lavish contributions by the Astors of England, lineal descendants of John Jacob Astor, the New York mogul whose wealth and aspirations gave birth to Astoria; the magnificent Astoria Column, atop the green mane of windswept Coxcomb Hill; gusty Fishermans Wharf; the lacey bridge spooled across the Columbia; and the profuse views of the Washington shore beyond the broad and restless stream. Look in the mist of morning, when the hills of Washington are pea green washes snorted up by the currents of the river, and at sundown, when the hills roll away in pure and lustrous waves.

Astoria's fishing fleet, which city boosters claimed was the largest on the Oregon Coast, had a saltwater authenticity which I found more dramatic and colorful than the avocational elegance of yachts. The brine of labor and the smack of robust love had been rubbed into fishing boats so that when you touched one you touched a man to the bone. The sea is no playground to the small-boat independent fisherman; it is his dark camerado and wily adversary; the meat on his table and the gasoline in his car come from the sea; if it fails him he is grounded upon hard times. Forever fickle, the sea will yield gladly nothing but death and those who put out to the deep six in frail crafts for livelihood walk and sleep with fatalism. Yet, so has the world turned, every fisherman I know feels safer on the swells of the ocean than driving on a highway.

The fishermen came home to many kinds of houses, from sour-faced slatted coops built on stilts to pretty bungalows garlanded by potted flowers. Art Paquet, who had 50 years of fishing behind him, lived in one of the many redone 19th century houses. From his rear window he could see in panoramic sweep the waterfront and the Columbia River bridge.

Paquet wasn't home but his wife was. She told us of other 19th century homes and from people at some of these dwellings we learned of still more old houses. After we had photographed a dozen or so we gave up, convinced that Astoria had more 19th century houses than any city its size in the state and perhaps more than any other city, of whatever size, in all Oregon.

Many of the old houses had been redone, retaining their original design and flavor. Bruce Berney, the city librarian, and his mother, bought an ancient dwelling for $6000 and spent $20,000 redoing it. It was pretty handsome when we saw it, probably a lot fancier and more comfortable than when originally built.

Sometimes you look for one person to typify a town, someone who reflects the intrinsic character of the community or who, in his life span, is a chronicler of change. Gordon Sloan, who was a justice of the state supreme court, and had come out of Astoria, urged us to talk with William B. Wootton, who Sloan thought not only had seen many richly-textured years but was more representative of Astoria than anyone he knew.

"He can tell you everything about the fishing industry," Gordon Sloan said, so when we were in Astoria we paid a call upon Mr. Wootton. He and his wife lived in a neat, comfortable and unpretentious frame house on a quiet hilltop street and the morning we arrived Wootton and his son, an army colonel who had just retired from the service, were out front washing windows, the older man with a methodical briskness and his tall soldier son with a blare of gusto.

You could tell at a glance that William Wootton, a crisp, gray-haired fellow with a nailfile salt-and-pepper mustache, was the kind of fellow who had come up from the ranks: he exuded the sure and controlled confidence of a man who had made many top-level decisions and he retained the unstudied posture of the hand laborer. He had started his fisheries career as a cannery worker and had left its day-to-day functionings as a corporation executive.

Wootton was born in Seattle on the second day of April, 1893, the son of a bricklayer who came to Puget Sound three years earlier. In 1897 the family moved to Hungry Harbor, across the Columbia River from Astoria, where his father worked at the George and Baker North Shore Cannery.

"Could I have been anything different?" he pondered. "It was really a combination of the Seattle fire and the depression of Cleveland's administration that made my father come out here. Otherwise I'd probably have been a bricklayer."

In 1899, with the establishment of Columbia River Packers, the Woottons settled in Astoria and there William grew up. It was a burly, raw-boned, steamy, folksy town, and he remembered it with affection.

"Oh, it was a great place, a wonderful place," he began, talking about the changes he had seen.

"At one time, in the early days, all downtown streets were on pilings. From the waterfront up past Duane was all on piling, fir plankings, three by twelves.

"I remember very well the fire of 1922 which practically destroyed Astoria. I was home when it started. It was early in the morning. I ran down, like any other person, and watched it. There wasn't anything anybody could do about it. The way the streets were built and laid out, if you were fighting one building in front of you, you looked around and saw a building behind you on fire. Dynamiting was all that stopped the fire."

In his youth Astoria was ethnically divided into four

sections. The Finns lived in Uniontown (which tells a little about the Finns); Scandinavians were the principal occupants of Uppertown, or "Yammerdahl—Valley of the Tears"; Alderbrook was a conglomerate of Scandinavians, Italians, Yugoslavs and some Greeks; and the center of town was "a mixture of Nordics—Englishmen, Scotchmen, Welsh all kinds."

The ethnic settlements developed when owners of canneries began importing experienced fishermen from their own and other lands. Now, Wootton said, the ethnic groups were in the third generation—"and all Americanized."

It was a shame, I thought to myself, for Americanization to have defoliated the rich rainbow flora of so many national cultures. I remember that in the 1930s the Finns had a hall, choral and dramatic groups, a cooperative, and Finnish dances were held regularly. Not too many years before I first passed through the town, I have been told, street signs were printed in both English and Finnish, and a Finnish daily paper was printed. It collapsed when the federal government deported the editors for possessing unsanitized political views.

Mr. Wootton talked on about other changes he had witnessed. "In the early days Clatsop County had one-fifth of all the prime standing Douglas fir in the state of Oregon, and they thought it would last forever. But it didn't, and there aren't many loggers in town now.

"There used to be quite a lot of sailors in town—from the sailing ships—to load up wheat for the United Kingdom. Five or six sailing ships anchored in the river, waiting to be towed to Portland to pick up cargoes, including wheat —but no more sailors today.

"A ship wreck was a big event in Astoria. Many heroic rescue efforts were made by life-saving crews from the stations near the mouth of the river. The crews had boats that were supposedly unsinkable. People hurried to the wreck on horse, on bicycles, on wagon, or they walked. A lot of people just took off from what they were doing and made tracks for the wreck. It seemed like the whole town poured out.

"I remember very well the first automobile in Astoria. It belonged to a Dr. Henderson. I think it was a Reo, though I'm not sure. Oh boy, did it create a fuss! We'd run for blocks just to see it pass. He could get down to Seaside."

Seaside was 17 miles from Astoria when we chatted with Mr. Wootton. It was five or seven miles farther when I first traveled the route. The distance must have been even greater when Dr. Henderson steered his new-fangled contraption down there, thumping and squishing and rubbing over roadbeds that were wood, dirt, grass, bog and sand. A fleet horse could probably have outraced the Reo with ease.

"At one time," Wootton continued, "we had 42 saloons and 12 churches. The town was full of loggers then and it seemed like they were all drinking.

"Astoria had its own Barbary Coast, on Astor Street. The nickname of the Red Light district was Swilltown. Governor Os West shut it down but it came back after he left office, in 1915, and ran open until 1941."

What seemed to have made the deepest impression upon Wootton were the characteristics of the people: their salty independence, stubborn pride, trust in each other, and a willingess to lend a helping hand without expecting to be repaid in inflationary interest rates.

"Those were the days," Mr. Wootton sighed with relish. "No one ever had much money and no one was ever busted. If you were short a couple of bucks you would walk into Danny's saloon and say to Sam, 'I need a couple of bucks,' and you got it.

"I can illustrate that by one yarn," he said, bending forward and holding up a finger. "There was a Christmas when a minister suggested that people donate food for buckets to the poor but when the buckets were made up nobody could find any poor people.

"It's only a story," he added, without smiling, "but I believe it."

For a moment there was something that puzzled him. Fifty years ago, he said, Astoria had more people and less houses. "We had 14,000 people then and there weren't too many houses, it seems; now there are 10,000 people and the town is full of houses."

After a bit of cogitating on it he thought he had found the answer. "The merchants downtown had one or two stories above their stores and they rented these as flats and a lot of people lived in these flats."

That made sense, I observed. Mr. Wootton frowned a bit, focused his mind inward, on the past, and declared firmly, "I think that's the way it was." He was not a man to adopt a statement as fact simply because someone agreed with him. He had to do his own verifying.

In 1910, when he was 17, William Wootton spent the first of many Alaska cannery-working summers. "I went up on the old *St. Nicholas,* a wooden three-masted full-rigged sailing ship," he recalled. Between 1910 and 1923 he made 15 round trips on the *St. Nicholas* and then, until 1928, five round trips on a steel sailing ship, the *Chillicothe.*

The trip to Alaska took from 25 to 64 days. "We came home faster—going downhill," Wootton joshed dryly.

In 1918 the *St. Nicholas* was frozen for 21 days, in the later part of May and the early part of June. "The Arctic ice pack came down farther than usual, because of the push of the wind," Wootton explained. The ice was frozen so solid the men could walk on it, and one of them walked far enough away to take a photo of the *St. Nicholas* stranded in an agglutinated northland sea. Wootton showed us a picture of the immobilized vessel, and added: "There were other ships out there, too, stuck like we were. One of them, the *Tacoma,* was crushed in the ice and and 125 men were taken aboard our ship."

Until 1925 Wootton worked with his father in the Bristol Bay canneries. "We turned to at four-thirty in the morning and if we were real lucky we got finished up after dinner, from seven to eleven p.m. The work was real steady because we had to make preparations. Our first job was to make the cans—and that was very involved because all the work was done by hand—and prepare the fleet to go fishing. We made up nets, put supplies on board, got the apparatus out—all these things. When the boats came in we unloaded the fish and put them in cans."

In 1925 he was at Chignik, on the Alaska Peninsula, as superintendent for the Columbia River Packers. Six years later the company placed him in charge of all its Alaska operations. He retired from the firm, which was now called Bumble Bee, in 1958, but since he was still on the board of directors he continued to make annual trips to Alaska.

"I've been up there every year since 1910 except for two years," he declared proudly. "I go to Alaska now because I like it and on inspection trips and for trout fishing. The most wonderful trout fishing in the world. On the Kvichak River, that flows out of Lake Iliamna, which, as far as I know, is, outside the Great Lakes, the largest lake on the North American continent, and is the greatest spawning area for red salmon in the world."

He noted these changes at Bristol Bay since his early salmon cannery days: Power fish boats, automatic canning machines, air transportation, fleets no longer owned by the canneries, supplies now delivered by commercial freight, and less fish.

But he didn't think the fish would some day run out. "In 1965," he asserted, with the conviction of a man who does not deal in ifs and buts, "50 million salmon came up Bristol Bay, the largest total entry on record."

His affinity for the sea was as strong now as it had been more than 70 years ago, when as a boy he had fished at the mouth of the Columbia and looked with awe and love upon the illimitable Pacific.

"Oh yes, definitely," he murmured. "But how do you measure the strength of an affinity?" He mused silently for a moment and continued in oddly rapturous tones that grew younger as he spoke.

"I love it. In the good old sailing days, when you had good sailors, and a fair wind and a following sea, and all the sails are up and she lays on her side and it's real gentle, and you can make miles—that's heaven."

I remarked that there was a nice chunk of poetry in him. He smiled shyly. Anyway, I commented, you're glad you spent your life in the fish business.

"Very much so," he replied staunchly. "It was the most disappointing and the most rewarding experience in the world." And he told with vibrance how he remembered the drama of the Alaska canneries:

"The run peaks in 10 days and you get 60 or more per cent of your pack in those 10 days and when there's a heavy run everything jibes. The cannery is running to full capacity, 16 to 18 hours a day, each line kicking out 250 one-pound cans a minute, and scows receiving the fish from fisherman out in the fishing grounds coming in, full loaded, fish boats loaded to the gunwhales. Oh, it's exhilarating—and everything comes out smelling like money."

He laughed and so did we and I thanked him for his time and words. He nodded, and said, "This will probably bore you but I once wrote a poem on being a fisherman. I don't suppose you'd care to hear it." We assured him we would and asked him to first give us the background for the poem.

All right, he said, and began, falling quickly into the casual prose of his young manhood:

"I was workin' these long hours in the cannery and I got tired of doin' it, and I had a little boat which took food out to the scows which were anchored out in the bay, and I went out for the mail which came in once a month, and we'd gone out after the mail and with me were two Norwegian fishermen, and I missed the mouth of the slough—very crooked slough this cannery was on—and took a homestead on the mud flats, and while waiting for the next tide in order to get off, I had some San Francisco *Examiners* as I remember—the union used to send up mail bags full of all sorts of papers—and I took one of these and just thinking—I'm not a poet but I learned a lot of Robert W. Service—and I was sitting there waiting for the tide, and had a pencil, and inscribed upon the edge of this San Francisco *Examiner* a poem about our fishermen and it went, as I remember it, something like this:

"Alaska, the land of romance,
Her tales are oft retold;
The grandeur of her mountain peaks,
Her valleys rich with gold;
Of the silver horde which comes and goes,
Of fortunes made in a day;
The romance of the miner
Who mucks in the earth for his pay;
   The romance of the mushers
   That hit the cold, cold trail,
   Bleary-eyed and frozen-stiff
   To get through the Dawson mail.
   I've read her tales by the thousands,
   From Cape Nome to Ketchikan,

But never a note, nor never a poem
About the fisherman.
No weakling here can take a chance,
They're weeded out like chaff;
No beardless youth nor city dude
Can stand the hard, hard gaff;
Lads with lots of guts, my boy,
Lads that never cry;
They have to fight from dawn 'til night
Or else lay down and die.
With a thirteen-foot oar and the old lee shore,
You have to pull like sin;
The roaring waves will be your grave
If ever you give in.
You fight like hell with never a yell
To get in a fathom of the net;
You've had no sleep and nothin' to eat
And your clothes are wringin' wet;
You fish the sands to beat the band
Till your very soul is sick,
And your mouth's red hot and your eyes blood-shot
But it's pick, you buggers, pick.
So here's to all the boys again,
Here's to the miner bold,
And to the musher on the Arctic trails
When they are icy cold;
The trapper, too, and the skinner,
For all of them have sand;
The last and loudest cheer we give
To the fisher-man."

When I had typed the poem I sent a copy to Mr.
Wootton with a note requesting that he correct what I
had transcribed from the tape. This he did, and enclosed
a letter which he gave us permission to use:

"The verse makes no pretense of being a literary gem.
'Fishermen' was written by a 17-year-old kid, an admirer
of Robert W. Service's works, trying to tell the story in
rhyme of a special breed of men, the Bristol Bay gillnet
Fishermen. Theirs was a tough and cruel occupation.
They went out in all weather in the wide open, in a 29-
foot open sail boat propelled only by sails or oars. A
considerable number of them came from the Lofoten Is-

lands off the coast of Norway. There, when a boy was large enough to see over the gunnels of the boat, he went out with his Dad to fish in the North Sea.

"The nets they fished with was, at the time this was written, some 200 fathom gill nets. This, at times heavily laden with fish, had to be pulled back into the boat by strength of arms and was backbreaking work. Then the fish had to be disengaged from the net, calling picking fish.

"In reference to lee shore and sands. The salmon would school along the lee shore or edge of sands. Therefore, if the men wanted to make a good catch they had to fish in these locations regardless of the weather conditions, which at times was a pretty tough place. For example, in Kvichak Bay, one of the most productive fishing locations was to fish 'Deadman Sands.' "

Mr. Wootton need not have apologized for his verse. I have seen less heroic contributions from men with college degrees. *Fishermen* tells a lot about William Wootton and about the spirit of Astoria he knew as a youth, when all those redone 19th century homes were flamboyant monuments to maritime wealth and, in no lesser degree, to the bravery of those who daily risked their lives on the inconstant sea.

One more summer

Summer was almost at an end and I was angry with myself. I had waited so long for summer, for the long days and for the heat that would rub the pain out of my neck and shoulders and for the weekend and vacation mornings I would spend carefree in the open and the evenings I would sit on the porch and watch the feathers of sunlight curl into twilight.

I had waited hungrily, almost desperately, for the summer, as though it would be my last to live, and now it was late August and in the high hills autumn was creeping into the pines.

Since the close of October last year, when we went off Daylight Time, and suddenly afternoon was telescoped into dusk, I had been waiting for summer. The hardest months were November and December—that is, until December 21st, when time turned back in my favor. Every day was a little shorter, a little grimmer, splashing away from summer in a dank, spongy gait. One bowlegged piddly step at a time, refusing to be hurried, obstinate that each day be a full 24 hours, and if most of the hours were dark and chill and stinging wet, why, that was part of the plan, and no show of irritation could change that fact.

Then came the winter solstice and with it the earth turning toward sunlight. But there came also the storms and the avalanches of snow and the streets so slick with ice that few drivers dared take to them, and the airport down to a single scrap of runway. We were the last plane in from the south (or anywhere else) that night, and four hours late, and I had the feeling as the plane catpawed stiffly toward the airport terminal that I was watching an old World War II film about someone escaping from the Nazis on the last plane from Norway and landing on a desolate field in Iceland.

There were about 200 people on the ground floor of the terminal, rooted and shaking behind the big glass doors that led to the taxi apron, waiting for taxis that didn't come. It was an unprofitable situation, so I opened my suitcase, put on an extra sweater, telling my wife and child I had to make an effort, and pushed outside.

The wind had such numbing power I soon forgot my anxiety and watched with blank curiosity, as though in a death-ordained scene, the eerie world of civilization marooned on a night of collapse.

Every time a taxi—there must have been two or three in three-quarters of an hour—slithered to the curb, a few people from the inside poured out and charged for the cab door. I might have reached them if I hadn't been so cold that I had become a spectator, watching the drama as though I were home in front of a television set, knowing I should turn the tube off but too sleepy to move.

The driver of the third or fourth cab had ruddy cheeks and a walrus mustache that reminded me of pictures I had seen years ago of a cossack general and I asked myself one of the silly questions that come when your mind is benumbed: What's a young cossack doing driving a taxi on the frozen steppes of Portland?

"Ralph!" someone shouted. "What the hell are you doing here?" The taxi driver had taken my hand and was pumping it.

"What are you up to?" I mumbled, trying hard to remember this fellow.

"Driving a cab," he laughed. He laughed lustily, as though wrestling with a storm was just the exercise he needed to keep him in good spirits.

"Do you like it?" I mumbled, groping wildly for a clue to his name. It couldn't be Budenny; that was the cossack general.

"It's a living," he grinned. "Going home? Where's Phoebe and Amy?"

"Inside," I said, quickly now, thawing to the warmth of salvation. "I'll get them."

So I ran to the doors and brought out my wife and daughter and our bags and hustled and carried and prodded them all to the middle of the platform, where the taxi driver shouldered forward to meet us.

"Jim Farrell!" my wife cried. "What are you doing here?"

So I knew it was Jim Farrell, whom I have known for

years, seeing him at least once a year, but never with a mustache, walrus or any other kind.

Jim took three other people in his car, two of whom he deposited at a motel about a mile from the airport. The third lived up on the West Hills, which Jim wasn't going to try to attempt that night but he would take the fellow downtown, so it was now a job getting us home.

"I don't know why the company doesn't put chains on the tires," Jim wondered, as we skidded down a street that looked like a sugar-coated block of ice and wasn't any more negotiable. "These snowtires aren't good enough in this kind of weather. But," and two fingers shot up in a reassuring smile, "we'll get there."

The streets were primitive alleys of white hell. Cars had been abandoned in the middle of them, snow had accumulated into hills and ridges and sharp cliffs that blocked intersections, soft troughs ran into hard monoliths. Any way you looked at it, it was a miserable situation.

Jim wheeled his car as though he were riding a highly disciplined and sure-footed cutting horse in a corral full of mean, bawling steers. Zig-in, zig-out, twist, dodge, bounce, slither. He miraculously pulled out of troughs, bent around white buttes, caromed off drifts, bounced over ridges and slid down hills, missing the cars in our path by no more than a frozen eyelash.

If he couldn't get through or across an obstacle the first time he'd back up and gun the motor. It sputtered and jolted and the cab staggered forward until the next resisting hurdle. Sometimes it took him three tries at a hill before he bounced over it. But two blocks from our house he came face to face with a churning wasteland of white waves higher than anything we had seen.

"Give it a try, cowboy," I urged.

"I don't dare," replied Jim, pale for the first time. He clenched his lips and rubbed his nose. "Tell you what," and he was breezy again. "I'll take you to our place. The folks will be glad to see you. They'll put you up. Things'll be better tomorrow and I'll take you home."

So we wheeled down less precarious streets, traveling in a round-about way, until we came to the Farrell house, about a mile from where we live.

"Now, that's fine," called Jim, as he helped us lug our suitcases inside.

"What does the meter say?" I asked. Jim bent his head inside the cab and emerged with a figure. I paid him and he lurched back out of the driveway with a blast that sounded like a tank booming into battle.

Three of Jim's family were home: father Russ, mother Lorine and sister Sharron. They were cordially willing to accommodate us, on a cot, on a couch and in a sleeping bag on the floor, which was very generous of them, with us barging in unannounced and late at night, but frustration was beginning to eat in my bones. So far to have come and then be held away from your home virtually in the same neighborhood.

Sharron must have been reading my thoughts. "I've got chains on my car," she announced. "I'll bet Dad could get through."

"It would be a rugged go," I doubted, hoping Russ wouldn't feel discouraged.

"Oh," he said, with his crackling terseness that belies a soft heart, "I think we kin give her a try."

Sharron scrounged up long woolen stockings for me to pull over my low-cut shoes and then Russ and I waded into the arctic night to find her car.

"If we git stuck we kin always walk back," Russ assured me. "I wouldn't worry about it."

I wasn't worried. Old Russ the logger, the construction worker, the lineman. Solid Russ, the true proletarian. He might get a little rattled and hot-tempered sometimes, when a discussion on political theory got a bit frantic, but Russ on the job was pure steel for nerves, and Russ was on the job now.

We made it almost to the house and we pushed on foot through mounds of snow, that under a milky grey sky looked like big scoops of glazed ice cream, until we pulled our way up the stairs and stomped across the porch to the door. The key worked, by God, and the door opened, and I didn't give a hoot about all the snow cascading inside.

The lights worked, too, beautiful, beautiful lights, which meant we had heat, which I could feel anyway, almost instantly. "Better wait to see if the pipes got frozen," I cautioned. "I think they're in good shape," Russ said.

Always the optimist. He was right. The water flowed evenly.

"Do you think you can bring Phoebe and Amy home?" I asked.

Russ shrugged. "I don't see why not. We made it once, didn't we?"

By the time he returned I had built a fire, swept out the snow, and shoveled a clearing down the stairs. I handed Russ his long woolen stockings and the worst of winter was over.

It was over because every day was a chicken's step toward spring, a seed planted to make summer grow.

Came more winter, temperatures below zero, heavy snow, harsh rains, days dismal and murder on arthritis. When I walked my dogs at night the trees shivered in the wind, which had galed through the Columbia Gorge and was bending even the stoutest boughs of the thickest trees. I worked, taught, researched, wrote, ate and slept and laughed and argued—and longed for summer.

I don't know why I yearned so much for this summer. I have seen more than half-a-century of summers—seen them in Norway, France, England, Mexico, New York, New England, Texas, Nebraska, California—well, as a matter of fact, seen summer in every state of the Union, including Alaska.

Why this summer was different I cannot explain. Perhaps it is because I had been so busy writing the last few summers that I felt I had missed them completely, and this one I did not want to drift by, as in a shadowy dream, so that when it is over you try to grasp at fragments that tell you something did happen, though the sounds and smells and touches are missing.

Longing for summer had become an obsession. This one I wanted to savor: to bite into and hold the taste from leaving until crawling exhausted, with the odor of sun still in my nostrils, into a cool bed.

It was this way through spring. And then we went to Hawaii for two weeks. We swam and walked bareheaded in the lavish sun and looked upon mornings aflame with soft orchid fire and watched twilight dance down the mountains and skim over the seawaves on velvet surfboards. We did all that, but not enough. Mostly we worked—taking pictures and jotting notes into stenographic pads.

Every day was a lost race against time. "Someday," my wife said, "we ought to come as tourists." It was a good visit, a beautiful trip, but the first days of summer slipped past us while I was heedful of other things.

All summer it was the same—but more so. Weekdays I worked and wrote. There was no time to sit on the porch with my wife and talk slowly about the many things that always need talking about. No time to frolic with my daughter and the dogs, except for a forced hike in the park when I came home from the office. I was always behind schedule. It was the typical life of a moonlighting free-lance writer. Editors brooked no excuses, a book could not wait. Summer slid down the channel of time and I was not even on the bank to see it pass.

This is not to say that, except for work, I did not leave the house. We were often weekends on the road. We drove so frequently to Hood River, to cover an assignment for a national publication, we began to feel like commuters. Our chores took us to The Dalles and Tygh Valley, to Government Camp and Sandy, Eagle Creek and Molalla, down the Oregon Coast and all through the Willamette Valley, and in mid-August we set off on a journey that carried us to the Idaho border and back across the state to Klamath Falls and Medford. But it was completely work: photos and interviewing and note-taking and planning and worry and fighting time and miles. It got so I looked at the sky only to see how much was left of the day.

Now summer was almost at an end and I felt like kicking myself. The golden days had gone down the drain. Soon it would be autumn and the nagging wait until the winter solstice and then the grains of added daylight until spring, the long approach to another summer. And I would be a year older and two years slower and three years sadder and summer five years away.

Summer means hot days but I like to remember those days when rain sweeps the streets, pounding the pavements like the hooves of charging cavalry. Summer may be trying to suck a cool breath of air out of a world that is a humid cellophane bag but I can take one of those days for three in December or January when every breath is a bubble of steam hung on an icicle.

Summer is the hell with suits and neckties and long

sleeved shirts. I don't like neckties, never have, they make me feel I'm being garroted, but I wear them because I don't think they're important enough to fight about in the business world. On hot days, though, you can get by without a necktie and no one will say: "What's the matter with Friedman? Has he become a hippie?"

Summer is the first probing rays of sunlight at Jordan Valley, flitting on the meadows above the river like field mice darting through the screening blades.

Summer is a stallion in the John Day Valley, sniffing the first flat blue of morning, deciding it will be a good day, and jogging from fence to fence, across the long pasture, every once in a while breaking into a sprint.

Summer is an old cowpoke in the Catlow Valley rubbing the sleep out of his eyes as he feels the cool of night being pushed down the Steens. It's going to be a firecracker today, another scorcher when you can fry eggs on rocks, but it'll start the juices flowing and pull the stiffness out of those busted legs.

Summer is the Portland floorwalker gulping the briny air of the deep sea from the starboard side of the charter fishing boat out of Warrenton and telling himself that even if he doesn't haul in his limit of salmon it's been a good day. Nothing to make a man feel manly like a few hours on the deep six, the wind blowing down from the north, and the salmon showing spirit.

Summer is the kid who gets stranded at Juntura and needs to hitch it into Beaverton today. He'll make it for sure, because there will be at least 14 hours of light, and if he averages 20 miles an hour he'll be O.K.

Summer is the crab fisherman at Newport waking up in the middle of the night to get to his boat and yawning to his wife, on the way out, "See you," and she mutters, "Yeah," and he means, "I hope the catch is good," and she means, "I hope there's no trouble out there."

Summer is when the morning sun sends the fog on the Coast Range up in puffs so that it looks like a hundred bonfires are burning on the ridges.

Oh, I know that summer is also dust and rusty lawns and parched trees and creeks bled white and the choking that comes when the seed fields are burning. And summer is a crowd of trailers and campers at Scott Lake and Lost Lake and Clear Lake and a lot of other lakes in the folds of the Cascades or webbed to its foothills and lines of tourists waiting to find space in state parks that are jammed to the gills. And mountain trails so crowded that from a distant peak the traffic resembles an army of ants.

All true, all true, and yet on the balance sheet I like summer for all the reasons I've given.

I was pondering the balance sheet as we wound around the south end of Klamath Lake. It was a clear golden day, the waters only slightly ruffled, and peace walked the shore.

"It's a beautiful lake," I told my wife.

"It is," she affirmed.

"We really ought to stop here for a few hours and enjoy the scenery and contentment," I said.

"We should," she agreed, in a sort of absent sigh.

"Someday," I said, as I drove on.

The conversation repeated itself at Lake of the Woods, where this time we paused for a moment.

A few days later, as we turned onto the street where we live, I asked, in the whisper one uses to look into fate, "Do you think I'll ever see summer? I mean, really see it, like I really want to see it?"

"I hope so," my wife said, tight-lipped. "I hope so, for all of us."

And that night I began looking ahead to the winter solstice.

Index

217